HOPKINS & GRAHAM.

V. WEAVER.

FRIEDLANDER & GUTTE.

LANGTON & Cº

RESIDENCE OF Wᴹ S. SPEAR.

RESIDENCE OF J. J. MUSSER.

MATTHIESEN & THOMAS.

R. ANDREWS & Cº

...ILDING.   A. S. HAXTER.

COURT HOUSE.

RESIDENCE OF T. H. FLETCHER.

REIS, BROˢ

Printed by Britton & Rey

...LLE, 1856.

...ALIFORNIA

P9-BJK-834

B068092LA

917.9403   Jackson   795
            Anybody's
    √   ─   gold。

192128

SANTA CLARA VALLEY LIBRARY SYSTEM
Mountain View Public Library
Santa Clara County Free Library
California

		(Calaveras
Alum Rock	Milpitas	(Community Center
		(Sunnyhills
Campbell	Morgan Hill	
Cupertino	Saratoga	(Quito
Gilroy		(Village
Los Altos	Stanford-Escondido	

Central Research Library - Headquarters
For Bookmobile Service, request schedule

LOS ALTOS   MAR 31 '7

175

Jackson, Joseph Henry, 1
Anybody's gold : the story of
California's mining towns.
[c1970]
33305210559245
cu   05/04/15

Anybody's Gold

The Story

of California's

Mining Towns

Joseph Henry Jackson

with a foreword by

Wallace Stegner

192128

Chronicle Books
San Francisco

SANTA CLARA COUNTY LIBRARY

3 3305 21055 9245

Publisher's Note

All of the scenes of the Gold Towns contained in this book are reproduced through the courtesy of the Bancroft Library, University of California. The publisher is especially grateful for the endless patience and good taste of John Barr Tompkins of The Bancroft Library, who assisted in the selection of Lithographs to be used, and to Director James D. Hart of The Bancroft Library for his permission to reproduce these examples of their priceless collection of early California art.

COPYRIGHT 1970, BY

CHARLOTTE C. JACKSON

All rights reserved. This book, or any part thereof, may not be reproduced in any form without the written permission of the publisher.

Library of Congress Catalog Card Number: 70–133990

Contents

v

Introduction

JOSEPH HENRY JACKSON was a gentle man, whether you spell it as two words or one. I never saw him nervous, upset, irritable, or rude. He met all situations with composure, he never raised his voice when other people were raising theirs, he suffered fools with infinite patience, he was kindness itself to a man with a talent and a problem.

His addictions were friends and books and California history. He loved company, a good story, and (discriminatingly) California wines. He was a good listener and a good dry talker. The fact that his enthusiasms were built upon evidence, and were always under control, did not mean that they were either tepid or tentative. He helped struggling, unrecognized, and hard-up writers as naturally as Boy Scouts help little old

vii

ladies across streets. As a critic he was catholic and kind. His eyes were always a little tired from excessive reading, his hair was smoothed back on his neat head, his suits were always pressed. He looked a little like a self-contained and prosperous banker.

But there were several things about him that were special.

1) He conducted the best-known and most respected newspaper book page in the United States outside of New York. If there was one single thumbtack that marked San Francisco's position on the literary map, it was Joe Jackson's "Bookman's Notebook" in the *Chronicle*.

2) He did the work of three men, did it for years, and did it well. Besides his daily column and his Sunday book page in the *Chronicle's* This World section, both of which went on without a break from 1930 to 1955, he did a weekly radio book program that ran for eighteen years and achieved a national audience through the Pacific Coast Network of CBS. There was hardly a year in which he did not serve as a judge in some major literary competition—Pulitzer Prize, Atlantic Prize, Harper's Prize, Bender and Phelan Awards, Commonwealth Club medals. Once he was on a panel that gave a short story of mine a prize in the O. Henry Memorial Awards, and though I liked the prize fine, what I loved and treasured was Joe's comment that accompanied it : he understood what I was trying to do, he took me seriously. To every visiting writer, editor, and publisher he was West Coast greeter. He spoke at banquets, he entertained nabobs, he answered letters from junior high school girls panning the local gravels for the dust that would make a term paper. He promoted high jinks at the Bohemian Grove and fine printing at the Book Club of California. His interest in California literature was such that before his death he was made honorary curator of the California fiction section of the University of California library. In odd

viii

moments, and they must have been odd indeed, he found time to become an authority on California history, especially the history of Gold Rush outlaws, to write six full sized books and two pint-sized ones, to edit a half dozen (including two anthologies of California writing, the stories of Ambrose Bierce, some Gold Rush journals, and a series of Book Club keepsakes on historical California vineyards) and to contribute introductions and essays to a half dozen more.

3) Though he was a regional shoot of an industry rooted in New York City, he got by on one New York trip a year—not the sort of trip that a provincial makes to the capital, but the sort of visit that equal pays equal. On that single trip, which in later years always coincided with the festivities accompanying the National Book Awards, rumor said he sold enough book advertising (though he was not a salesman) to run the *Chronicle's* This World section for a year, and I have never heard rumor contradicted. When the business and revelry of that annual pilgrimage had run their course, he returned quietly to the Bay Area, and the rest of the year New York came to him.

4) He was a man apparently without vanity, pretension, or ill will. So far as memory can attest or research discover, he had hundreds of friends and not a single enemy.

Naturally, being so good a Californian, he was not a native son. He was born in Madison, New Jersey, in 1894, attended the Peddie School in Highstown, and went on to Lafayette College, from which he dropped out to help organize an ambulance unit in 1917, thereby allying himself with Hemingway, Dos Passos, Malcolm Cowley, and two dozen other American college boys who later made literary reputations. Discharged at the end of the war as a lieutenant of infantry, he spun his wheels for a while and in 1920 went west.

From the beginning his jobs and associates were literary. He was associate editor, then managing editor, and finally editor

ix

(1926-1928) of *Sunset Magazine,* and when he left *Sunset* he spent one year as literary editor of the *San Francisco Argonaut* before settling into the literary editorship of the *Chronicle,* where he remained for the rest of his life.

His work for Californian magazines and his friendship with Californian writers such as George R. Stewart were influential in turning his attention to California life and California history. His uninterrupted residence in the Bay Area did what it does to so many: it made a convert of him. The East had had him for his first twenty-six years; contrary to all Jesuitical educational theory, it never left a mark on him. Everything that mattered to Joe Jackson in his mature life—his home and family, friends, writings, affiliations, historical and literary enthusiasms—centered not simply in the West, but in a small and consciously restricted section of it.

Not inappropriately, his chosen country coincided neatly with the sphere of influence of the San Francisco *Chronicle.*

A little after his death in 1955, a number of his friends led by George Stewart and James Hart began raising money for a memorial. From the beginning it was clear what his most fitting monument would be; he had helped so many writers that he ought to be remembered through a fellowship to a young writer of promise. Prose or poetry, it didn't matter; Joe had a history of liking and assisting both. But the geographical territory from which these fellows should be drawn *did* matter, and the committee of his friends had some discussion about it before they made up their minds.

Joseph Henry Jackson was Mr. West Coast Books to everybody in New York. Did that mean that the winner of the annual Joseph Henry Jackson Award could come from anywhere on the west coast? We didn't think so; Joe's interests and his influence both stopped considerably short of that. The state of California, then? The "Bookman's Notebook" was syndicated in the Los Angeles *Times,* and had devoted readers south as well as north. But a little consideration convinced us that Joe's personal affections didn't really reach down south of Tehachapi. He was a bird of a more northerly range. Should we limit the competition to the Bay Area? Joe lived in Berkeley and worked in the City, and he knew every literary personality and landmark from the Valley of the Moon to Salinas. But we had to decide that the Bay Area, even broadly interpreted, was too narrow for our purposes. As we talked about where he was known and read, and where his own interests were concentrated, we concluded that though the Bay Area was his center, he extended through all northern California and Nevada. He knew, loved, studied, and wrote about the wine country of Mendocino, Napa, Sonoma, Contra Costa, and Santa Clara counties; the gold country of the Sierra Nevada, including the Nevada side; and the Bay Area proper, with a special bow to San Francisco as its cultural heart, market, and counting house. A boundary line that took in California as far north as Santa Rosa and as far south as Monterey, and that reached into Nevada as far as Carson City, Virginia City, and Reno, would include not only most of Joe Jackson's closest friends and most faithful readers, but practically all his abiding intellectual interests and all but a couple of his books.

His non-Californian books were his first two: *Mexican Interlude* (1936) and *Notes on a Drum* (1937), accounts, respectively, of travels in Mexico and Guatemala. Once he found his true metier in *Tintypes in Gold* (1939), he never abandoned it except to write the Mexican short story, "The Christmas Flower," published as a booklet, with illustrations by Tom Lea, in 1951. The rest of his work is all Californian, and most of it is Gold Rush. The best of it is in *Bad Company,* a centennial-year history of Gold Rush highwaymen that incorporates the earlier and briefer *Tintypes in Gold,* and especially in *Anybody's Gold.*

Long before the centennial-miners had panned and repanned Gold Rush history, and well before tourist-oriented antiquarianism and jumping frog contests had made the towns along Highway 49 familiar, Joe Jackson had read the diaries and letters, studied the drawings, consulted the newspapers, visited the places. He knew a lot of local lore, and he knew enough, as most tourists do not, to be able to separate local lore from local history. He knew the sources, and which ones were dependable, which merely colorful. He was amused and delighted by what the old gold towns had been, he was charmed by what time had done to them.

There have been, at a guess, a hundred Gold Rush and Gold-Country books since *Anybody's Gold,* but if I were making a visit to the Mother Lode tomorrow, this is the book I would reach for first, and be most sure I took along, and consult most often. Other histories supplement Joe Jackson's; none that I know of seriously modifies his general picture of life in the mines. Other books on the gold towns may have details that *Anybody's Gold* lacks, but none, to my knowledge, approaches those towns with such a combination of knowledge and delight.

A modest man, Joe Jackson never claimed to be a literary critic. He said he was a book reviewer. Nevertheless, in his column he managed to tell all sorts of people from the literarily naive to the literarily sophisticated what was in the books he reviewed, what if anything was good about them, and where they stood in some hierarchy of literary value; and he never fell into the common reviewer's disease of hating books publicly, or treating an unsuccessful book as a public offense.

In the same way, while denying that he was a historian, he

COURT HOUSE.

Anybody's
Gold

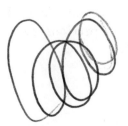

state of California, then? The "Bookman's Notebook" was syndicated in the Los Angeles *Times,* and had devoted readers south as well as north. But a little consideration convinced us that Joe's personal affections didn't really reach down south of Tehachapi. He was a bird of a more northerly range. Should we limit the competition to the Bay Area? Joe lived in Berkeley and worked in the City, and he knew every literary personality and landmark from the Valley of the Moon to Salinas. But we had to decide that the Bay Area, even broadly interpreted, was too narrow for our purposes. As we talked about where he was known and read, and where his own interests were concentrated, we concluded that though the Bay Area was his center, he extended through all northern California and Nevada. He knew, loved, studied, and wrote about the wine country of Mendocino, Napa, Sonoma, Contra Costa, and Santa Clara counties; the gold country of the Sierra Nevada, including the Nevada side; and the Bay Area proper, with a special bow to San Francisco as its cultural heart, market, and counting house. A boundary line that took in California as far north as Santa Rosa and as far south as Monterey, and that reached into Nevada as far as Carson City, Virginia City, and Reno, would include not only most of Joe Jackson's closest friends and most faithful readers, but practically all his abiding intellectual interests and all but a couple of his books.

His non-Californian books were his first two: *Mexican Interlude* (1936) and *Notes on a Drum* (1937), accounts, respectively, of travels in Mexico and Guatemala. Once he found his true metier in *Tintypes in Gold* (1939), he never abandoned it except to write the Mexican short story, "The Christmas Flower," published as a booklet, with illustrations by Tom Lea, in 1951. The rest of his work is all Californian, and most of it is Gold Rush. The best of it is in *Bad Company,* a centennial-year history of Gold Rush highwaymen that incorporates the earlier and briefer *Tintypes in Gold,* and especially in *Anybody's Gold.*

Long before the centennial-miners had panned and re-panned Gold Rush history, and well before tourist-oriented antiquarianism and jumping frog contests had made the towns along Highway 49 familiar, Joe Jackson had read the diaries and letters, studied the drawings, consulted the newspapers, visited the places. He knew a lot of local lore, and he knew enough, as most tourists do not, to be able to separate local lore from local history. He knew the sources, and which ones were dependable, which merely colorful. He was amused and delighted by what the old gold towns had been, he was charmed by what time had done to them.

There have been, at a guess, a hundred Gold Rush and Gold-Country books since *Anybody's Gold,* but if I were making a visit to the Mother Lode tomorrow, this is the book I would reach for first, and be most sure I took along, and consult most often. Other histories supplement Joe Jackson's; none that I know of seriously modifies his general picture of life in the mines. Other books on the gold towns may have details that *Anybody's Gold* lacks, but none, to my knowledge, approaches those towns with such a combination of knowledge and delight.

A modest man, Joe Jackson never claimed to be a literary critic. He said he was a book reviewer. Nevertheless, in his column he managed to tell all sorts of people from the literarily naive to the literarily sophisticated what was in the books he reviewed, what if anything was good about them, and where they stood in some hierarchy of literary value; and he never fell into the common reviewer's disease of hating books publicly, or treating an unsuccessful book as a public offense.

In the same way, while denying that he was a historian, he

reported historical facts with a minimum of distortion, and on certain matters, such as the lives and exploits of the legendary bandits Joaquin Murieta and Tiburio Vasquez, and the somewhat better documented Black Bart, Rattlesnake Dick, Dick Fellows, and Tom Bell, he made himself the ultimate authority.

And that is a strange thing, that this gentle, kindly, generous, and highly civilized man should have been so fascinated by the violence in California history. Not only did he write two books on the Sierra highwaymen, but he made a collection of famous San Francisco murders and edited the Viking Portable Murder Book. It was the colorfulness of those outlaws, one supposes, that attracted him. He could not resist a good story; and mayhem, so long as it was historical and in costume, made some of the best stories.

Yet as any reader can discover by dipping into *Anybody's Gold*, Joe Jackson was not one to let his love of a story blur his historical understanding. He was an intensely interested spectator, and he liked to look the whole length of the road, from where he stood in the present, let us say under the ailanthus trees of Volcano, or in the old cemetery at Murphys, clear back to the energy and unrest that tore up those foothills and planted the beginnings of a civilization there.

He wanted to understand events in the terms of the men who lived them. When he presents us with the vast gallery of characters who live the events in *Anybody's Gold,* he is doing essentially what he did in his book column. He is *giving a hearing,* he is listening respectfully to what these characters out of history have to say. In the end he judges, not harshly. Rereading him now, I get from this best and most representative of his books the impression I always got from him in person. I feel that I am in the presence of a man who knows what he is about and enjoys what he is doing, a professional, a man of letters whose craftsman's conscience cannot inhibit or stifle his capacity for delight.

And what historian, fascinated by people, places, color, yarns, humorous and heroic action, ever had a better subject than the Gold Rush? *Anybody's Gold* is a mine, a Mother Lode, of stories and personalities, and of places that started out Golgotha and wound up Sleepy Hollow. It is high time, nearly thirty years after its first publication, that so rich and amusing a book should be back in print.

WALLACE STEGNER

COURT HOUSE.

Anybody's Gold

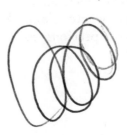

Prologue:

Before the Gold

CALIFORNIA and its gold were born together in the brain of a second-rate yarn-spinner who knew very well he was telling a thumping lie.

It was a hack romancer, one Garcí Ordóñez de Montalvo, writing a cheap sequel to a famous fifteenth-century Spanish novel of chivalry, who invented both. *The Exploits of Esplandián* was his book, and in it Montalvo told a tale of a strange land inhabited by Amazons, a land known as "California," so he said, ruled by the black Queen Calafía. He was most explicit about the gold: "The weapons were all of gold," he wrote, "and the island everywhere abounded with gold and precious stones, and upon it no other metal was found."

3

Where Montalvo found the name "California" still puzzles the scholars. There are several theories about it, some mildly plausible. No one really knows. But the point here is that the idea of a land abounding in gold, not to mention precious stones, was precisely the kind of idea to take root in the minds of the Spanish generation that had begun to reach out restlessly toward new worlds. When Cortés first saw what he supposed to be an island off to the west of Mexico, he thought that perhaps at last he had found the golden land he sought. When he stepped ashore in Baja California and took possession in the name of His Most Catholic Majesty Charles the Fifth of Spain, the spot he named Santa Cruz was to him merely a gateway to what he hoped were "mighty treasures, and the vast city of Cibola." When he sent Ulloa voyaging northward, it was so that he might spy out just such a treasure city, Cibola or another. Ulloa found no gold, no precious stones. He did learn that California was not an island but a peninsula. But because he brought back no evidence of treasure, because he failed to find even the least of fabled Cibola's Seven Cities, he got scant credit. It may have been the mutineer, Jiménez, who first applied Montalvo's romantic name, "California," to the new country; it may have been Cortés himself or Ulloa or any leather-jacketed soldier of the lot. One of the Conquistadores did; that much is fairly certain; the "Esplandián" story was widely read at that period and they must have been familiar with it. To be sure, Montalvo had written that there were griffins in California, too, but the conquerors were not interested in griffins. Gold was what they were after. If there were some odds and ends of precious stones lying about, then so much the better. As for the rest of it, for the wealth of Cibola a man could believe in as many as a dozen griffins before breakfast.

The notion of gold in California never quite died. Sir Francis Drake was too hard-headed to take any stock in fabulous cities, but when he sailed from Plymouth in 1577 to "annoy the King of Spain in his Indies" it was gold he sought. Drake was well aware of the political significance of harrying the Manila galleons. But the privateer—the pirate if you prefer—does not sail the seas just because his country's Ministers of State think it a good thing to have him go out and annoy the enemy. He makes his perilous voyages to grow rich if he can. Drake knew all about the galleons and their burdens of silk and jewels, musk and amber, the ivory, apes and peacocks of far Cathay, and it was their golden cargoes he wanted. He was not familiar with the "California" myth; Spanish novels of chivalry had no wide circulation in England; there was no Mudie's then. When he landed briefly on the Pacific Coast, he called the place "New Albion" in his insular English way. Yet the tale of gold was told again when Drake returned to England. Gold, reported the old sea-dog—doubtless with his tongue in his cheek—was to be found in quantity in this marvelous new country he had claimed for his Queen. How, after all, should Elizabeth know better?

For a time the myth languished, the fable was forgotten. When Vizcaíno explored the California coast in 1602, found the fine ports of San Diego and Monterey and named them, gold was not in his mind. He had been a merchant trader; he knew that the wise man makes his money by shrewd buying and selling, not by looking for mines in the moon. An experienced voyager, too, he must have felt the fascination of discovery for its own sake. And after Vizcaíno's time the viceroys in New Spain thought less and less about exploration to the north. Aztec, Maya, and Inca had been conquered by Cortés and Alvarado and Pizarro. Their vast volcanic ranges held both gold and silver; the new city of Mexico that had sprung up on the ashes of Moctezuma's Tenochtitlán had become a place of comfort, even of luxury. Life for Spain's representatives in the new hemisphere had been an affair of sleeping with sword and musket at hand; now it had turned into a matter of palaces, retinues of Indian slaves, a soft and softening existence. Why bother about the little-known country to the north? Some captains had come back with stories of a lovely wooded land, sheltered harbors, pleasant rivers and valleys filled with flowers. Yes, but others had tales to tell of fiery deserts, harsh and rocky coasts, storms and starvation. For a century and a half Spain, old and new, forgot about California.

Then whispers began to come down to Mexico from above. The Russians were nosing about up there; Bering's voyages had stimulated his countrymen's interest in Alaskan furs, and who knew how much farther southward these fur-seekers might want to move? The English had Canada now, and were moving steadily westward. There was even a rumor that the Dutch had an eye on the Pacific, that they had gone so far as to gather information on Spanish shipping and settlements. There had been this kind of talk before, but now it appeared that something had to be done.

Something was done. José de Gálvez, who had been sent to Mexico to bring some order into its financial affairs, happened to be a man of action. When, in the first month of 1768, a letter came from Spain to the viceroy telling him that the Russians seemed to mean business, he and Gálvez talked it over. There was no gold in this California, of course; that was an old fairy tale and sensible men maintained a healthy skepticism about such things. But gold or not, the land had to be held, or Spain would have Russia on her new-world door-step, England looking over her shoulder and perhaps the Dutch at her elbow.

Between them, Gálvez and the viceroy resurrected the old colonizing plan for the settlement of Vizcaíno's two good ports in Upper California. They outlined their scheme. Four divisions would start, two by sea and two by land, the four

6

to meet at San Diego and proceed to Monterey. Because it was the Spanish way, sword and cross would march together. Aside from the souls brought to salvation, missionaries seemed to understand how to subdue the heathen with a minimum of expense and trouble; old Bartolomé de las Casas had demonstrated the technic in Guatemala some two centuries earlier. Moreover, the Franciscan fathers, lately supplanted by Dominicans in Lower California, had long wanted a chance to bring the Indians of the north into the fold. Franciscans would be just the men to send. It was so decided, and the choice fell upon Fray Junípero Serra as leader of the group. On the military side the appointment went to Don Gaspar de Portolá, a Catalonian of noble descent and an able soldier. Spain's first attempt to hold California was under way. Once more the thought of gold was the moving force, though this time indirectly. If the Russians or English or Dutch once got a foothold so close at hand, it would be no time at all until Spain would lose her treasure-house of Mexico, perhaps Peru as well. So far, at least, the idea of gold was bound up with the new conquest.

It was to be another seventy-five years before gold would mean anything to California or to Californians.

Now and then, as the missions grew and prospered, an Indian would come to one of the Fathers and show him a quill or perhaps an acorn-cup full of yellow dust. Whenever that happened—and the records show it did, more than once —the good priests discouraged the Indians, hinted at punishment if the story got about. They had troubles enough without their converts turning gold-hunters. There were all too few mission Indians to take care of planting the grapes, herding the cattle, slaughtering, rendering the tallow and curing the hides, harvesting the grain. And as the nineteenth century wore along there were other things to think of. The province of California was forced into a series of adjustments that kept

7

Sutter's Fort, Sacramento, California, 1847
Before the gold, Sutter's Fort was the heart of the great
central valley. Sutter's land holdings were vast and he was

the friend and patron of all the valley and those adventurous
immigrants who were beginning to appear from beyond the Sierra.

everybody busy merely getting used to what was going on.
From Spain the United States acquired the Oregon region.
Then suddenly Mexico became an independent empire under
the ill-starred Iturbide. Almost immediately that empire ceased
to exist and Mexico was a republic. By the time Californians
had grown accustomed to the new order, the missions were
secularized and there was a fresh scheme of things. The old
romantic dream of gold had died; Californians had found a
new kind of riches. The great land-grants, made to encourage
settlement, were developing into fine cattle ranches, and California was well pleased with the way of life that had come
into being; her people wanted no change.

Change was closer than any one thought. Perhaps it might
have been postponed a few years; in the normal course of
things, pioneering takes time. To be sure, the American
wagon-trains across the mountains were growing longer each
year, following more closely on each other's heels, but there
was plenty of room. California could absorb the fresh hundreds, even thousands, and still keep its spacious pastoral
character for a long time. It might have been like that.

It was not like that. The gold was there, little as the Mon-
talvos, the Vizcaínos, the Drakes had believed it. Back in the
Sierra foot-hills, up from the great central valley, the icy
rivers held more gold than the new world had ever seen.
Buried in the quartz lodes strung along the ridges for three
hundred miles and more, was even greater wealth, uncounted
and uncountable millions in gold. No one had found it. No
Californian ever went into the foot-hills unless perhaps on
an Indian hunt, some small punitive expedition to recover
stolen horses and teach thieves a lesson. There was nothing
else to take a man up there. Down in the valley and in the
lesser mountains of the Coast Range there were tens of thousands of empty acres, pasture for everyone's cattle and to
spare. As for the Americans who made their painful way

across the Sierra, they were thinking only of cheating the far deserts and the winter snows, dreaming only of how quickly they might get down those slopes into the fair land below; the thought of gold never entered their heads. Nearest to the incredible treasure was a man named Sutter, a Swiss who had been given large grants in the Sacramento River country. But like his fellow Californians he was a rancher at heart; he thought in terms of cattle, farm land, now and then a bit of trading or fighting, and always the delicate diplomacies necessary to keep solid with the governors sent up from Mexico. Yet it was through this rancher, trader, small politician, that the discovery of gold was to come. Already, in the middle 1840's, events were shaping themselves. The moment was not far off.

California's last decade before the days of gold has been called the happiest period through which any country ever passed.

Perhaps it was. At least it saw life lived graciously, largely, simply, easily. Americans were filtering in, more every year, but they were scattered and there were not enough of them to affect the Californian way of living. Many of them married into old families, settled into ranch life and found it good. It was good, too; far better than a counting-house stool in Boston, for example, far easier than trying to scratch out a bare existence from stony New England soil. Back east, a man had a good-sized farm when he could say he owned a quarter-section of land. Here in the new California land-grants were made by the league, and a league was almost 4,500 acres. There was Francisco Pacheco, for instance, owner of the San Felipe and San Luis Gonzales ranchos which sprawled over something like 90,000 acres of valley and hill. On that vast expanse Don Francisco pastured 14,000 head of cattle, 15,000 sheep and about 500 horses and mares. There was the Estrada

9

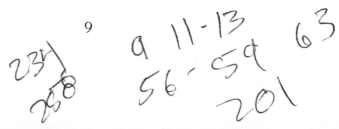

family with its Buena Esperanza rancho, a matter of 25,000 acres or so; an American, David Spence, had married a daughter and was as good a Californian as any of them. So was Henry Fitch whose wife was a Carrillo and whose Rancho Sotoyome was another eleven-league parcel. There were dozens more. It was said that General Mariano Guadalupe Vallejo actually did not know how much land he had, nor how many cattle and horses.

For that matter, no Californian kept very careful check on what he owned. How would a man be sure, when all animals multiplied so fast in this new country with its gentle climate and fine feed? The great landholders counted roughly; so many head, more or less. Estimates were made at the yearly rodeos when the cattle were rounded up and branded, but they were rough guesses, no more. It did not matter much anyway. Sometimes, indeed, the rapid growth of herds made trouble; in dry years when the feed was light, the *vaqueros* were sent riding to cut out and kill the older beasts, drive them over cliffs, shoot them on the gallop. Hides could always be used; hides were currency; deals down at ship-side in Monterey were consummated in terms of hides; hides bought anything and everything. As for the carcasses, Indians might take those where they lay, or the packs of half-wild dogs might snarl and fight over them. Who cared? There was plenty.

And plenty was enough for the Californian. He had no particular inclination to grow rich; to accumulate money for money's sake was alien to his nature. On his rancho his word was law or very near it. He looked after his land, devoted himself passionately to horse-flesh, spent his days in the saddle and his nights gambling a little and dancing a great deal, played the gracious father to all his servants but especially to his *vaqueros,* and did his best generally to be a man of good will. If he was a trifle touchy in matters concerning his honor, his fellow-Californians understood him perfectly. They had

shall for a saw-mill to be erected on the American Fork.
John Bidwell, Sutter's great friend, admirer, and right-hand
man, drew up the agreement and Sutter, and Marshall signed
it. The contract provided that Sutter was to furnish building
materials, all supplies and board, and to pay the men employed
on the project. Marshall was to build and manage the mill,
receiving one-fourth of the lumber as compensation for his
services. Nothing could have been more businesslike. But,
had Sutter been able to hear it, that contract was the second
distant trumpet-note heralding his downfall, a little closer
than the first, a little clearer, the call of history on the march,
the warning of the thousands of tramping feet headed westward to overrun and destroy his empire.

Sutter had no hint of what was so soon to come. All through
that autumn of 1847 his diary records with satisfaction the
progress of Marshall and the mill. Members of the Mormon
Battalion drifted up to the Fort and Sutter hired them; there
was plenty to do; his enterprises were growing, expanding.
That energetic Latter-Day Saint, Sam Brannan, opened a
store at the Fort. The harvesting went on, the scheme for
milling flour developed; Indians, trappers, immigrants, and
soldiers came and went. By the end of September the sawmill
was well under way. Sutter notes: "I dispatched a wagon with
provisions and 3 yoke of oxen to the saw-mill site; also six
men whom I have engaged to manufacture shingles, clap-
boards, etc." A week later there is the entry: "Sent 40 sheep
to the saw-mill site; also a wagonload of provisions." By
December, so well had Marshall managed things, the sawmill
was nearly ready. In a postscript to a letter written that month
to Lieutenant H. W. Halleck, acting Secretary of State who
had asked for some census information, Sutter wrote: "One
of my flour-mills, driven by water power, is now in operation;
the other and the saw-mill are erected and will be in operation within thirty days." All unknowing, John Sutter had set

their own honor to think about. It was the grand manner that
was important. The lord of a dozen leagues might have to
nudge a chicken or pig out of the way before he could enter
his house, but after all California was a province, and in the
provinces one expects life to be provincial. If his children were
flea-bitten, well then so were those of his richer neighbor with
forty leagues of land. It was ranch life. A flea has nothing
to do with honor. There was something in knowing you could
trust your neighbor utterly, whether it was a matter of a
simple promise, a debt or a fight. As the 1840's drew to a
close the Californian was content. He was living in the free
and natural state to which he had become accustomed, and
he was certain in his heart that it was the only way for a man
to live. Gold? Well, there was usually a sack of Spanish gold-
pieces somewhere about the house for the rare occasions on
which it was needed. But that was unimportant. The passing
stranger was welcome to help himself if he lacked money.
Close as he was to it, gold was the last thing the Spanish-
Californian thought about.

In many ways John A. Sutter, Swiss immigrant and man of
destiny, was a Californian like his friends and neighbors.

He had come to the new land a decade earlier, made the
right friends, settled beside the Sacramento River on his first,
eleven-league grant which he called New Helvetia as though
it were a whole country in itself. To this vast holding he had
added from time to time in the 1840's; first the great Sobrante
Grant, then Fort Ross and Bodega Bay over on the coast,
bought from the Russians who had tired of their venture.
Over his valley empire Sutter pastured cattle, grew grain,
busied himself in much the same way as his fellow Californians. But there was a difference. Sutter was ambitious. He
had, in a way that other Californians did not have, a burning

urge to get ahead. He was forever looking round for new opportunities, considering new ways to acquire more property, employ more Indians, add to the tremendous principality that was already his.

On a slight rise of land near the river, he had built himself a fort which served as the center for all the activities related to his holdings. There were still hostile Indians scattered about, and anyway the Fort made a good hub for his wheel, a place to bring together his blacksmith shop, his store-rooms, his granaries, his miniature arsenal. Every one knew the Fort; immigrants aimed for it, travelers stopped at it. Sutter was invariably generous, hospitable, kindly. Often he went to all sorts of trouble and expense to aid the new Californians who were drifting across the Sierra, give them food and clothing and good advice. It was men from Sutter's Fort who went to the aid of the tragically snow-bound Donner Party in the dreadful winter of 1846-47. It was to the Fort that men came for flour and supplies of all kinds. Settled in its neighborhood was a floating population of trappers and hunters, bad eggs many of them. Sutter had his worries, especially in the early summer of 1846 when Frémont's men conducted that comic-opera performance known as the Bear Flag Revolt. If this kind of lawless procedure was going to be the order of the day, who could tell when the Fort might have to defend itself in all seriousness?

The revolt had no immediate disastrous consequences for the Fort or for Sutter. There had been an expedition or two and Sutter had actually become an American officer with a commission from Commodore Stockton. But none of this commotion was close to his heart. What interested him, first, last and all the time, was his farming. It was something he understood, something that was in his cautious European blood. When you had land, you took care of it, developed it, watched it, made it prosper.

By the spring of 1847 Sutter was in full swing again with his plans for New Helvetia. His diary is crowded with entries concerning the details of management: "Started the tannery to-day, after invoicing everything. . . . Bray went with six hands to cut poles for the threshing-floors. Some of the Walla-Wallas dropped in to trade. . . . Sent my vaqueros to slaughter some cattle at Rancho del Paso. . . . A visit from General Kearny. At my order 11 guns fired a salute. The garrison paraded. Harvest has begun with 50 reapers. . . . Stopped cradling to-day because of the high wind. Building begun on the new bake-oven. We are gathering and threshing the peas. Much curing of the sick and their treatment to-day. . . ." It is easy to see where Sutter's interests lay. He was the owner of a great property, and he was going to take care of it as a sensible man should.

Then, on July 21, 1847, appears the entry that sounds the first faint note of what was to come. "Marshall and Nerio left for the Mts. on the American Fork to select the site for the sawmill."

That, though he did not know it, was the beginning of the end for Sutter. All he wanted was lumber, good clear pine and cedar. The fertile plains of the Sacramento Valley were all very well for wheat, for peas, for pasture, but they did not grow the kind of timber he needed so badly. Sutter had plans for expansion, and they involved lumber and plenty of it. What more logical than that he should send his best carpenter, James Marshall from New Jersey, up into the hills to find a place where there would be water to run a mill and timber within reach to keep it busy? How could he know that though Marshall would find the very spot for him he would also find the gleaming yellow flakes that were to spell his destruction?

He could not know. Just a month later, the Sutter diary carries this note: "Made a contract with James Wilson Mar-

down the number of his days of grace. One more month and the cataclysm would be upon him.

It is interesting to look briefly at Sutter and his empire in these closing days of his greatness. One of his duties as the old year died was to write to his brother Jakob Friedrich, so many miles away across the sea. A pioneer brother is privileged to boast; it is one of his rewards for the hardships he has undergone. Sutter never missed a chance to brag a little, and he was more than willing to let his relatives know that he had got along in this New World. He wrote: "My holdings are extensive. In truth I have not yet beheld them in their entirety. I named my new home New Helvetia in honor of the ancient Roman title of our fatherland. ... A crude stockade and fort were my first concern, since the savages were at times none too friendly. The venture improves steadily now, and Sutter's Fort may still live in history."

Sutter did not exaggerate. The venture had improved. The crude stockade had become the heart of the whole region. The Fort stood on a slight rise of ground from which it overlooked the broad sweep of field and pasture. Horses and cattle grazed over the lush plain, rested and found shade in the groves of sycamore, cottonwood, elm, and live-oak. Down by the river was a small *embarcadero* at which boats from San Francisco discharged and stowed their cargoes, Sutter's own twenty-ton sloop, *Amelia,* among them. Closer to the Fort was a ten-acre garden and orchard where peach, apple, pear, olive, almond, and fig trees marched in rows. Beneath the trees and between them, Sutter's Indians hoed and irrigated the vegetables. There were even two acres of roses of Castile, raised from cuttings Sutter had got from the Mission fathers. But it was the Fort itself, with its brass cannon, that focused everything. Citadel, home, and office in one, it was Sutter's place wherein he sat, the friend and patron of all the Valley.

It was roughly finished, with great hewn rafters and un-paneled walls. Sutter's office was perhaps a trifle more impressive than most of the rooms; in it were a redwood table and some chairs and benches made in his own shops. There was a set of furniture of California laurel; Sutter had acquired it in the Fort Ross purchase from the Russians. There was a fireplace, too, and a small table held a stack of paper, with pens and ink and sand for the records. A wooden candelabrum furnished light, and the floor and chairs were covered with Indian blankets woven on the Fort's crude looms. Perhaps the candles were burning on the dark, rainy afternoon of Friday, January 28, 1848, when James Marshall came bursting into Sutter's office. "He was soaked to the skin and dripping water," Sutter carefully wrote in his diary. "Very much excited," he added.

James Marshall had reason to be excited. Four days earlier, up there in the hills, he had risen at dawn to inspect the mill-race and plan out the work for the day. As he walked along the ditch his men had dug, he noticed some particles of yellow mixed with the reddish earth. He picked them up and turned them over in his hand. Tiny grains, they were, not much bigger than a pin's head. Could they be gold? He did not know. He had never seen raw gold. But they might be. He looked further, found more, and sent an Indian to his cabin to fetch a tin plate. With this he washed out handfuls of dirt until he had gathered something like half an ounce of the stuff. Then he went about his business. Probably it would be better to say nothing to anybody until he knew more about it.

The next morning he was up early again and at the tail-race, looking eagerly around him. Yes, there were more of the yellow flakes, sluiced out and washed by the water of the day before. Was it gold, or was he all wrong? It could be fool's gold; Marshall knew about pyrites. Yet it seemed like the real thing; it was heavy, soft when he pounded the particles between two stones. This time he collected three ounces of the stuff, whatever it was. His mind was made up. He would go down to the Fort and find out what Sutter thought. But he was sure he knew. It was gold.

Sutter was astonished to see the dripping, excited Marshall in his office that afternoon. Only the day before he had sent him all the supplies he needed, bought from Elder Sam Brannan's store. What was he doing here?

He was even more surprised when Marshall said that he must talk to him alone, in his living quarters, not in the office where they might be interrupted. Marshall was an odd, moody man, but he was not usually as odd as this. Still, he might as well be humored. Sutter took him into his private suite of bedroom and parlor and asked him what was the matter.

Marshall said only that he must have two bowls of water and a pair of scales, and continuing to humor him Sutter got these. Then—but let Sutter himself tell it: "He drew out a rag from his pocket. Opening it carefully, he held it before me in his hand. It contained what might have been an ounce and a half of gold-dust—dust, flakes and grains. The biggest piece was not as large as a pea, and it varied from that down to less than a pinhead in size."

Sutter made this statement later. But at the moment he did not know what to think. All he knew was that the thing to do was to try out the particles Marshall had brought. Together the two men applied all the tests they could think of. They weighed the specimens and found them heavy enough for gold. They hammered them and saw that they did not splinter; they were malleable as gold was. With some acid from the apothecary shop they touched the grains; they did not tarnish or stain. In the end, they came to the only conclusion left to them. Marshall had discovered gold.

Now the warning rang clear and unmistakable, and Sutter heard it plainly. Marshall, nervous and feverish with excitement, would not wait; storm or no storm, he was heading back to the hills. Sutter let him go. He wanted time to think. Whose was this gold, after all? Not his. He had built a sawmill in a valley in the foot-hills, that was all. A sawmill and some vague timber rights were one thing; a gold mine was something else. How much gold was there? Did it lie scattered all through those mountain regions? If it did, then to whom did it belong? To anybody. It was anybody's gold. That was the trouble.

What Sutter could have done about it is anybody's guess. Probably nothing could have saved him, but he made one try. Gathering the Indians of the little valley of Coloma where Marshall had set the sawmill, he made a treaty with them. For shirts, handkerchiefs, shoes, and flour, he leased the twelve-mile square of the valley for three years, drew up a document vaguely mentioning the possibility of minerals in the soil and had it decorated with a flourish of Indian marks. There was no way to register such a lease. The days of Mexican grants were over, and nobody yet knew whether California would really be part of the United States or not. But it was all Sutter could do. He doubled the wages of the men at the mill site, cautioned them again to say nothing and rode back to the Fort. There he chose a messenger, one Charles Bennett, and sent him with the paper down to Monterey to Governor Mason. If the Governor would confirm the lease, Sutter had at any rate a chance to keep the discovery private.

But the Governor would not confirm. He said he could not. California was still a Mexican province, held by the United States as a conquest. No laws of the United States could apply to it, much less land laws which could go into effect only after a public survey. The Governor was sorry, but there it was.

The decision was a blow to Sutter. More clearly than ever, he saw that the gold spelled trouble for him. His workmen would leave; his grain would go unharvested, his timber

their own honor to think about. It was the grand manner that was important. The lord of a dozen leagues might have to nudge a chicken or pig out of the way before he could enter his house, but after all California was a province, and in the provinces one expects life to be provincial. If his children were flea-bitten, well then so were those of his richer neighbor with forty leagues of land. It was ranch life. A flea has nothing to do with honor. There was something in knowing you could trust your neighbor utterly, whether it was a matter of a simple promise, a debt or a fight. As the 1840's drew to a close the Californian was content. He was living in the free and natural state to which he had become accustomed, and he was certain in his heart that it was the only way for a man to live. Gold? Well, there was usually a sack of Spanish gold-pieces somewhere about the house for the rare occasions on which it was needed. But that was unimportant. The passing stranger was welcome to help himself if he lacked money. Close as he was to it, gold was the last thing the Spanish-Californian thought about.

In many ways John A. Sutter, Swiss immigrant and man of destiny, was a Californian like his friends and neighbors.

He had come to the new land a decade earlier, made the right friends, settled beside the Sacramento River on his first, eleven-league grant which he called New Helvetia as though it were a whole country in itself. To this vast holding he had added from time to time in the 1840's; first the great Sobrante Grant, then Fort Ross and Bodega Bay over on the coast, bought from the Russians who had tired of their venture. Over his valley empire Sutter pastured cattle, grew grain, busied himself in much the same way as his fellow Californians. But there was a difference. Sutter was ambitious. He had, in a way that other Californians did not have, a burning urge to get ahead. He was forever looking round for new opportunities, considering new ways to acquire more property, employ more Indians, add to the tremendous principality that was already his.

On a slight rise of land near the river, he had built himself a fort which served as the center for all the activities related to his holdings. There were still hostile Indians scattered about, and anyway the Fort made a good hub for his wheel, a place to bring together his blacksmith shop, his store-rooms, his granaries, his miniature arsenal. Every one knew the Fort; immigrants aimed for it, travelers stopped at it. Sutter was invariably generous, hospitable, kindly. Often he went to all sorts of trouble and expense to aid the new Californians who were drifting across the Sierra, give them food and clothing and good advice. It was men from Sutter's Fort who went to the aid of the tragically snow-bound Donner Party in the dreadful winter of 1846-47. It was to the Fort that men came for flour and supplies of all kinds. Settled in its neighborhood was a floating population of trappers and hunters, bad eggs many of them. Sutter had his worries, especially in the early summer of 1846 when Frémont's men conducted that comic-opera performance known as the Bear Flag Revolt. If this kind of lawless procedure was going to be the order of the day, who could tell when the Fort might have to defend itself in all seriousness?

The revolt had no immediate disastrous consequences for the Fort or for Sutter. There had been an expedition or two and Sutter had actually become an American officer with a commission from Commodore Stockton. But none of this commotion was close to his heart. What interested him, first, last and all the time, was his farming. It was something he understood, something that was in his cautious European blood. When you had land, you took care of it, developed it, watched it, made it prosper.

12

By the spring of 1847 Sutter was in full swing again with his plans for New Helvetia. His diary is crowded with entries concerning the details of management: "Started the tannery to-day, after invoicing everything. . . . Bray went with six hands to cut poles for the threshing-floors. Some of the Walla-Wallas dropped in to trade. . . . Sent my vaqueros to slaughter some cattle at Rancho del Paso. . . . A visit from General Kearny. At my order 11 guns fired a salute. The garrison paraded. Harvest has begun with 50 reapers. . . . Stopped cradling to-day because of the high wind. Building begun on the new bake-oven. We are gathering and threshing the peas. Much curing of the sick and their treatment to-day. . . ." It is easy to see where Sutter's interests lay. He was the owner of a great property, and he was going to take care of it as a sensible man should.

Then, on July 21, 1847, appears the entry that sounds the first faint note of what was to come. "Marshall and Ncrio left for the Mts. on the American Fork to select the site for the sawmill."

That, though he did not know it, was the beginning of the end for Sutter. All he wanted was lumber, good clear pine and cedar. The fertile plains of the Sacramento Valley were all very well for wheat, for peas, for pasture, but they did not grow the kind of timber he needed so badly. Sutter had plans for expansion, and they involved lumber and plenty of it. What more logical than that he should send his best carpenter, James Marshall from New Jersey, up into the hills to find a place where there would be water to run a mill and timber within reach to keep it busy? How could he know that though Marshall would find the very spot for him he would also find the gleaming yellow flakes that were to spell his destruction?

He could not know. Just a month later, the Sutter diary carries this note: "Made a contract with James Wilson Mar-

shall for a saw-mill to be erected on the American Fork."
John Bidwell, Sutter's great friend, admirer, and right-hand
man, drew up the agreement and Sutter, and Marshall signed
it. The contract provided that Sutter was to furnish building
materials, all supplies and board, and to pay the men employed
on the project. Marshall was to build and manage the mill,
receiving one-fourth of the lumber as compensation for his
services. Nothing could have been more businesslike. But,
had Sutter been able to hear it, that contract was the second
distant trumpet-note heralding his downfall, a little closer
than the first, a little clearer, the call of history on the march,
the warning of the thousands of tramping feet headed westward to overrun and destroy his empire.

Sutter had no hint of what was so soon to come. All through
that autumn of 1847 his diary records with satisfaction the
progress of Marshall and the mill. Members of the Mormon
Battalion drifted up to the Fort and Sutter hired them; there
was plenty to do; his enterprises were growing, expanding.
That energetic Latter-Day Saint, Sam Brannan, opened a
store at the Fort. The harvesting went on, the scheme for
milling flour developed; Indians, trappers, immigrants, and
soldiers came and went. By the end of September the sawmill
was well under way. Sutter notes: "I dispatched a wagon with
provisions and 3 yoke of oxen to the saw-mill site; also six
men whom I have engaged to manufacture shingles, clap-
boards, etc." A week later there is the entry: "Sent 40 sheep
to the saw-mill site; also a wagonload of provisions." By
December, so well had Marshall managed things, the sawmill
was nearly ready. In a postscript to a letter written that month
to Lieutenant H. W. Halleck, acting Secretary of State who
had asked for some census information, Sutter wrote: "One
of my flour-mills, driven by water power, is now in operation;
the other and the saw-mill are erected and will be in operation within thirty days." All unknowing, John Sutter had set

down the number of his days of grace. One more month and the cataclysm would be upon him.

It is interesting to look briefly at Sutter and his empire in these closing days of his greatness. One of his duties as the old year died was to write to his brother Jakob Friedrich, so many miles away across the sea. A pioneer brother is privileged to boast; it is one of his rewards for the hardships he has undergone. Sutter never missed a chance to brag a little, and he was more than willing to let his relatives know that he had got along in this New World. He wrote: "My holdings are extensive. In truth I have not yet beheld them in their entirety. I named my new home New Helvetia in honor of the ancient Roman title of our fatherland. . . . A crude stockade and fort were my first concern, since the savages were at times none too friendly. The venture improves steadily now, and Sutter's Fort may still live in history."

Sutter did not exaggerate. The venture had improved. The crude stockade had become the heart of the whole region. The Fort stood on a slight rise of ground from which it overlooked the broad sweep of field and pasture. Horses and cattle grazed over the lush plain, rested and found shade in the groves of sycamore, cottonwood, elm, and live-oak. Down by the river was a small *embarcadero* at which boats from San Francisco discharged and stowed their cargoes, Sutter's own twenty-ton sloop, *Amelia,* among them. Closer to the Fort was a ten-acre garden and orchard where peach, apple, pear, olive, almond, and fig trees marched in rows. Beneath the trees and between them, Sutter's Indians hoed and irrigated the vegetables. There were even two acres of roses of Castile, raised from cuttings Sutter had got from the Mission fathers. But it was the Fort itself, with its brass cannon, that focused everything. Citadel, home, and office in one, it was Sutter's place wherein he sat, the friend and patron of all the Valley.

It was roughly finished, with great hewn rafters and un-paneled walls. Sutter's office was perhaps a trifle more impressive than most of the rooms; in it were a redwood table and some chairs and benches made in his own shops. There was a set of furniture of California laurel; Sutter had acquired it in the Fort Ross purchase from the Russians. There was a fireplace, too, and a small table held a stack of paper, with pens and ink and sand for the records. A wooden candelabrum furnished light, and the floor and chairs were covered with Indian blankets woven on the Fort's crude looms. Perhaps the candles were burning on the dark, rainy afternoon of Friday, January 28, 1848, when James Marshall came bursting into Sutter's office. "He was soaked to the skin and dripping water," Sutter carefully wrote in his diary. "Very much excited," he added.

James Marshall had reason to be excited. Four days earlier, up there in the hills, he had risen at dawn to inspect the mill-race and plan out the work for the day. As he walked along the ditch his men had dug, he noticed some particles of yellow mixed with the reddish earth. He picked them up and turned them over in his hand. Tiny grains, they were, not much bigger than a pin's head. Could they be gold? He did not know. He had never seen raw gold. But they might be. He looked further, found more, and sent an Indian to his cabin to fetch a tin plate. With this he washed out handfuls of dirt until he had gathered something like half an ounce of the stuff. Then he went about his business. Probably it would be better to say nothing to anybody until he knew more about it.

The next morning he was up early again and at the tail-race, looking eagerly around him. Yes, there were more of the yellow flakes, sluiced out and washed by the water of the day before. Was it gold, or was he all wrong? It could be fool's gold; Marshall knew about pyrites. Yet it seemed like the real thing; it was heavy, soft when he pounded the particles between two stones. This time he collected three ounces of the stuff, whatever it was. His mind was made up. He would go down to the Fort and find out what Sutter thought. But he was sure he knew. It was gold.

Sutter was astonished to see the dripping, excited Marshall in his office that afternoon. Only the day before he had sent him all the supplies he needed, bought from Elder Sam Brannan's store. What was he doing here?

He was even more surprised when Marshall said that he must talk to him alone, in his living quarters, not in the office where they might be interrupted. Marshall was an odd, moody man, but he was not usually as odd as this. Still, he might as well be humored. Sutter took him into his private suite of bedroom and parlor and asked him what was the matter.

Marshall said only that he must have two bowls of water and a pair of scales, and continuing to humor him Sutter got these. Then—but let Sutter himself tell it: "He drew out a rag from his pocket. Opening it carefully, he held it before me in his hand. It contained what might have been an ounce and a half of gold-dust—dust, flakes and grains. The biggest piece was not as large as a pea, and it varied from that down to less than a pinhead in size."

Sutter made this statement later. But at the moment he did not know what to think. All he knew was that the thing to do was to try out the particles Marshall had brought. Together the two men applied all the tests they could think of. They weighed the specimens and found them heavy enough for gold. They hammered them and saw that they did not splinter; they were malleable as gold was. With some acid from the apothecary shop they touched the grains; they did not tarnish or stain. In the end, they came to the only conclusion left to them. Marshall had discovered gold.

Now the warning rang clear and unmistakable, and Sutter heard it plainly. Marshall, nervous and feverish with excitement, would not wait; storm or no storm, he was heading back to the hills. Sutter let him go. He wanted time to think. Whose was this gold, after all? Not his. He had built a sawmill in a valley in the foot-hills, that was all. A sawmill and some vague timber rights were one thing; a gold mine was something else. How much gold was there? Did it lie scattered all through those mountain regions? If it did, then to whom did it belong? To anybody. It was anybody's gold. That was the trouble.

What Sutter could have done about it is anybody's guess. Probably nothing could have saved him, but he made one try. Gathering the Indians of the little valley of Coloma where Marshall had set the sawmill, he made a treaty with them. For shirts, handkerchiefs, shoes, and flour, he leased the twelve-mile square of the valley for three years, drew up a document vaguely mentioning the possibility of minerals in the soil and had it decorated with a flourish of Indian marks. There was no way to register such a lease. The days of Mexican grants were over, and nobody yet knew whether California would really be part of the United States or not. But it was all Sutter could do. He doubled the wages of the men at the mill site, cautioned them again to say nothing and rode back to the Fort. There he chose a messenger, one Charles Bennett, and sent him with the paper down to Monterey to Governor Mason. If the Governor would confirm the lease, Sutter had at any rate a chance to keep the discovery private.

But the Governor would not confirm. He said he could not. California was still a Mexican province, held by the United States as a conquest. No laws of the United States could apply to it, much less land laws which could go into effect only after a public survey. The Governor was sorry, but there it was.

The decision was a blow to Sutter. More clearly than ever, he saw that the gold spelled trouble for him. His workmen would leave; his grain would go unharvested, his timber unsawed. Strangers from San Francisco, from the Valley, even from the southern parts of California maybe, would squat on his land, steal his cattle, destroy his crops. He could see it all. His only chance was that his men would take their double pay and keep quiet as he had told them.

Men do not keep quiet about gold. Bennett, Sutter's messenger, talked. One of the workmen down from the sawmill told Sam Brannan in the store all about it when he settled his account in gold-dust. More gold trickled down to the Fort and more people heard about it. Now and then a workman would disappear. When that happened, Sutter simply noted in his records that the man had gone to the mountains to look for gold; it was the obvious thing.

Yet the news took a curiously long time to filter down to San Francisco, and still longer to gain public acknowledgment. It was the middle of March before Mr. B. R. Buckelew's *Californian* printed an item about gold, the first notice any newspaper took of a discovery that was to shake the world. Along with a brief bit on the quicksilver mines and an enthusiastic squib about "immense beds of copper ore" up near Clear Lake, Mr. Buckelew noted that gold had been discovered in the "newly made raceway of the Saw Mill recently erected by Captain Sutter on the American Fork." That the worthy editor hadn't the remotest notion of the true magnitude of the find is evidenced by his rather perfunctory additional note—taking more space than the notice of the actual discovery—to the effect that California "no doubt" was rich in mineral wealth and that there were "great chances here for the scientific capitalist." That was good, sound newspaper promotion, just as it has been ever since.

Though the news spread slowly, it spread. As April passed, the entries in Sutter's diary began to show how the word was getting around. The master of the Fort was making a determined effort to stay with his ranching, but fate was against him: "Finished shearing sheep. Ploughing. . . . Willis and Martin arrived from the Mts. with a great deal of gold which they brought to the store. . . . Rain all day, getting cargo from the launch. Men passing through to the gold mines." Then the significant note: "Brannan and Smith returned from the gold mines."

Sam Brannan, like the bear, had gone over the mountain to see what he could see. The Mormon Elder was a business man, and he kept his eyes and ears open. By the middle of May, he was satisfied. He had built a fine new store and stocked it well; down at Sutterville it was, right on the river and three miles or so below the Fort. Customers were what he needed, and now he knew how to bring them. He took Sutter's launch for San Francisco. When he landed there, he lost no time. Swinging above his head a bottle filled with glittering gold-dust for all to see, he shouted: "Gold! Gold from the American River!" All day he walked about the town telling his tale, showing his proof. And he sold the citizens what he had set out to sell them—gold, and Sam Brannan's store. On May 23rd Sutter's diary reads, "Hosts arriving by water and land for the Mts. Fine day." On May 24th he wrote, "Loaned to Mr. Harlan three horses and two saddles to go to the Mts." On May 25, 1848, the entry consisted of just six words: "Great hosts continue to the Mts." It was the last entry he made. The slow, easy-going, routine-filled days were gone. There was no time for diary-writing any more. The stampeding hosts, the trampling feet, had caught up with Sutter.

Now that the news was out, it spread with incredible rapidity. Four days after Sutter had made the last entry in his diary the San Francisco *Californian* suspended publication. Mr. Buckelew, the publisher, got out a curtailed issue on May 29th, not much more than a sheet of paper on which he noted plaintively: "The majority of our subscribers and many of our advertisers have closed their doors and places of business and left town.... The whole country, from San Francisco to Los Angeles and from the seashore to the Sierra Nevada, resounds with the sordid cry of Gold! *Gold!* GOLD! while the field is left half planted, the house half built, and everything neglected but the manufacture of shovels and pickaxes." Having thus done his duty by such subscribers and advertisers as remained to him, Mr. Buckelew went up to the mountains to have a look around on his own account. The record does not state whether he borrowed horses and saddles from Captain Sutter.

In Monterey it was just as bad. Walter Colton, alcalde of the town and a conscientious if somewhat imaginative chronicler, wrote: "The blacksmith dropped his hammer, the carpenter his plane, the mason his trowel, the baker his loaf, the tapster his bottle. All were off for the mines, some on horses, some in carts, some on crutches and one went on a litter. The fever has reached every servant in Monterey; none are to be trusted in their engagement beyond a week."

The soldiers, too, began to grumble and desert. Sailors, more expert in such matters as the taking of French leave, departed from their ships by the hundreds. One bold group from the United States sloop-of-war *Warren* calmly lowered one of the ship's boats and rowed ashore, led by no less a personage than the master-at-arms himself. That particular lot nearly missed its chance. Monterey looked so attractive that they all decided to have just one drink before heading for the hills to make their fortunes. The next morning found them asleep on the beach, in full sight of the ship they had so recently deserted. But they got away. Everybody was too busy making his own arrangements to bother about arresting a handful of men who were only trying their best to get rich.

21

The Volcano Diggings

The beautiful valley around Volcano was astonishingly rich.
Miners got as much as a hundred dollars in a single pan of

gravel. The camp flourished and became a city of imposing homes, stores and hotels. Some ninety millions in gold came out of Volcano before it played out in the middle sixties.

Everybody was busy, that is, but one old man in Monterey and another to the north, across the Bay from San Francisco. The old man in Monterey comes down anonymously from the past only because the scrivening alcalde, Colton, records his eccentricity as unique. That ancient would have nothing to do with the gold excitement, it seems, because he was convinced the whole thing was a hoax. Even when he was shown actual flakes and lumps of gold from the mines, he refused to believe. It was all hocus-pocus, he claimed, nothing but a sly Yankee invention got up to reconcile the people of California to the change of flag. The second old man knew well enough what had come to pass in California. He was Don Luis Peralta, owner of the great Rancho San Antonio, a man who had seen much of the world and grown wise in its ways. While other Californians joined the dervish-dance for gold, he called his sons about him and told them how he felt. There was gold in California, one could see that. But it was plain also that God had given this gold to the Americans. If He had intended the Spanish Californians to have it, He would have let them find it long before. Therefore it was the part of wisdom to let the Americans go after it. The fields of Rancho San Antonio were still their own to plant and to harvest. The Peralta family would find its gold in those fields, since all must eat while they live.

But these were only two men. The rest of California caught the gold hysteria as men have always caught it. By the first of June there were two thousand greenhorn miners digging and washing for thirty miles in both directions from Sutter's mill. Some of them paid Sutter for the privilege; for a time his priority was recognized. But as the excitement spread it was forgotten. So was his right to the land below the Fort on the river; miners camped everywhere along the banks, and before long it was taken for granted that they belonged there. By the end of July four thousand eager men had spread into the hills and fanned out, north and south. Sutter's empire was overrun, his flour-mill was deserted, his *vaqueros* had ridden off and left the herds to take care of themselves. Sutter himself tried mining for a while; with a group of hired Indians he prospected to the southward and worked a small area near what is now Sutter Creek, down in Amador County. But it was not his game. All the money he made seemed to be gone before he had so much as looked at it; there was the large debt to the Russians for Fort Ross, and there were all kinds of other expenses at his own Fort and farm. Besides, how could you run a ranch when workmen kept coming and going at such a rate, leaving the leather to rot in the vats, the grain to mildew in the fields? You couldn't. After a time, he gave up and retired to his place at Hock Farm up near the Feather River. It was the end for Sutter. He tried desperately to salvage something from his great properties, but it was no use. California had changed overnight. A frenzy had taken possession of the country, and Sutter and his kind were doomed.

There was no peace and quiet in California anywhere, for that matter. With amazing energy the Californians pushed their way up the rivers and creeks, dug into every nook and cranny of the hills. A transplanted Australian called "Yankee Jim" worked his way up the North Fork and one of the richest diggings in the region took its name from him. A Frenchman, one Claude Chana, found gold in a dry ravine farther down the stream; a settlement which was to become Auburn sprouted there in less than a week. To the south a man named Daylor discovered other waterless deposits which were called Old Dry Diggings. Afterward, for good and sufficient reasons, the name was changed to Hangtown; to-day it is Placerville.

Up on the Middle Fork of the American River a rich spot was named Spanish Bar; it eventually produced something over a million dollars' worth of coarse placer gold. Down in the Valley of the San Joaquin, Captain Charles Weber founded Tuleberg, changed its name to Stockton, saw his chance there and let his associates go ahead with their prospecting while he stayed to watch his real estate. It was Weber's men who really opened the Southern Mines, and it was evident almost immediately that the Stanislaus, Cosumnes, Mokelumne, and Tuolumne rivers and their tributary creeks were just as rich as those farther north. To-day's place-names show the penetration of the pioneers of 1848; Murphy's, Angel's, Jamestown, Carson Hill, Wood's Creek—all of them were settled in the summer and autumn of that year.

Some of those early diggings were immensely rich. One Californian reported that he had visited bars on the better creeks where each spoonful of red earth yielded as much as eight dollars in gold. On the Stanislaus, one John Sullivan took out $26,000 from his small claim before he moved on. They were always moving on, those first scratchers and washers; there might be another better bar just around the next bend. Why not? Major Reading, who moved as far north as the Trinity River, was said to have accumulated dust to the amount of $80,000 by the time a party of Oregon men coming down from the Willamette Valley drove him off because they did not approve of white men mining with Indian labor. The Yuba River bars were fabulously wealthy. In July a Sonoma company including Jasper O'Farrell and Jacob P. Leese, noted for their part in the Bear Flag trouble, took out $75,000 in three months. There was a report that a man on the Middle Yuba had loaded his saddle-bags with thirty pounds of gold from a claim four feet square in less than a month. Nor are these isolated or exceptional examples. There were hundreds who could make claims as good and substantiate them. No accurate check was ever made of this first year's outflow from the new El Dorado, but Bancroft estimates it at ten million dollars. Frank Soulé and his co-workers who put together the *Annals of San Francisco* quote an extreme figure of forty-eight million dollars. The official report was two million dollars. To-day's reader can take his choice. But there was no doubt about one thing. Gold had been found in quantity, and there was plenty more where it came from. If eastern newspapers would just realize what was going on, if Washington would only pay attention to the letters that Thomas O. Larkin, Consul in Monterey, had written to the government, there would be a real gold rush westward.

It took a little time, but at last the eastern seaboard woke up. By November the New York papers were full of the extraordinary news. Companies were formed, ships chartered and the mighty surge to California began. Horace Greeley declared in his best oracular manner, "We are on the brink of an Age of Gold!" and his New York *Tribune* opined that within the next four years the California fields would add "at least one thousand millions of dollars to the general aggregate of gold in circulation and use throughout the world." In case any one might be inclined to doubt this fantastical statement, the editorial writer added, "This is almost inevitable!" That clinched it.

As 1848 drew to its close, in New York, Philadelphia, Boston, and New Bedford ships put out to sea crowded to the limit for the perilous journey round the Horn. Some sailed for the Isthmus of Panama on the chance that there might be ships on the Pacific side ready to take passengers northward again to California, provided they got across through the jungles without dying of fever, snakebite, or Indians. If all went smoothly such fortunate men would be far ahead of their fellows who sailed the long way. Thousands more gathered along the Missouri waiting for winter to pass and the grass to show. Still other thousands headed south and west to follow the ancient Santa Fé trail. *"Oh, Susannah!"* they sang, and paraphrased the last line of the refrain, *"I'm off for*

25

Californy with my washbowl on my knee!" So far, the golden
hills of California had been mined by California's own people.
It had been a community affair, a matter of friends, fellow-
citizens, people who knew a good deal about each other even
if they didn't know each other's first names. Now it was to
be different. The Forty-Niners were on their way, a hundred
thousand strong. Not one but was sure he would strike it
rich! Not one but planned to go home just as soon as he had
made his pile. They did not know that they were to-morrow's
Californians, that they would build a new State, a new civilization. They were on their way, hopeful, enthusiastic, exultant, by land and by sea. *"Oh, Susannah, don't you cry for me!"*
They sang it to mothers and wives and sweethearts; they
sang it to themselves as they went, to keep up their spirits
through hurricanes and snow, through dust and heat and
drouth, through swamp and jungle. They sang it in full-
throated chorus, confidently, young men about to open the
oyster of the world: *"Oh, Susannah!"*—the brassy, nasal,
cock-sure, triumphal overture to Gold.

The northern Sierra passes were closed tight under a dozen
feet of snow; none could come that way in winter. A few
began to trickle in by the Santa Fé trail, across the southern
deserts and up through the little pueblo of Our Lady, Queen
of the Angels, which one day was to become Los Angeles.
But the dramatic entrance was reserved for those who had
been lucky enough to choose the sea. On February 28, 1849,
the steamship *California* stood through the Golden Gate to
the accompaniment of thunderous salutes ordered by Commodore Jones whose Pacific Naval Squadron was anchored
in the Bay. The first Forty-Niners had arrived. The curtain
was rung up. California's "early days" had begun.

1.

"Off to Californy..."

HIRAM PIERCE of Troy, New York, had a wife and seven children when the news of gold in California electrified the Atlantic seaboard.

He had done reasonably well in business, considering the fact that he had made his way from scratch. He owned a blacksmith shop, had served as city alderman (Russell Sage was on the board at the same time), had been president of the fire department and was an elder of the Second Presbyterian Church of Troy. He and his wife, Sarah Jane, honored God, did their best to bring up their children to be good citizens of their homespun up-state town. Perhaps Hiram worked too hard at his many tasks; certainly he gave more than a fair share of time to the church of which he was so devout a mem-

ber. At any rate, his health began to fail and his doctor suggested a long sea-voyage. In those early months of 1849 there
was only one sea-voyage in anybody's mind—the voyage to
California.

It may have been that Hiram Pierce secretly longed for adventure; his young manhood as apprentice to a farmer, helper
in a blacksmith shop, and finally owner of the forge, head of a
family and pillar of the church, can have left him little time
to indulge such tastes. Or perhaps he saw the plain Yankee
logic in combining the pursuit of health and wealth when one
could. Whatever his reasons, the bare fact remains: he joined
a mining company booked to sail from New York City on the
S.S. *Falcon,* 700 tons burthen, for San Francisco by way of
Panama. On the eighth of March, Hiram Pierce was off on the
greatest adventure of his life, an adventure shared in its essentials by tens of thousands more in that year. It was a diary-
keeping time; all sorts of people were overcome by a positive
passion for recording events and thoughts in careful, close-
written pages. Hiram was no exception. His journal is one
of the best records of the average Forty-Niner's experience
on the Isthmus trek.

The first leg of the journey, on the *Falcon,* went along very
nicely. They stopped briefly at Charleston to take on a few
more passengers; at Havana, where Mr. Pierce went ashore
to take a ride in an omnibus and to acquire somewhere the
information that "Moora Castel and the Fortifications" cost
thirty-eight million dollars; at New Orleans to take on coal and
still more passengers; and on the twentieth day disembarked
at Chagres on the Isthmus of Panama, where the party was
left to make its own bargain regarding ways and means of
crossing the Isthmus to the Pacific. As for the settlement of
Chagres itself, Mr. Pierce observed its squalid huts and mixed
Spanish, Indian, and Negro population and noted somewhat
dryly in his journal that the little town with its old Spanish

fort was "a romantic looking place & in dry weather passable." The weather was dry, and it seemed that things were going to go well enough; the members of the company were in the best of spirits as they made arrangements for a small boat, the *Orus,* to take them up river on the second leg of their journey to the West.

The little vessel performed its duty faithfully, while the party gaped at the strange scenery, the extravagant, lush growth, the curious trees and plants, and stared in fascination at the brilliant tropical birds that swooped and screeched about them. It was a new and different world they were entering, no doubt of that. Some of them wondered audibly about it. Things could happen in a wild land like this; a man couldn't be sure he was safe when there was no part of his own kind of civilization to put a finger on.

The *Orus,* small as she was, could negotiate only some seventeen miles of the Chagres River; after that it was shallow water cut up by rapids, and the company had to take to small boats. The captain helped them there, or they thought he did. After an hour or two of bargaining they arranged for five "bungas," flat-bottomed native boats poled upstream, sometimes dragged when the water was so shallow they scraped on the stones. Boatmen, so the captain told them, came to ten dollars a head for the trip up to the village of Gorgona whence all would have to make their way to the Pacific by land. It was not until later that they learned what the true wage was. The helpful captain had paid the standard wage of six dollars to each native; the extra four dollars was his "squeeze" for making the deal.

This part of the journey was much more difficult. Now the little company was closer to the strange, frightening new country they had entered. It is one thing to sit on the deck of a vessel, no matter how small, and quite another to be poled up river while you sit in the bottom of a boat, near enough to the water to trail your hand in it. The half-caste boatmen poled slowly, the air was heavy and full of odd scents, the heat was unbearably oppressive. Monkeys chattered in the trees; parrots and many kinds of water-fowl darted along the water's edge, dipping and shrieking. Alligators slid off mud banks, disappearing into the brown water with scarcely a ripple, and bubbles rose slowly through the slime, dispersing unpleasant smells as they burst. Mosquitoes plagued the travelers constantly. This was not at all like Troy, New York. It was not like what they had heard of California, either. That first night, the company slept under the trees. After conducting prayer, Hiram Pierce stood guard for the first four hours. In the morning he wrote in his diary, "I heard wild animals howl."

The second day real trouble began. Toward evening they reached the village of Gorgona, and there the boatmen refused to do more, saying that they had been hired to pole the boats, not to unload baggage. It was a matter of more pay, of course—pay and the persuasion of a pistol which Hiram Pierce "happened to have" in his pocket. It was not loaded, but the Indians did not know that. They brought the boxes and bags sullenly up the bank and then vanished with their boats. The next step was to bargain for the overland journey, twenty-four miles to Panama. Something had to be done, too, for the women of the party and for one sick man. They settled down to spend at least a day or two in Gorgona while the deal was made. In the meantime Mr. Pierce and some others went out to see what they could bring in for food. It was a curious assortment of meats that supplied the makeshift table under the tropic stars that first night. Hiram lists the bag in his diary: "Two wild Turkeys, one Monkey, one Anteater, some Pigeons and one Iguana." It was less than ever like Troy, New York.

Within three days the matter had been more or less settled.

For the sum of two hundred and fifty dollars a pack train was put together, two natives slung a hammock for Mrs. Newcomb, who had fallen ill, and the other two women and the sick man were perched on mules. While this sorry cavalcade started for Panama, the rest set out behind it on foot through the jungles.

The trip was hard, even for the strongest. Moreover, several of the members were confessing to headaches and general malaise. Over that kind of terrain it was impossible for them to walk the full twenty-four miles without a stop. Insects bit them, the sun struck them down, they were drenched in sweat, bone-weary, bone-chilled after sundown. Once they passed an American who had made himself a little camp by a running stream. When they went over to chat with him they found out why he was there. Maybe there was gold in the California hills, maybe not. Meanwhile he was content to make his profit where he was. He was selling coffee to all who chanced to go by; the price was one shilling for a small cup. Hiram Pierce and a few others bought coffee, for they needed the stimulant.

There was no real rest that night, either. One man shot a "tiger" near the camp; another man fell sick in the night. The jungle was alive with the cries of birds and beasts. Before sunrise, the party shook itself together and began the march again. At eight in the morning, half dead with fatigue, they arrived in Panama where they had expected to find a ship to take them at last to California. What they found was a ragged, malarial, cholera-ridden crowd of nearly two thousand fellow-adventurers who had been waiting for weeks in the same vain hope.

Hiram Pierce and his company waited thirty-five days before they could get passage in any kind of vessel. At first, being a man of inquiring disposition and lively intelligence even if his spelling was done on an original model, Hiram busied himself with learning a few words of Spanish, looking at religious processions, discovering how the natives lived. He heard that one of the priests had lost five hundred dollars betting on a cock-fight the week before, and records the fact rather primly in his journal. But there was soon too much to do to be examining into the lives and habits of the Panamanians. Everywhere around him men shook with chills and burned with fever. News came that the ship *Crescent City* had arrived at Chagres with several cases of cholera aboard, and the next day a fresh batch of arrivals struggled through the jungles to bring word that among the passengers on the *Colonel Stanton,* out of New Orleans, there had been seven deaths from the dread disease before they had made Chagres. More men came down with strange fevers every day; Hiram notes that he himself felt "weak & unwell," that he had severe headaches, and that it was depressing to see the frequency with which Americans were dying. Nevertheless he hustled around, nursing, cooking, scouting for fresh fruit to feed his patients, doing his best to play his part in the venture. For the first time, however, he began to doubt the wisdom of the enterprise on which he had so hastily embarked. On the second Sunday, a Congregational minister preached from the text, "The wages of sin is death." Hiram does not write it down in so many words, but clearly it was his opinion that a Presbyterian divine would have had more tact under the circumstances. The sermon, though, had its effect. That night Hiram noted in his diary: "Whatever may be the result of this enterprise, I am satisfide there is more Folley in this world than I supposed before leaving home."

Still no ships arrived, and Panama was growing more and more choked every day. Very sensibly Hiram swam in the Pacific when he could, avoided walking about in the heat of the day, wrote letters, and faithfully kept up his journal. It did not encourage him to hear that a group of Americans had got into a fight with some natives, and that two had been stabbed to death. Neither was it pleasant to learn what had happened to another party of gold-seekers who had grown so impatient with the delay that they had bought an old life-boat, calked and painted it, and set out in their ignorance to sail the frail cockle-shell all the way to California. These foolish adventurers had been out two months, soaked to the skin most of the time, and had gained a point some three hundred miles above Acapulco, Mexico, but had been forced back to that harbor by storms. There they had taken passage on a French vessel which dragged her anchor before leaving port and was driven on the rocks. Twenty of the company had been lost in the disaster. Once, when some more men from York State had come into Panama, there was "an evening of good singing," and Hiram's spirits rose a trifle. But sickness spread, men continued to die, the "Chagres fever" killed two more of the original *Falcon* company, and the church bells began to get on Hiram's nerves. "They jingle and jangle incessantly," he writes with some bitterness, "continually there is the sound of hammering kept up on a cracked Bell, which sounds much like work on a Boiler." It would not have been long before his nerves let him down entirely, but one morning he awoke to find the whole city of Panama in a ferment. Two ships had arrived at sunrise. Still better, another anchored during the day. Now things would go well again. One or two members of the company even attempted a feeble, *"Oh, Susannah!"* By Wednesday, May 9th, Hiram Pierce and his party had arranged for passage, boarded their ship, and were headed for the open sea. At last they were going to get to California.

Whether they would have started at all, if they had known what that voyage was to be like, is a question Mr. Pierce himself does not care to answer, though his journal hints that he at least might have been only too glad to point back for Chagres and home. They did not know, of course. It seemed

33

only that they were finally free of this poisonous land and were practically in the gold fields.

It was not at all like that.

The ship was "wretched dirty," overcrowded and not too well sailed. Food was even worse than they had been able to forage in Panama; Pierce writes:

Our fare for Breckfast, coffey, hard bread and molasses. For Dinner, pork, Corned Beef & beans or rice some times. Supper, Bread and Sugar. Butter is served, but the sight is sufficient without the Smell. Meals are taken in Hand when we can & when we cannot we go down on the deck.... Our mode of living is truly brutish. For meals we form ourselves in two lines when we can, on that small part of the Deck that is clear. A man passes through with the Coffey. Another with the Sugar. Another with a basket of Bread. Another with a pan of boiled Meat. Another with a bottle of vinegar and one of Molasses & then the grabbing commences. We ketch a piece of Meat with the fingers & crowd like a lot of Swine. The ship perhaps so careened that you will need to hold on or stagger & pitch like a Drunken man. Many behave so swineish that I prefer to stay away unless driven to it by hunger.

There was more sickness, too, though the ship's doctor was of little help, since he drank whisky most of the time instead of eating. Pierce writes:

The Dr. got beastly drunk & got down betweene Decks & the passengers were determined to get him out from there. So they got a rope round him & with a great heveing hoisted him on deck, & took him to his hammoc & lashed him in. His hammoc was slung verry high, & in the night he got out & was found suspended by his feet. The same worthy took a dose of Medicine to a patient & haveing a bone in his hand knawing, he took the Medicine & gave the bone to the patient.

Once there was a storm in which the ship lay for thirty hours at the mercy of the waves:

To see the fury of the Ocean, hissing, boiling and heaveing like a Cauldron, the roar of its waters & of the tempest & the storm, the roar of the wind through the rigging & pitching of the ship combined to make a Sene truly appauling. For my part, in the fore part of the storm I felt

34

to look up to my Heavenly Father & commit to Him my Family & my Soul & bid adieu to the Senes of Earth, but when I saw the ability of the Ship to ride it, I thought we should be Saved.

Conscientiously, Hiram adds "Lat. 16:30 Long. 116."

By that time they had spent two months at sea and were still a thousand miles from San Francisco. There was water for twelve days, and the ship's captain estimated that it would take another fifteen to complete the run. It may have been the stale water or it may have been badly cooked pork that did it, but Hiram and his companions began to suffer from a stomach complaint that culminated in a "severe Cholic pain & a Diarea discharging a bloody Slime with severe Headache." Even though the doctor stayed sober long enough to prescribe pills of opium and camphor from the ship's medicine chest, one member of the party succumbed. Mr. Pierce's account of the event is well worth preserving here:

This morning at 6 Mr. Bristol expired. Not withstanding it is the blasting of all his worldly hopes & prospects, yet in view of his sufferings it seemed a sweet releaf. His request was that his boddy might be sent home & we comenced to make preperations accordingly. We ascertained that spirits could be obtained at $2 per gallon. We got a cask of the Captain. It would take about 40 gallons. A meeting of the passengers was called & it appointed a committy composed of the Phisicians aboard to concider & report the best mode of preservation. They reported it could best be done in spirits, & then it was decided by the Surgeon of the Ship & other Phisicians that his heart & vitals be taken out, otherwise it would burst the Cask. To this his friends objected & a majority of our company voted against opening him, & that rather than have him cut to pieces we would bury him in the deep. So a committy was appointed to make the necessary preperations, & at 6 p.m. he was brought to the waist of the Ship, sewed up in canvas with his face exposed, while the English Service was gone through in a Solom manner, after which all was sewed up & he was commited to the deep. The Ship passed on & in one moment he was hid from mortal eyes until the morning of the resurrection. The sene was a Solom one & many eyes were sufused with Tears. Thus perished one of our most active & usefull members before we had reached the field of operation. It took place in Lat 33.33. Long. 130.28.

35

Shasta, Shasta County, California, 1856

Shasta was as rip-roaring a camp as any the mines ever boasted. It was a transfer point where the wagon road stopped and

transport from there northward and westward to Weaverville
was a matter of packtrain.

The burial of Mr. Bristol was the last untoward incident of the voyage. In another ten days they were off the entrance to San Francisco harbor, though it was too foggy to attempt an entrance. But at noon on July 26th the fog cleared and the little band of Argonauts from Troy saw their promised land. It took the captain two hours to find a good anchorage among the 175 ships Pierce counted in the bay. The members of the little company were ill, weary, downcast, and homesick, but their drinking water had not quite run out, and they had made California at last.

The Isthmus was somewhat easier after those enterprising gentlemen, Aspinwall and Law, worked out their mule-transport route, but it was no less expensive, and the ships were still incredibly crowded. In the meantime the passage around Cape Horn had its advocates, particularly among European Argonauts to whom the news of gold began to get through. There was less risk of dying from malaria, snakebite or "Chagres fever," to be sure, but the passengers on the Horn voyage took their chances of wind and weather and the far longer time at sea. There was the stop at Rio, too, where yellow fever sometimes made its way aboard mysteriously, and the long months on the water took their natural toll. Sometimes ships would slip through the Golden Gate loaded with men and woman who had come by way of the Sandwich Islands. Small coastwise vessels brought South American Argonauts by the hundreds. It didn't make much difference where they came from; to the American miner they were all Chileños—that is, unless they were Mexicans. The men from "the States" knew about Mexicans; after all there had been a Mexican War only a few short months before. If they didn't know a Mexican when they saw one, there were plenty of ex-soldiers to tell them, men who had been mustered out after the Treaty of Guadalupe Hidalgo and had come north to California instead of going back to the Atlantic seaboard or the Missouri hills and valleys. The widely known Stevenson Regiment, made up chiefly of New Yorkers, sent many an adventurer to California months before the rush began. But though these various methods of reaching the diggings accounted for large numbers, most Americans still came by the two main routes—the Isthmus and the plains.

The plains crossing had its special features, its own trials, hardships and dangers; it was different from the voyage by sea, but it was no less difficult. Sometimes the covered wagons rolled southward, by way of the old Santa Fé Trail; sometimes the caravaneers chose the more northerly way, risking the inhospitable desert that was a prelude to the great Sierra wall. Relatively few, at first, came by way of Oregon, though occasionally tales of the fine land to be had in the northwest changed the minds of men who were farmers long before the notion of gold entered their heads. Whichever route they chose by land, there were experiences shared by all, common adventures and perils and difficulties. And they kept journals, too, those land-voyagers, though they had less time for it than those who came by sea. There was, for instance, Mrs. Royce, mother of Josiah Royce who became one of America's great philosophers and educators.

Sarah Eleanor Royce and her young husband had already broken ties with their eastern home when they heard the story of gold; they had come west into Iowa in their vague, undefined search for the "something better" that was moving all America so strongly in those restless days. Now a new Never-Never Land beckoned them still farther to the west. The curious mingling of romanticism and materialism that colored the current American dream had its way with them, too, and all unconscious of what drew them into the stream, they

37

merged with the great human river that began to flow across the plains. In the late spring of 1849 they loaded their wagon with provisions, hitched their three yoke of oxen, brought along two cows whose milk was to feed the one child they then had, and headed for Council Bluffs which was to be their jumping-off place for the journey proper. Like thousands of other hopeful pioneers, they knew nothing of where they were going, were utterly without experience in the technic of camp life, had little else but the spirit of adventure to carry them through. Perhaps the Royces were the least bit better prepared; they had read Frémont's *Travels,* and carried a copy of the book with them. Somehow they would get there. They were sure of that.

Mrs. Royce's diary was a very sketchy affair, broken and desultory, interrupted by the thousand and one exigencies of the hazardous journey. But she was an intelligent woman, and thirty years later when her California-born son, then a young lecturer in philosophy at Harvard, asked her to write for him an account of the trip across the plains, she produced the classic manuscript on which Josiah based his *California.* A record of hardship and travail and high courage, it is also a reflection of a point of view, a mirror held up to the America which produced the pioneer generation. It is significant that Josiah Royce gave his *California* the subtitle, *A Study of American Character.* Mrs. Royce, a devout woman whose simple religious faith was her greatest support and comfort all the way, reflects the best in the American character of the time. Nor was it a rare best; many thousands of women—and men too—had been molded as she was, had grown to maturity under the same code of faith made manifest in works. If Sarah Royce was more the mystic than some, had a better mind than many, she was no less typical of thousands who moved West to make the new America. Her journey was theirs, and her story is in essence theirs as well.

38

The Missouri, swollen with the rains of that wet spring of Forty-Nine, was the physical and spiritual point of departure for the strange new land that held the Royces' hopes. It took the plodding oxen a solid month to reach the little town of Council Bluffs, perched above the river, a month in which every day brought a new lesson in the kind of life they would have to lead on their great adventure. Late storms lashed at the canvas covering of their home on wheels, the soft ground caught and held their heavy wagon. "I cooked as well as I could by a log fire in a strong north-east blow," wrote Mrs. Royce as late as May 3rd. She was learning how to "make do," as all pioneer women must. Sometimes they traveled no more than three miles in a whole day and camped exhausted after hours of levering the hubs out of the mud, cutting brush, even trees, to form a corduroy over which the wagon might pass when the ground was swampy. After a week or so they had company; at Cedar River they fell in with three other wagons, all bound for California. No one needed to be told the value of coöperation on that hard trail; every one welcomed additions to the train. Together, in a community of interest that has rarely been so strongly felt since, the travelers made their way across streams, uniting teams to save time, helping each other in a hundred ways, joining for Sabbath services, keeping up each other's spirits. Wrote Mrs. Royce with sound common sense, "It soon became plain that the hard facts of this pilgrimage would require patience, energy, and courage." She was a woman who could look hard facts in the face, meeting them with inexhaustible courage and patience, never letting her husband see that she was afraid. She was also a shrewd analyst of her own emotions; she could recognize and note the "mildly exultant feeling which comes from having kept silent through a cowardly fit, and finding the fit gone off."

It was well that she could, for there was more to discourage the travelers than the physical difficulties they were meeting.

Already the weaker spirits among those ahead were turning back, and with them came rumors, stories that the dreaded cholera was raging among the emigrants camped at Council Bluffs, that supplies were running out, and that it was impossible to replenish stores of provisions at the Missouri, that such an immense number had already passed through that the grass was all eaten up and no more animals could live on the great plains. "All this we heard," writes Sarah Royce, "and all this we talked over. But still we went on." Then at last they came to Council Bluffs and the thousands of gold-seekers gathered there waiting their chance to cross the river. A ferry was working but it could not begin to accommodate the anxious thousands. The Royces had to take their turn with the rest.

Mrs. Royce's description of this great temporary "city of wagons," as she called it, is interesting for its vivid picture of the thronged and busy river-banks, ant-heaps of bustling, impatient humanity anxious to be about its business and fidgety at the delay. But its chief value for to-day's reader lies in its correction of one of the most popular conceptions concerning the gold-rush. It is true that a little later the gold fields drew to them all kinds of rascally adventurers from the four corners of the earth, the scum of the continents. But the early Forty-Niners were not of this stamp, or at any rate most of them were not. Good, solid citizens they were, anxious to better themselves, not perhaps quite aware of the toil and trouble they would encounter before they were done, many of them poorly equipped by nature for the hard struggle they were facing, but sound, respectable Americans for all that. Indeed, what first struck the observant Mrs. Royce was the absence of quarreling and strife. She writes:

Notwithstanding the crowd of people, most of them strangers to each other, thrown together in such new and inconvenient circumstances, with much to try patience—and all standing necessarily more or less in the position of rivals for the local conveniences which campers so soon learn to look for and prize—still the utmost quiet and good humor . . . prevailed. The great majority of the crowd were men, generally working men of ordinary intelligence, farmers and mechanics accustomed to the comforts and amenities of domestic life, and most of them evidently intending to carry more or less of these agreeable things with them across the plains. Occasionally these men were accompanied by wife and children, and their wagons were easily distinguished by the greater number of conveniences and household articles they carried, which, here, in this time of prolonged camping, were often, many of them, disposed about the outside of the wagon in a homelike way. And where bushes, trees or logs formed partial enclosures, a kitchen or sitting-room quite naturally suggested itself to a feminine heart, yearning for home.

A great section of America was on the move, taking along its bureaus, its pots and pans, its seedlings and its planting-corn, its crayon enlargements, too, and its small mementos of home with which to make a new kind of dwelling in a new kind of land. Adventurers they were, these people, but of the same pioneer strain that had followed the Kentucky Trace, that had moved into the valleys of the Cumberland and on to the plains of Indiana and Iowa a generation before. With their Bibles and their banjos they kept back the fears of the unknown that must have beset them, and while the womenfolk sat in the still wagons and found comfort in the Book of Job, the men gathered by fires down near the river and sang:

> "For seven long years I courted Nancy
> *Hi-oh, the rolling river!*
> She would not have me for a lover,
> *I'm bound away for the wild Miz-zou-rye!"*

or perhaps the rousing wagon-song, a favorite of the time,

> "Oh, don't you remember sweet Betsy from Pike,
> Who crossed the big mountains with her lover, Ike,
> With two yoke of cattle, a large yellow dog,
> A tall Shanghai rooster and one spotted hog?

41

Saying good-bye Pike County
Farewell for a while,
We'll come back again
When we've panned out our pile!"

or, if they were in an especially sanguine mood,

"We've formed our band, we are all well manned,
To journey afar to the promised land;
The golden ore is rich in store
On the banks of the Sacramento shore.
Then ho, boys, ho! For California, O!
There's plenty of gold, so I've been told,
On the banks of the Sacramento!"

They knew they were facing peculiar dangers, many that they had heard about and others that they could not imagine. But the spirit of the frontier was in them, the urge to go forward, to pass beyond the borders of to-day into a new to-morrow. What they would find they didn't know, but they knew they were not afraid and they knew that they could learn.

All of them learned much while waiting for the ferry at Council Bluffs, that "fag-end of the American continent" as Mrs. Royce calls it.

From stragglers they discovered that this was truly an outpost of empire, that they would see no house again until they came to Fort Laramie, miles to the west, and after that not until they reached the Mormon settlement at Salt Lake City in Utah. They discovered, if they had not realized it earlier, that they were going almost immediately into Indian country; in fact, Council Bluffs itself was infested with Indians who begged and stole, swarming about the campers, refusing to be driven off by anything less than physical violence. They were told that the only way for a company to get along was to elect a leader, a "Captain," and to draw up a set of rules and by-laws for their governance. In the Royces' company a few extra-devout souls tried to include in the by-laws a provision that every Sunday should be a day of rest, but there were enough practical men to outvote them; the rules mentioned merely that there was a general assent to camping on Sundays when the necessities and dangers of the way did not demand steady traveling. As a matter of fact, the rule was tested almost as soon as it was made. The season was well advanced, and it was imperative for their own sakes that their small company keep as close as possible to the larger groups that had preceded them. So it happened that they set out on a Sunday, the tenth of June, 1849, on the journey from which, notes Mrs. Royce, "we all knew from that hour there was not the least chance of turning back."

Their first bad moment came within a week or two, when their wagon train was suddenly surrounded by what seemed to be hundreds of Indians. On the Mormon Trail which followed along the north side of the Platte to Fort Laramie, they were in the midst of the plains country where the Indians followed the herds of bison over the grasslands. Emigrants here might meet many tribes; there were bands of Poncas, Sioux, Cheyennes, Pawnees constantly on the move everywhere on the plains. When these were not actively hostile they were ready to bully travelers who might be frightened by paint and feathers. Sometimes, too, they were ready to kill. Fortunately for the little cavalcade, these first dark marauders that lined the trail were after money, not scalps. From the traders the Indian had learned the white man's tricks, and now they were demanding toll from this latest emigrant train to pass through their country. So much per head, or the train would have to turn back. It did not come to a battle. At their Captain's order, the men of the company showed their arms and the command to move was given. It may have been touch and go for a few minutes; the Indians sat their wiry ponies sullenly, ready for some incident which might bring on a fight. But the drivers shouted to their oxen, none of the whites was foolish enough to fire a shot, and the wagon train moved slowly on out of sight of its first hostile Indians.

There were other enemies, too, and the first point of attack was in the Royces' own wagon. An elderly man riding with them complained of intense pain and sickness and was soon unable to sit up. When convulsions seized him, the train was halted, and the Captain administered some home remedies which helped very little. There was a large company ahead not more than a mile or two, at the forks of the Elkhorn River, and a rider galloped forward to bring back the doctor they knew was with that group. But the physician could do nothing. It was Asiatic cholera, and the old man died in a few hours. That meant disinfecting the wagon, and, of course, a halt while the job was done. With her small daughter Mary wrapped in a blanket on the only cot available, Mrs. Royce sat the night through, hoping and praying that their little family had not been infected. They were not, though two more of the company died within the next three days, and Mrs. Royce prayed anew: "I poured out my heart to God in the full assurance that He would not afflict us beyond our strength to bear.... I said from my heart, 'Thy will be done.' Then peace took possession of my soul and in spite of threatening ills, I felt strong for duty and endurance."

Mrs. Royce needed her strength many times in the long four months of the journey. Sometimes Fate seemed to pursue them all with a special malignancy. One night when they had camped, with wagons in a circle as plainsmen had taught them and the cattle all inside this temporary corral, a thunder-storm broke and frightened the beasts into a concerted rush toward one side, breaking the wagon-wall. The cattle were rounded up safely enough, but three wagons had had their wheels smashed, and the camp was fifty miles from timber. Hard necessity suggested ways and means. There was a blacksmith in the company, and the wheels were eventually patched up. But it meant a loss of two days, and time was precious.

There were storms in plenty that summer to wet the trail and hold back the wagons. There was sickness in the natural course of things; now and then other bands of roaming Indians would give them a fright, though none actually molested them. For a time the Royces were almost alone, for the company had to be divided, most of the men ranging up likely valleys and creeks with the cattle in order to find feed away from the trail where the animals of earlier emigrants had cropped the ground clean for miles. For some weeks the group consisted of two men, two women, and four small children; the rest of the men were sometimes ahead, sometimes behind with the beasts, but always separated from their companions. Yet they managed to make their way, mile by slow mile, and early in August they reached the South Pass of the Rockies, and the point at which they passed from the Atlantic to the Pacific slope. Mrs. Royce, who knew her Bible, records her irresistible desire to mark the spot, her Ebenezer, with a small monument; nothing any one else would see or recognize, but a little private token of her thanks that she and her family had safely come this far. But in that desert spot there was no stone, no pebble, not even a stick or a bush or tree within sight. She had to be content with a small prayer of gratitude, made quickly before her friends went on too far for her to catch up.

Now they were finding a new kind of travel. This high northern end of the great Colorado Valley was almost entirely desert. There were springs, but many of them were so strong with alkali as to be poisonous, and the grass near them was so saturated as to be useless for feed. One of their oxen died there, and the indomitable little company had to yoke up and travel all night in order to get to safer feed and water. At Fort Bridger they were forced to make a decision. There was

the Fort Hall route available, a fairly safe course that skirted
the desert country west of the Salt Lake. But that meant more
miles to travel, and there were all too few weeks before the
snow would begin to fly. The steep ranges of the Sierra still
lay ahead, and every one knew the story of the Donner Party
that had been caught in the terrible snow on those rocky
heights. There was only one choice possible after all. They
would take the desert route. Even though at Salt Lake City,
where they stopped to rest a few days, they were told of still
another more southerly route, they did not feel they could
chance it. They knew they had to make time, and they stuck to
their original plan to follow the trail from the Great Salt Lake
west by way of the Humboldt and the Carson desert to the
Sierra. Though the Mormon fathers shook their heads and
warned them they would perish, on August 30th the Royces set
out. Now the group was whittled down to four; one man,
beyond middle age and not well, was anxious to go straight
through and agreed to join forces with the family. They had a
"guide book" consisting of two sheets of note-paper sewed
together and lettered on the first page, "Best Guide to the
Gold Mines: 816 Miles." There was no printing-press in Salt
Lake City then, and the instructions were written in longhand.
Worse, it was precise about the trail only as far as the sink of
the Humboldt. After that, the directions grew less and less
definite. There was a new track, supposed to have been made
the previous autumn, which "might be better." The travelers
might meet a train of Mormons which should be returning
about that time; if they did, these Mormons would tell them
about the trail over which they had just come. With this kind
of vague information they set out on the most perilous stage
of their journey, with their single wagon, three yoke of oxen,
and no more provisions than would see them barely across the
Sierra, if they made it in reasonably good time.

Amazingly they made it, though they were virtually the last

party of the overland Forty-Niners to get through. Once they fell in with two young men, scarcely more than boys, who helped them hunt game, though they brought in less meat than would balance the flour and other supplies they asked for. Once the travelers were surrounded by a band of the despised Digger Indians of the dry central basin, a wretched lot and cowardly, but in this case armed with rifles. It was another ticklish situation, but Mr. Royce bluffed them and got through. They met their Mormon party and received exact and complicated directions which did not work out as well as it seemed they should. Somewhere some one went wrong, for where there was supposed to be water and feed there was neither, only sand and sage-brush. Mrs. Royce's account of those desperate days is a record of amazing fortitude and patience. Because the last of the fodder had been fed to the oxen and it was necessary to conserve all their strength, only the children rode. Mrs. Royce walked in the lead, sometimes even ahead of the team in her anxiety to get forward, to find the meadow for which they were searching, the spring without which none would live very long. "My imagination acted intensely," she writes. "I seemed to see Hagar in the wilderness, walking wearily away from her fainting child among the dried up bushes and seating herself in the hot sand, and when my little one, from the wagon behind me, called out 'Mamma, I want a drink' I stopped, gave her some water, noted that there were but a few swallows left, then mechanically pressed onward again, alone, repeating over and over the words, 'Let me not see the death of the child.' "

Sarah Royce did not have to see her child die. They found their grass and water at last, and just in time. But she had known they would. Only a few hours earlier they had passed a spot where a fire left by some Indians or emigrants had burned a wide circle in the brush. Smoke was still curling up here and there, but no fire was visible when Sarah Royce was given her sign from Heaven. "Suddenly just before me, to my

47

right," she records, "a bright flame sprang up at the foot of a small bush, ran rapidly up it, leaped from one little branch to another, till all, for a few seconds, were ablaze together, then went out, leaving nothing but a few ashes and a little smoldering trunk. It was a small incident, easily accounted for, but to my then over-wrought fancy it made more vivid the illusion of being a wanderer in a far off, old-time desert, and myself witnessing a wonderful phenomenon. For a few moments I stood with bowed head worshiping the God of Horeb, and I was strengthened thereby." It was this message from her burning bush that made Sarah Royce sure they would be saved. A mystic by nature, she was an even more devout mystic from that time forward.

Other trials were ahead of them. More than once they passed the dead bodies of cattle, sometimes wagons abandoned by emigrants who had given up the fight and made their way back. At one such scene were several beautifully finished trunks of various sizes standing open among the deserted wagons, their contents strewn about them. In one was a little book, bound in cloth and illustrated with a number of small engravings, a story called *Little Ella*. Mrs. Royce took it. Many years afterward she was pleased to recall that her Mary and many another child had been enthralled by its pages. By the time they reached the foot-hills that marked the Sierra they must still conquer, it was almost the middle of October, dangerously late in the year for even the most experienced hand to tackle the mountain passes. Luckily for them, the Government had sent out relief companies of experienced mountain men to help late emigrants over the Sierra, and the Royces fell in with one such party, leading two mules in case they were needed. Even with the help of these trained men, each day was a long and weary struggle. The precipitous passes seemed to fight back at the traveler, to challenge him to come through. Writes Mrs. Royce:

The men had hard work to drive the cattle and mules over the boulders at the frequent stream-crossings and in between the great masses of rock where the trail sometimes almost disappeared. As the canyon narrowed, the rocky walls towered nearly perpendicular, hun dreds of feet; and seemed in some places almost to meet above our heads. At some crossings it was well nigh impossible to keep the trail, so in numerable were the boulders, and the scraggy bushes so hid the coming-out place. The days were shortening fast, and in this deep gulch darkness was beginning to come on early. The animals became restive with the roughness of the way, and it was hard work to keep them from rushing into a narrow ravine that occasionally opened, or up one of the steep trails which appeared now and then, suggesting unpleasant ideas of Indians and wild beasts.

With the help of the government guides they gained the summit in seven days. On the last night before they were to reach the high point they slept within a few yards of snow which lay in a ravine; the water froze in their pans not far from the fire. But the morning was bright and sunny, and Sarah Royce, at least, exulted in their success.

On that day, the blessed 19th of October, [she writes] we were to cross the highest ridge, view our promised land and begin our descent into warmth and safety. So, without flinching I faced steeps still steeper than yesterday's; I even laughed in my little one's upturned face, as she lay back against my arm while I leaned forward almost to the neck of my mule, tugging up the hardest places. I had purposely hastened, that morning, to start ahead of the rest; and not far from noon I was rewarded by coming out, in advance of all the others, on a rocky height whence I looked *down,* far over constantly descending hills, to where a soft haze sent up a warm, rosy glow that seemed to me a smile of welcome; while beyond, occasional faint outlines of other mountains appeared; and I knew I was looking across the Sacramento Valley!

It seemed like a brutal bit of irony when two nights later their little camp was attacked by Indians in the middle of the night. But the guards frightened off the savages before much harm was done. One man was wounded by an arrow, though not badly, and no one else was even scratched. In another three

49

Weaverville, Trinity County, California, 1856
Weaverville was the most isolated of the mining towns and
thus became self-sufficient. In addition to its several
banks, hospital, three newspapers, two theaters and Republican

and Democratic Clubs, it had a Lyceum which sponsored debates
and similar intellectual get-togethers for those preferring
to stay away from its numerous "fandango halls."

days they reached their first mining settlement, a huddle of a few tents called Pleasant Valley. Slightly farther on was Weaver Creek and on its banks a camp Mrs. Royce calls "Weaverville." It was actually named for the same Captain Weber who was later to found the city of Stockton, but some tongue had corrupted his name to "Weaver" and the misnomer stuck. "Weaverville" or Weberville, it was a haven of relief for the Royces who pitched their tent, gathered their goods about them, and once more began to feel that they had a home. Four days later it rained heavily, and a Californian told them the significance of the storm. What it meant was that the mountain passes over which they had just come were now solidly blocked with snow. There would be no more Forty-Niners over the mountains.

By ship and Isthmus, around the Horn, by the southerly Santa Fé Trail or across the plains, the journey was an undertaking to be entered upon in grim earnest, as those knew who arrived at length in the gold fields. Yet the stories that filtered back to the east coast did not discourage the Forty-Niners. More wanted to go than the ships would accommodate; the parade of wagons on the transcontinental trails did not diminish in that year until the most reckless fortune-hunter knew that there was no chance to beat the snow. Perhaps it was this extraordinary eagerness on the part of the populace that led Mr. Rufus Porter, Editor of the *Scientific American,* to launch a scheme he had been mulling over for some years.

This astonishing proposal was no less than a plan to fly passengers to the gold diggings, and Mr. Porter put it forward for public consideration in a prospectus grandly entitled, "Aerial Navigation: The Practicability of Traveling Pleasantly and Safely from New York to California in Three Days." A subtitle made it plain that the scheme was "Fully Demonstrated" in the prospectus, and that the reader might find between its covers a description of a perfect Aërial Locomotive, together with careful estimates of its capacity, speed, and cost of construction.

Some of the details of this lighter-than-air California Locomotive are worth quoting. Its total weight was worked out by the ingenious Mr. Porter at 14,000 pounds. It would require 20,000 feet of spruce rods which would form the framework of a spindle-shaped bag that was to be covered with 8,000 yards of prepared cloth to hold the gas. Something like 12,000 feet of "cast steel" wire would suspend the passenger saloon, which was to be constructed of thin boards and painted cloth. The whole would be propelled by steam engines capable, Mr. Porter declared, of driving the machine at a speed estimated at 100 miles per hour. As for safety, though it was to be inflated with hydrogen, the bag would nevertheless be perfectly protected against lightning because of the many steel wires. However, passengers would have added protection; the prospectus noted that "It may sometimes be requisite to throw out one end of a small copper wire to earth, to discharge electricity from the machine."

The inventor had thought about storms, too. "In case of the approach of a real tornado," the brochure explained, "the locomotive may either rise above it, or a grapple may be thrown out by which the machine may be brought to safe moorings."

The cost? Mr. Porter believed he could manufacture his Locomotive for $1,750. The prospectus adds that "If the engine is omitted, the cost will be $850 less," which is a trifle puzzling. Perhaps Mr. Porter counted on his passengers taking turns at a crank. In any event, he came down frankly to brass tacks in the matter of expenses. The fare to California was set at a flat $200, take it or leave it. There would be only one exception—the grand trial trip on which no more than 300 passengers would be taken at a reduced rate of $50 each, for advertising purposes.

What became of Editor Porter's scheme? Despite the fact that more than 200 persons were advertised as having put up their money for tickets, the Porter Locomotive never flew. Indeed, there is no record to show that it was ever built. It may be that "Sherwood's Pocket Guide to California" helped to kill the enterprise. Wrote Mr. Sherwood, after outlining the Porter plan with his tongue very obviously in his cheek, "We advise our readers to *look out* for the fast line!" Or perhaps some professor of the physical sciences showed Mr. Porter the errors in his aërodynamics, with especial reference to his failure to estimate correctly the resistance to be encountered from the passage of his craft through the air. Many years later, an American naval officer commented that, take it all in all, Mr. Porter might have done worse. But the little matter of air-resistance, together with the traditional "pounds per shaft horse-power" problem, which still worries the aircraft designer, were too much for him. His eager passengers made their way to the diggings by ship or across the plains, or else they changed their minds and stayed at home. Some of them may have consoled themselves by thinking of the day when Mr. Porter's splendid dream might come true, and by reading over again the closing rhetorical flight of the editor-promotor-inventor's appeal for clients. "Suppose," wrote Mr. Porter, (and it does not sound so silly to-day), "suppose yourselves leisurely cruising along by the steep and rugged sides of the Rocky Mountains, and laughing at the astonished countenance of the harmless grizzly bear, or at the agility of the frightened antelope; and then descending to the extensive prairie to watch the prancing of wild horses or the furious rushing of hordes of buffalo. These things indeed are but fancies at present, but in a few months they may become pleasant realities in America, while the proud nations of Europe are staring and wondering at the soaring enterprise of the independent citizens of the United States!" It was a fine flag-waving climax, and it is almost too bad that Mr. Porter's dream could not have become the pleasant reality to which he looked forward.

The venture collapsed, however, and that was that, except for a postscript by Mr. Nathaniel Currier, lithographer of Nassau Street in New York City. Mr. Currier, with the flair for news and the talent in draftsmanship that were later to make him and his partner famous, produced a fine burlesque print of the Porter Air Line taking off for the mines, leaving behind a crowd of disappointed Argonauts and soaring handsomely over a mere slow sailing ship. As it happens, it is not the Aërial Locomotive that first catches the eye, but a boldly printed sign across the sailing vessel's stern. Mr. Currier was shrewdly counting on the rough-and-ready humor of the time when he painstakingly lettered the legend, "Passage, $125 and Found (If Lost)."

2.

The Age of Innocence

THE first gold strike on the rich Feather River was made by a Californian who had lived in the state seven years before any one ever heard of gold in the foot-hills.

John Bidwell was a man of ambitious character. He had grown up in New York State, made his way west by gradual stages, and in 1841 had almost decided to teach school in Missouri for a living. But the swelling tide of migration was washing too close to him to be ignored. Bidwell wanted elbow-room and independence, and this combination of qualities did not fit too well with school-mastering. He was a young man of adventurous temperament, too; he always liked to see what was around the next corner. Emigrants were drifting steadily toward Oregon, and stories came back about that fertile, well-watered land. Certainly Oregon on the Pacific was around the corner; quite a long way around. For the matter of that, there was a good deal of talk about California, too. Boston skippers were trading in Monterey in spite of the restrictions put on their goods by the Mexican law, and most of them came back with fabulous yarns about the immense grants of land to be had, the Americans who had become Californians, the bland and gentle climate. And John Bidwell grew restless. When he heard about the plan of some of his fellow-citizens to organize the Western Emigration Society he threw himself into the scheme with enthusiasm.

At first the idea took hold like wild-fire. Five hundred Missourians joined the Society and it looked as though there would be a small army of them to tackle the long journey across the plains. It was a little different when the organizers actually came down to it. One man was perfectly willing to go, most anxious indeed, but unfortunately his wife was not as well as she might be and perhaps he would do better to give his place to some one else. Another would leave in a minute if it were not for a business deal that was hanging fire; he was very sorry, but any one could see how that was. And so on, through a long list of pioneers-in-spirit who preferred not to translate the wish into the fact. The truth was that these hardy souls had used up what adventurous qualities they had. Most of them had already put in their quota of pioneering; they had come as far as Missouri, and that was enough for one lifetime. Here, after all, were good farm land and not too many restrictions to keep a man down. It was all very well to talk about enormous ranchos in California, but some consideration ought to be given the bird in hand. So it happened that by the time they were ready to start, the Western Emigration Society had shrunk from its original five hundred enthusiasts to a mere sixty-nine hard-bitten men who meant what they said.

Because they were far less traveled, the plains were even more dangerous for the white man then than half a dozen years later when Sarah Royce and her little family took their chance. But the small party of sixty-nine pushed on bravely, knowing little about the actual geography of the territory they were planning to conquer and even less of the conditions they might encounter on the way. Fortunately for them, they fell in with a party of missionaries led by the saintly Father De Smet. These good men thought in terms of Heaven rather than of this earth, but they had their practical side as well. They had had the sound common sense to arrange for a practiced guide, a trapper named Fitzpatrick who knew the trail to Oregon and engaged to get the missionaries as far as the Flathead country in what is now Idaho. For many miles the Bidwell party's route coincided with that of the missionary group, and Trapper Fitzpatrick brought them safely to the Great Salt Lake. There almost half these emigrants changed their minds. Fitzpatrick, they said, knew how to get them to Oregon, and to Oregon they would go; probably the whole California idea was a kind of mirage anyway, a rosy dream, too good to be true. Bidwell, however, had not torn up his Missouri roots easily, and he would not switch. California was his goal and it was to California he was going, no matter what. Thirty of the Society saw it his way. They said good-by to the rest and turned resolutely to the conquest of the desert and the precipitous Sierra beyond.

They suffered, that courageous little group, but they won through. Their wagons left behind, and such provisions as they could take packed on the few animals strong enough to get through the mountains, they struggled over the summit and down into the warm California valleys. John A. Sutter, lord of Sutter's Fort, took to John Bidwell immediately. A mild, intelligent, hard-working, imaginative, loyal youth, he was the opposite of everything Californians had come to expect of a

"Missouri adventurer." Before long, Bidwell had become Sutter's right-hand man and manager of his great outlying principality at Hock Farm. Indeed, Sutter thought so well of his manager that he wanted to marry him off to his daughter, Eliza. That was a difficult situation for Bidwell, and there still exists his reply to Sutter, manifestly written in utter confusion at the unexpected offer. Because it reflects so well the kindly, careful, generous yet firm nature of John Bidwell, the letter is worth including here, with all the crossings-out and changes that show the panic into which the writer had been thrown by his former employer's notion of bringing him into the family.

My dear Sir, [wrote Bidwell] Having spent a considerable portion of my life in your service; having partaken of your hospitality when a stranger in a strange land; having been with you under variable circum-

                              & misfortune

stances through which it has been your fortune/to pass since I came to this country; and on all occasions, whether in prosperity or distress, finding

found you the same kind, gentlemanly, agreeable, generous even to a fault, enterprising person, man and manifesting the most unbounded confidence in myself; and finally to crown all your acts of attention and esteem you made me an offer—and I know it must have been from the fullness of an affectionate heart and a sincere desire for my happiness— of the hand of an only daughter—Capt. Sutter I am not ungrateful, but I often want either means or ability to display my gratitude. I have fel the deepest interest in your welfare on all occasions, whether in your employ or not, and I hope you will believe me sincere when I tell you

                              grateful

that in spite of all the changes of time my/affection and friendship which began with my first interview with you and have grown up and become a part of myself and nature will ever be with you and your family

57

can never be obliterated. I shall ever cherish the warmest regards for you and your family. During my recent calls at your farm on business, your family have shown me the politest attentions. I felt bad because they ~~they desired~~ tried so much to make me comfortable—for I was afraid they would discommode themselves.

Eliza speaks English very well & I was pleased with her accomplishments. I regretted much that I could not converse with Mrs Sutter, but her attentions were unceasing and kind. Now Capt. Sutter, I am at a loss to know what to say. My determination is made. I desire to prove to you on all occasions my gratitude— In matters of business you have only to say what you want done and it shall be done, so far as I can do.

or

Whatever assistance I can render yourself ~~and~~ family in all time to come, I shall consider a first duty. You~~r name~~ are ~~is~~ identified with the history of California and your enterprise will form a theme for the historian, which shall transmit your name to all succeeding generations till the end of time.

But you are known not in California alone, but in almost every other quarter of the Globe. I saw no intelligent person during my visit to the U. States last year who did not inquire about Capt. Sutter, and I was really proud to answer that I have the honor of being intimately acquainted with him.

I desire to see you frequently, and to live, so long as we both may live, on terms of intimacy and friendship. I should be happy to visit you frequently—have you do the same to me when convenient, and try and make life as pleasant as possible—But I cannot persuade myself to marry. ~~Your I shall keep this offer a profound secret~~ I hate the name of an old bachelor, and yet I do not know that I shall ever marry. Let this be a secret between you and me.

I remain, Capt. Sutter, with the greatest affection & esteem, ·

Yours
J. Bidwell

It is impossible to read that letter without a smile. Bidwell was so plainly fond of Sutter, so clearly aware of his obligations to him and so obviously admiring and respectful, yet so manifestly determined not to marry Eliza. Undoubtedly it was a difficult letter to write, but Bidwell did not shirk difficulties. He simply did the best he could.

But this came later. By 1847 John Bidwell had acquired his own land, the Rancho Chico near Butte Creek. He was an established Californian and a man of property when James Marshall brought the news of gold down to Sutter's Fort on that stormy day in January, 1848.

As it turned out, Bidwell was one of those whom Sutter trusted with the secret of Marshall's find. Sutter was frankly worried about the discovery and made no bones about his fear that gold-seeking would be the ruin of his vast lands. Yet his mercurial temperament made him incapable of keeping even so important a matter entirely to himself. It was only five days after he had gone up into the hills to the mill Marshall had built for him at Coloma and verified the strike, that he inserted in a letter to General Vallejo the comment that "there has been the discovery of a gold-mine which, as we have since experienced, is extraordinarily rich." Bidwell seems to have been the messenger who took Sutter's letter to the General, for he records that Vallejo acknowledged the information with characteristic Spanish grace. "As the water flows through Sutter's millrace," he said, "so may the gold flow into Sutter's purse!" It was a pleasant and polite expression of good will, though it bore no fruit. It may or may not have contributed to Bidwell's own notions about gold mining. At any rate, he was sufficiently interested to think about the matter seriously, and within a few weeks to make a trip up to Coloma and have a look at the ground. Isaac Humphrey, the Georgia miner, may have been there at the time; there is a story to the effect that he instructed Bidwell in methods of placer mining, including the use of the cradle or rocker and perhaps the Long Tom. Whatever the facts, John Bidwell was convinced that this new gold-fever was no temporary excitement but the real thing. And being convinced he acted characteristically. If the American River's gravel held gold, then why not the sands of the Feather? On his way back he stopped overnight at the little settlement of Hamilton, resolved to see what he could find out. "On trying some of the sand in the river," he wrote later, "I found light particles of gold, and reckoned that if light gold could be found that far down the river, the heavier particles would remain near the hills." The reasoning seemed sound enough, and he went on back to Rancho Chico, called his neighbors together, and told them what he believed. It speaks volumes for Bidwell's character and reputation that none of them even thought to doubt him. If he said he had figured it out that there was gold in the Feather River, that was enough for them.

It took some time to organize the party, but at length the messengers returned from Peter Lassen's mill with flour for the prospectors; the meat was dried; the shovels, picks, and pans they had ordered arrived from Sacramento, and they set out, five new-style pioneers ready to get rich. They found gold, too, wherever they went. As they worked up river, the "colors" improved; sometimes they took out as much as an ounce of fine gold in an hour. But unquestionably there is something about gold; the sight of a little suggests more, and men do not remain long content with what would have seemed a fortune on some dull yesterday. The ounce of dust did not please two of the party—Messrs. Potter and Williams. What they had in their mind's eye was lumps and chunks of gold, big nuggets, some of those pansful of sand that yielded half a pound of gold at a washing. They came to the unscientific conclusion that the Feather River's gold was no more than "light" gold-dust, and that it would take too much of it to make a pound. Over on the American River, now, where Marshall had made his discovery—that was the place for "heavy" gold! And it seemed to them that the American was the place to go. Bidwell did not try to dissuade the sanguine pair. If they wanted the American River they were welcome to it. As for himself and the other two, Mr. Dickey and Mr. Northgraves, they would just work on up the Feather a little farther and see how it looked.

They found one of the incredibly rich deposits of those early days, a veritable set of natural riffles filled with gold. A less balanced man than Bidwell would have been frankly excited; Bidwell himself might be excused a mild "Hurrah!" But his own record of that fabulous find demonstrates that he took it calmly and in stride. He wrote just nineteen words about it: "Dickey, Northgraves, and I went to what is now Bidwell's Bar and there found gold and went to mining." He might have added, though he didn't, that the three had selected an excellent day to make their discovery. It was the Fourth of July, 1848.

There was gold enough in the new river for everybody. Throughout the remainder of 1848 California was constantly being thrown into fits of excitement by news of fresh strikes in the cañons of the Feather. When the Forty-Niners arrived, the forks of that river were famous for their richness. They were famous also for the high cost of living in the settlements along their banks. Bars and provision-stores sprang up like mushrooms, and old diaries record some of the fantastic prices. A pinch of gold-dust for a drink of whisky was a standard rate, and the bartender did the measuring; hence the question saloonkeepers used to ask of prospective employees: "How much can you raise in a pinch?"

Food of any kind brought almost anything the vender chose

to ask. So did clothing and sundries of all sorts. One Forty-Niner wrote in his journal, before he grew accustomed to the scale of values in this new El Dorado, that a jar of pickles and two sweet potatoes had cost him $11, that he had paid $7.50 for one needle and two spools of thread, and that onions sold as high as $2.00 each. Eggs were at a premium, commanding anywhere from fifty cents apiece to $3.00. Flour ran up to $800 a barrel, boots were $16 a pair, woolen shirts sold for $6.00 "and poor quality at that." Not that any one complained very seriously. They did not worry about to-morrow. Haphazardly and recklessly they played the game of gold, celebrated Thanksgiving with cranberry sauce from Boston at $16 a can, rented a wagon and team for $150 a day if they needed it, paid outrageous board bills if their claims were close enough to town for such luxuries. There was always more gold to be had for the trouble of washing it, and as long as they got what they paid for the miners took it all in good part. At Bidwell's Bar, as it happened, one enterprising storekeeper went just a little too far. Unfortunately the record does not name him or explain what happened to him. There is only the brief matter-of-fact note, "Last week a meeting of miners was called to take into consideration the action of a merchant who had been selling Dr. Stover's California Salve for butter."

When it came to Indians, however, strict honesty went by the board. The California Diggers could not understand the white man's passion for these foolish bits of shining rock and dust, and though they learned soon enough that the gold had value to the miners, they were easy to cheat. Old, worn blankets sold for their weight in gold to the Indians who saw some sense in a blanket that would keep them warm, but none in a handful or two of shiny dust. Even after the Indians discovered that white men weighed out their gold and insisted on bargaining likewise, they were still one move behind. The miners merely invented a new measure, the "Digger ounce," which was represented by a special lead weight sometimes running as high as five or six ounces.

It might seem, with gold so abundant everywhere along the forks of the Feather and the American, that no one would need to go farther afield. But gold-seekers were coming into California faster than any one or two rivers could take care of them. Working up the main bodies of the Sacramento and the San Joaquin, they fanned out into a network which doggedly followed the lesser streams and creeks that tumbled down out of the high Sierra granite. To the north, they spread out along the American, the Feather and the Yuba. Extending to the south, they found the Mokelumne, the Cosumnes, the Stanislaus (Bret Harte's "Stanislow"), the rushing, rocky Tuolumne, and the quieter, colder Merced. Hundreds of smaller creeks cobwebbed the hills, and these began to take the names of the men who first washed gold on their banks; Weber Creek and Wood's Creek, Ward's and Carson's and Knight's, even one called after General Sutter who made one pathetic effort to get some of the gold that was making other men rich while his great farms went to pieces without laborers to work them. Not that the Forty-Niners lacked imagination; they named their creeks and streams for all manner of things. There are still dozens that carry the original labels, Bear and Deer creeks in numbers, at least one each called for Antelope, Beaver, Otter, Wolf, Coyote, and Coon, even a Duck Creek and a Cow or two. Now and then a Spanish name stuck, in spite of the severer American nomenclature that threatened to sweep away such fanciness. Mariposa Creek is Mariposa yet, like the county and the warm and friendly little town near which an early settler first saw the clouds of soft yellow butterflies in a little valley. But in the main the American Way triumphed. For every Esperanza Creek there were twenty such plain and foursquare watercourses as Willow, Cottonwood, Rock, and Brush. Now and then a sensibly descriptive tag put

Angel's Camp, Calaveras County, 1857

In 1848, Angel's Camp had begun the growth that was to make
it one of the leading towns for miles around. Several famous
mines were developed here—the Marshall, the Lightner, the

Mother Lode Central, the Utica, and many more. But the chief fame of Angel's Camp came from Mark Twain's story of the Jumping Frog of Calaveras County.

a stream in its place; many a winter rivulet was known as Dry Creek because some miner who had not yet learned California's ways found it so great a disappointment in summer. Coarse Gold Creek logically called for Fine Gold Creek; both are still named that to-day. Either a very literal man who stumbled on a skeleton or else a Bible student with a muzzy sense of reference surely christened Jawbone Creek. And somewhere in that rush was a classicist, for up in the northern Sierra there is a Rubicon River where he must have debated his crossing and then cast his die.

Almost all these rivers, streams, brooks, and creeks held gold. Yet it needed only the slimmest rumor of a new strike to send men scrambling over the hills and ravines to try a greener pasture. One such whisper, which turned out to be a false alarm, indirectly brought about the discovery of the richest gravels found on the whole length of the Feather River. Like so many bonanzas, this one was the result of an accident and came on the heels of a bitter disappointment.

To this day, men argue about whether "Gold Lake" Stoddard ever saw what he said he did.

At any rate, his story convinced many. He had stumbled into a small settlement on the upper Feather, in his heel an arrow wound which he said he sustained in a skirmish with some Indians. He was half starved and on the brink of collapse. With a companion, he said, he had been prospecting back in the hills and had come upon a lake whose banks bore scattered chunks of pure gold. The two had drunk the water of the lake, which they found pure and sweet, had gathered a few specimens and tried to find their way back to the camps along the river. But they had somehow got lost. Wandering in the mountains, they had been attacked by Indians and Stoddard had managed to escape, even with his injured foot. He did not know anything about his companion, had never seen him again. But he had finally made his way down to the

Feather, and here he was. Could he find his lake again? He was not sure, but he thought so.

There was plenty of time to debate his story, since winter had set in and it was impossible to penetrate the snow-bound Sierra in which Stoddard said he had made his find. But the word spread from one camp to the next, and the River was agog with the new fever. Now and then a hard-headed citizen would suggest that Stoddard was crazy, that the whole affair was the dream of a frightened and starving man. To such skeptics the answer was made that Stoddard had specimens to substantiate his claim. There is nothing to prove that he had; it may have been just one of those tales that gain credence by being repeated often enough. But the whole story was like that. And by May of 1850 twenty-five stanch believers had organized a company to follow Stoddard's will o' the wisp into the mountains. They did their best to keep the expedition's starting-time a secret, but it was no use. When at length they began their journey it was with nearly a thousand other miners straggling behind them, determined to stake claims on the shore of the great Lake of Gold when it was found.

At first, Stoddard seemed to know exactly where he was going; for five or six days his demeanor was that of a man certain of himself and his goal. Then he began to waver. The lake was farther to the south. It was necessary to bear more to the west again. Or no, that wasn't right; it was over this next ridge, farther to the east. The credulous twenty-five bore with him for a time, but finally they lost patience and called a meeting to determine what should be done. They were joined by a strong representation of the hundreds who had been following their erratic course; in fact, by this time the search had become a common enterprise, shared by all who had set out from the River. Even those who had not been asked to join the search were angry at Stoddard's failure; indeed they were among the loudest in demanding that something be done.

The discussion was futile. Some chose to take the attitude that Stoddard had been crazy all along. Some suggested that he might have heard a story about such a lake and thought he could find it and claim credit. Others clung to the belief that he had really seen the lake, rocks of pure gold and all, but that he had simply grown confused as to its location. One miner offered the ingenious explanation that the lake Stoddard had seen might have been covered over by a landslide during the winter. No one thought much of that notion. In the end a committee was appointed to convey to Stoddard the sense of the meeting. He was to have twenty-four hours more to find his lake. If he could not find it he would be hanged to the nearest tree. Perhaps they didn't actually mean what they said, for apparently Stoddard was not very carefully guarded. In the night he managed to leave camp without being observed. Next morning there was no lake, no Stoddard, and very little hope of finding either.

That was the end of the stampede. There is a Gold Lake to-day, nestled high in the Sierra near the foot of Mount Elwell; but there is nothing definite to connect that body of water with Stoddard's dream. Somewhere along the years it was christened, perhaps because of the pyrites in its sands, and that is all any one knows. As for Stoddard, there was a rumor afloat that he reappeared after the miners had had time to cool off a bit, and attempted to get together another company to help him continue the search. If this is true, it came to nothing. Nobody went looking for a lake of gold again.

Yet the Feather River diggings gained from the foolish rush after all. For three German miners, disappointed in Stoddard's failure, made up their minds they would try to get something out of the wild goose chase if they could. On their way back to the settlements, they cut straight across the hills to the upper reaches of the Feather, farther east and north than prospectors had gone before. A few scattered colors rewarded them on their first day, and they decided to camp for the night near the mouth of a small stream that emptied into the river. It was while carrying water back from the junction, across the water-worn boulders lining the creek, that one of the men was stopped in his tracks by the most astonishing sight of his life. The cracks and crevices of all the rocks around him were filled with gold—shining flakes and grains of it, and siftings of fine dust. He and his two companions staked claims there and then, and sat long under the stars talking of what they would do with the fortune they were going to pick up to-morrow. The story is that they took out $36,000 in dust and nuggets in the first four days, without even having to resort to washing the gravels around them.

If they could have kept their strike hidden they might have made millions before they were done, for millions eventually came from the square mile in the middle of which they had pitched their camp. But the news leaked out, as such news always does. Down to Nelson Creek, Poorman's Creek, and all along the tributaries of the Feather the story traveled, and by early July the place was alive with eager prospectors. So rich were the diggings that it was agreed to limit claims on the bar itself to ten feet square; up on the hillsides forty feet square was the rule. Those early arrivals had little beside picks, pans, and shovels, but in a week or two cradles and Long Toms were built, and Rich Bar—the strike named itself—was in full swing. Half a mile or so to the east Smith's Bar came into being, and half a mile to the west there grew up another settlement called Indian Bar. It was at Smith's bar that one Enoch Judson staked a claim so high on a hillside that his fellow-miners laughed at his folly. They were especially amused to see him stagger down the steep hill on his first day of digging, with a flour-sack of dirt to be washed in the river. They stopped laughing almost immediately. Judson panned $750 out of that first sack.

That was doing exceptionally well for dry diggings on the hillsides. But in the first months' plundering of Rich Bar miners who were lucky enough to have claims directly on the river bank took out enormous sums. The highest yield from a single pan is reported to have been $2,900, but pans of $1,500 to $2,000 were fairly commonplace. One company of four men who had had experience in the Georgia mines took out more than $50,000 in one day's work. Yet, odd as it seems, there were few quarrels and no serious trouble at all. In that summer of 1850, men still understood that the safety of one depended on the safety of all. They recognized their common interest, held together against any kind of dishonesty, settled counter-claims by temporary courts which dispensed rough and ready justice based on equity and common understanding rather than on precedent and law. That is, with one exception. And even that single departure from reason was conducted in a reasonably orderly way.

The trouble began when a party of Americans and a party of Frenchmen arrived at the Bar simultaneously and attempted to stake out the same general area. It would be interesting to know whether the French or the Americans suggested the return to the days of chivalry; at any rate some one did. For it was agreed that there would be no pitched battle. Instead, each side chose a champion and agreed to abide by the result. The groups lined up on opposite sides of their Field of the Cloth of Gold, and the champions met in the center. There were no gloves, no rules; the man who survived to walk off the field would win for his side the contested claim, that was all. The battle lasted nearly three hours and the American won, though not until his adversary was so far gone that he could not get to his feet. It was a fair fight and a square fight, but by a fantastic quirk of fate it was the Frenchmen to whom the spoils went after all. They held honestly to their bargain, moved farther upstream, staked out new claims on fresh ground, and went to work. In less than a week they had opened up the richest diggings ever found on Rich Bar. The scene of their operations is still called French Gulch.

Rich Bar, however, did not last. In half a dozen years it was mined out, its gravels turned over time and again, the dry diggings on the hillsides sifted and washed through ten million buckets of painfully carried water. Yet Rich Bar has a fame of its own. In its short life it embraced all the stages of the typical California mining town, from the day of the solid, respectable, hard-working miner with no need for law, through the swiftly following years of gambling, debauch, and justice at the end of a rope, on into the later stages of settled law, failure of the gold supply, gradual depopulation, final collapse, and decay. Many another mining settlement suffered the same cycle; it was the expected thing. But Rich Bar differed from the rest in one important way. Rich Bar had a biographer. And that biographer, unconsciously penning in letters home the finest notes on early gold-rush days ever written, was a woman.

Louise Amelia Knapp Smith was born in Elizabeth, New Jersey, in 1819. On her mother's side she is said to have been related to Julia Ward Howe. Whatever the truth of that, neither Mrs. Howe nor her parents had anything to do with developing her talents, since she was orphaned at an early age and sent to New England to be educated. When she was twenty she was attending Amherst Academy, as good a school for young ladies as there was anywhere. Edward Hitchcock, afterward President of Amherst College, taught her there, as he was later to teach Emily Dickinson in the same school.

Those early-middle years of the nineteenth century were the great years of letter-writing. Louise Smith—her brothers, sisters, and friends had nicknamed her "Shirley" for some reason of their own—was as good as any of her contemporaries when it came to the business of correspondence, and far better than most. Modeling her epistolary style on that of the Transcendentalist great, Shirley established herself as a vivid letter-writer even in her girlhood. When she married the delicate Dr. Fayette Clappe and he decided that the climate of California might be good for him, her family and friends knew they could count on Shirley to keep them posted on the new land to which she was going. In 1849 she and her husband left for San Francisco, sailing around the Horn.

The Doctor did his best to adjust himself to the wind, the dust, and the fleas of the roaring new city, but by June of 1851 he concluded that he would have to give it up as a bad job. He might have gone sailing back again to the East but for a friend who brought him glowing reports of the fine dry climate and bracing mountain air of the gold-mining country. Doubtless he was skeptical as the invalid always is, more especially the ailing medical man. But there might be something in it. Maybe the altitude and the dryness might be good for the "fever-and-ague, the bilious, remittent and intermittent fevers" with which he was so sorely afflicted. And when another acquaintance, just returned from Rich Bar on the Feather River, sang its praises to him, he made up his mind that he would at least go up there and look at the place. If he liked it, then he would send for his wife, and they would see how life suited them in the mines. On the seventh of June, despite the fact that he had just recovered from a "brain fever," and was suffering from "excessive debility which rendered him liable to chills at any hour of the day or night," he started off on muleback, accompanied (as Dame Shirley records with some asperity) by "a friend who kindly volunteered to assist him in spending his money."

He made a hard trip of it. Spells of sickness continued to bother him; in places the mountain trail was still covered deeply with snow. But the air did precisely the wonders for him that his friends had promised, and by early September he was ready to send for his helpmeet. Indeed, he was genuinely enthusiastic about the prospects in Rich Bar for a man of his profession, so much so that he proceeded to build himself an office which, in its superior elegance, was a marvel to the miners for miles around. As he wrote his wife, in all that region, with the settlement at Rich Bar growing by leaps and bounds as the rich gravels continued to yield more and more gold, there were only three doctors. Plainly his chances for both health and profit were excellent. But Dr. Clappe seems to have been one of those unfortunate creatures who can always guess wrong. What he had not realized was that other physicians might have the same idea. By the time Shirley arrived in Rich Bar, in the middle of September, there were no less than twenty-nine doctors there, waiting for the salubrious mountain airs to allow them their quota of patients.

Shirley had passed most of the summer with friends near Marysville at the confluence of the Yuba and the lower Feather, and her journey from the haphazard little board-and-canvas town up into the mines was a procession of minor disasters. She began it by falling off the mule her husband had brought down to carry her. Next day the Doctor had one of his bilious attacks and kept his bed for several days while Shirley fretted to be going. Once up, he insisted that Shirley must not risk another slipping saddle; he would take the mules the forty miles to Bidwell's Bar, and she would follow by stage.

That conveyance Shirley called "the most excruciatingly springless wagon" it had ever been her lot to ride in, but its lack of comfort did not prevent her from taking a healthy interest in everything new she saw. Her first letter to her sister is full of bright bits about the rolling landscape, the Indian women with whom she talked and the fine baskets they wove, the narrow and fearsome road that led over the foot-hills and

71

down into Bidwell's Bar. Her behavior was exceptionally good, certainly, for the driver complimented her on being the first woman ever to ride over the road " 'thout hollerin'." She was thoroughly tired when she got in, but the Doctor had a new idea. Instead of staying in the Bar, where "there was nothing to sleep in but a tent, and nothing to sleep *on* but the ground, and the air was black with hopping fleas," they would ride on, he told her, to the Berry Creek House, ten miles farther, and spend the night there. It was really only a short trip and they would be so much more comfortable. They mounted mules again and rode off.

The Doctor must have been an inept sort in more ways than one. This time he experienced no fevers, no bilious attacks, no ague, but neither did he have a very good notion of the road. It was bright moonlight, and the hills seemed to Shirley a kind of fairyland spread around them. She writes, "We were in tip-top spirits. It seemed to me so *funny* that we two people should be riding on mules all by ourselves in these glorious latitudes, night smiling down so kindly upon us; and funniest of all that we were going to live in the Mines!" But the tip-top spirits began to fade when ten o'clock came and there was no sign of the Berry Creek House. Nor did another four hours of riding get them anywhere excepting, obviously, higher and higher into the mountains. There was nothing to do but camp where they were. Luckily it was a mild enough night, and though they slept little they rested until sunrise when they tried the trail again. The second day brought them more exhausting travel, up through groves of fir and oak and along the edges of deep ravines, then down again into dark cañons where the road, such as it was, often disappeared entirely. It was not until two o'clock that afternoon that they came out upon what appeared to be a main highway and at last met a traveler who might give them directions. Their questions were soon answered. They were just seven miles from Berry Creek House. As for where they had been, they had somehow got on to the trail that led down to the North Fork of the American River, more than thirty miles out of their way. Perhaps that was the only time in her California experience that Shirley broke down. "I sobbed and cried," she writes, "like the veriest child, and repeatedly declared that I should never live to get to the *rancho*." She recovered herself, of course, and managed to ride the rest of the way, though once there she wanted no food, nothing but sleep.

It is difficult to believe that even the muddled Dr. Clappe could have lost his way again, but he did. The journey to Rich Bar, which should have occupied five days, took them eight, and there was a second night of camping out. This time there were grunts and snufflings in the brush until daylight; later Shirley learned that the countryside abounded in bear, including grizzlies. Yet even her fatigue did not keep her from noting what was new and strange. Her descriptions of the hills and especially the approach to Rich Bar itself are sharp and clear. Wrote Shirley:

Hardly a living thing disturbed this solemnly beautiful wilderness. Now and then a tiny lizard glanced in and out among the mossy roots of the old trees, or a golden butterfly flitted languidly from blossom to blossom. Sometimes a saucy little squirrel would gleam along the sombre trunk of some ancient oak, or a bevy of quail, with their pretty tufted heads and short quick tread, would trip athwart our path. Two or three times, in the radiant distance, we descried a stately deer, which, framed by embowering leaves and motionless as a tableau, gazed at us for a moment with its large limpid eyes, then bounded away with the speed of light into the evergreen depths of those glorious woods. Sometimes we were compelled to cross broad plains, acres in extent, called *chaparrals,* covered with low shrubs which, leafless and barkless, stand like vegetable skeletons along the dreary waste. You cannot imagine what a weird effect those eldritch bushes had upon my mind. Of a ghastly whiteness, they at first reminded me of a plantation of antlers, and I amused myself by fancying them a herd of crouching deer; but they grew so wan and ghastly that I began to look forward to the creeping

73

across a *chaparral*—it is no easy task for the mules to wind through them —with a feeling of dread.

But what a lovely sight greeted our enchanted eyes as we stopped for a few moments on the summit of the hill leading into Rich Bar. Deep in the shadowy nooks of the far down valleys, like wasted jewels dropped from the radiant sky above, lay half a dozen blue-blossomed lagoons, glittering and gleaming and sparkling in the sunlight as though each tiny wavelet were formed of rifted diamonds. It was worth the whole wearisome journey, danger from Indians, grizzly bears, sleeping under the stars and all, to behold this beautiful vision.

The hill leading into Rich Bar is five miles long, and as steep as you can imagine. Fancy yourself riding for this distance, along the edge of a frightful precipice where, should your mule make a misstep, you would be dashed hundreds of feet into the awful ravine below. Every one we met tried to discourage us, and said that it would be impossible for me to ride down it. However, I insisted upon going. About halfway down, we came to a level spot, a few feet in extent, covered with sharp slate-stones. Here the girth of my saddle—which we afterward found to be fastened only by four *tacks*—gave way and I fell over on the right side, striking on my left elbow. Strange to say, I was not in the least hurt; and again my heart wept tearful thanks to God; for had the accident happened at any other part of the hill, I must have been dashed, a piece of shapeless nothingness, into the dim valleys beneath.

So Dame Shirley came to the mines.

The Rich Bar in which she was to spend her gold-mine year was neither worse nor better than a hundred such settlements, from Sonora to Shasta. Indeed, a comparison of Shirley's letters with the diaries and correspondence of others who saw the mining region in its first blossoming shows how remarkably the early development of one gold-rush town paralleled that of the rest. All were the same startling mixture of luxury and make-do. In all of them the miner lived his day-to-day life primitively, plainly, getting along on salt pork, beans, and granite-hard home-made bread or biscuit. And in all of them the miner who had been lucky made up for his week's work by allowing his soul to expand on a diet of canned oysters, brandied peaches, and the imported claret of which thousands of gallons were sold up and down the mines in those first years. For those who were so inclined there were splendidly fitted bars and opportunities in plenty to lose the week's take at monte, faro or *vingt-et-un,* which last clung to its French name for many years before becoming transformed into the commonplace "blackjack" that removed half its charm. Yet even these gilded palaces of week-end sin were the same curious blend of elegance and crudity that characterized all the miner's existence. As for the mere ordinary hotel—well, there was, for example, Rich Bar's pride, the Empire.

The Empire was the only two-story building in town; upstairs were three glass windows, the only ones in Rich Bar. It was built of planks of the roughest kind, roofed with canvas that sagged and flapped at the edges, no matter how the owners strove to brace and nail it. Canvas also formed the entire front of the building, and supplied an excellent base for the seven-foot lettering in brilliant red and blue paint which announced to the world the hostel's name. On a level with the dusty pathway called the street was the main entrance. It opened into the bar, of course; there was no point in wasting valuable space on a lobby. Sound psychologists in their field, the owners realized that rough plank walls would only remind the customers of their workaday surroundings, wherefore the Empire barroom was draped from ceiling to floor in scarlet calico, tastefully fluted and puckered into rosettes in the corners; "that eternal crimson calico," Shirley called it, "which flushes the whole social life of the Golden State with its everlasting red." The bar itself was planed and sanded pine; mahogany would come later. But behind it gleamed a really magnificent mirror in which were reflected the shining decanters, the squat vases of cigars and jars of brandied fruit that dazzled the miners' eyes while they drank. At the end of the room was a long table covered with green felt behind which sat a dealer who would take on all comers at whatever card game they chose. Beyond the dealer were stacked piles of paper-bound novels; true to her New England tradition, Shirley spoke of this reading matter as "a sickening pile of 'yallow-kivered' literature." Along the side wall of the room were rough counters littered with an extraordinary assortment of goods—velveteen coats, shoes, flannel shirts and calico ones, the latter, Shirley notes, starched to an "appalling state of stiffness," hams, preserved meats, oysters, potatoes, and onions, anything and everything from bullets to butter. Bar, store, gaming-room and hotel office in one, it was headquarters for the business of the town and never empty.

The proprieties had their place in the Empire, however. Four steps up from the barroom was the parlor, its floor covered with straw matting, its windows draped with purple calico, its walls lined with the same material in a delicate shade of blue. On the wall was a looking-glass which Shirley admitted to be "quite decent." The furniture consisted of a "sofa" fourteen feet long and a foot and a half wide, a round table covered with a green cloth, six cane-bottomed chairs, one rocker, and a cook-stove. In such a room, the proprietors seemed to say, the rare woman visitor to Rich Bar might feel at home. If the straw matting grew fungus in the rainy season and smelled a little like a disused stable—well, after all that was not the fault of a good hotel man who conscientiously provided for his guests the best the country offered. Upstairs the accommodations were limited but in the same style. There were four bedrooms, eight feet by ten, furnished with small tables covered in oil-cloth, bedsteads so heavy that only a giant could move them (Shirley wrote that she was convinced they were built, piece by piece, on the spot where they stood), and hard cane-bottomed chairs. As for the doors, they were merely frames covered with dark blue drilling and hung on leather hinges. That was the grand Hotel Empire, rough, crude, uncomfortable. "Such a piece of carpentering," wrote Shirley, "as a child two years old, gifted with the strength of a man, would produce if it wanted to play at making grown-up houses." Yet she saw, too, why this makeshift tenement was no better. "This impertinent apology for a house," had cost eight thousand dollars to build because every bit of material in it had to be packed up into the mountains from Marysville at the rate of forty cents a pound. It had been built originally by a pair of gamblers, Shirley explained modestly to her sister, "as a residence for two of those unfortunates who make a trade—a thing of barter—of the holiest passion (when sanctified by *love*) that ever thrills the heart of poor humanity. But to the lasting honor of miners, the speculation proved a failure. . . . These unhappy members of a class to one of which the tenderest words that Jesus ever spake were uttered, left in a few weeks, absolutely driven away by public opinion. The disappointed gamblers sold the house to its present proprietor for a few hundred dollars."

Dame Shirley wrote the truth in this respect, as far as those early years were concerned. The mining towns were still made up chiefly of solid, respectable men, most of them young, who thought of this California as an adventure only, who were quite sure that in six months or a year they would be back again in their Eastern homes, with their wives or sweethearts, rich in the easy gold that the mines would provide. They were beginning to learn that the gold was not quite as simply come by as they had thought. They were finding out that weeks of toil might be rewarded by no more than day-wages and sometimes not that. But there were still the fantastic strikes, the extraordinarily rich discoveries that kept their hopes high. And as long as there were still only a few thousands to share in the river Golcondas, any man might become dazzlingly rich. In the meantime a woman was a splendid delicate creature compounded of his memories of his mother and sisters to whom

Yankee Jim's, Placer County, 1857
Yankee Jim's was named for a fugitive from the Australian prison camps who had a penchant for other miner's horses.

The ground under the corral he built for his stolen animals contained enough gold to have made him an honestly rich man. He was hanged before his corral blossomed into this prosperous town.

he wrote long letters every Sunday, a being from another world to whom honor and respect were due, even if these were expressed in ridiculously extravagant terms. As for a woman with a baby—well, Bret Harte's tales have made clear the exaggeratedly romantic reverence which the miners exhibited toward a small child.

It was not to last long, this viewpoint. As a new element crept into the mines, as women became more commonplace, as the towns grew and flourished and buildings of brick replaced the plank and canvas edifices, women of the type Shirley calls "unfortunate, earnestly to be compassionated creatures" became common enough. That was a side of life in the mines that Shirley never saw. With her husband she stuck it out at Rich Bar for nearly a year. But Dr. Clappe was not up to the kind of life that his one spark of wilfulness had led him to try. Nor was he up to the spunky, lively, quick-witted Shirley. Somewhere along the line—the record is not clear—the Doctor passed out of her life, and she settled in San Francisco to teach in the public schools, to renew her acquaintance with the scholarly Harvard graduate, Ferdinand C. Ewer, and to give him her letters for publication in his magazine, *The Pioneer*. It is perhaps the best of all commentaries on the rapidity with which the California mining settlements passed through their early naïve phase and grew into the rough-and-ready, brawling, gambling, hard-drinking towns they became, that as early as 1854 Ewer found the Shirley letters worth publishing as a valuable record of a day that had passed.

Shirley did see the beginnings of the bad feeling between the Mexican miners and the new Americans. She witnessed a few drunken fights, a killing or two, the formation of a local "Committee of Vigilance" modeled on the first of San Francisco's famous Vigilante groups. But she left Rich Bar before she had a chance to understand the change that was coming over the face of the mining country. Even the single hanging that took place in Rich Bar while she was there partook of the nature of an execution for proper cause, and she so records it. The change was imminent, but Shirley was never a part of the new life; and because it never touched her at all, her letters will always remain the best picture of gold-rush California's age of innocence.

3.

The "Honest Miner"

ONE of our more charming misconceptions of the gold rush is our notion of the Forty-Niner as a graybeard accoutred in red flannel shirt, high boots, and black slouch hat.

Doubtless that was the way he was romantically remembered by the next generation when those sons and daughters grew old enough to be concerned with history. Perhaps, too, there were actually some red flannel shirts, though there were more of red calico and gray flannel or blue. Certainly miners who waded most of the day in mud and water wore high boots, and the black slouch hat was typical of the time. There were also beards in plenty; men after gold have more to do than to shave. But not many of the beards were gray. The voyage by sea and the journey across the plans were selective enterprises. The hardships were well known, and older men are never especially keen for bucking the wilderness in any era. California gold was something for the younger men to tackle.

The Forty-Niners, then, were young men. There is good authority for estimating the average age of four-fifths of them as between eighteen and thirty-five. They were also a pretty fair cross-section of the America of the day. Alonzo Delano, widely known "Old Block" of early California journalism and author of the "Pen Knife Sketches," notes the variety among them, which is another way of calling attention to the fact that the urge to get rich is found anywhere, and that the pursuit of gold at its source is a great leveler. Wrote Delano:

It was a common thing to see a statesman, a lawyer, a physician, a merchant or clergyman, engaged in driving oxen or mules, cooking for his mess, at work for wages by the day, making hay, hauling wood, or filling menial offices. Yet false pride had evaporated, and if they were making money at such avocations, they had little care for appearances. I have often seen the scholar and the scientific man, the ex-judge, the ex-member of Congress or the would-be exquisite at home, bending over the washtub, practising the homely art of the washerwoman; or sitting on the ground with a needle, awkwardly enough repairing the huge rents in his pantaloons or sewing on buttons.

The law of averages went further than this, too. It operated to balance the really rich strikes—the ones that have come down in story—against the thousands of claims in which the hardest working miner made no more than fair wages, no matter how long he toiled, and often not that much. There were enormously rich deposits, it is true; and many men made their pile from such discoveries, sometimes to keep it, often to lose it in gambling or in speculative investments, from new mines to real estate. But the general run took what they could get and were thankful, keeping up their spirits in the hope that to-morrow they would come upon another French Gulch, a

second Carson Hill. They didn't, most of them. But the miner
has always lived by such hopes; if he does not possess the
sanguine spirit, then he is no miner.

In those first years, then, the foot-hills were chiefly filled
with young men from decent homes somewhere on the other
side of the Missouri River, their instincts leading them to treat
their fellows honestly and straightforwardly, to form in
groups wherever possible, to arrange their conduct, as soon as
they could, in an approximation of the pattern to which they
were accustomed. The sense of responsibility to which they
had been brought up led them to deprecate crookedness, to
assume that the stranger was an honest man until he proved
himself otherwise, to help the down-and-outer when they had
the chance. Charles Shinn, in his recollections of the mining
camps, tells a characteristic tale of this willingness to aid a
fellow-creature who had been unlucky, a story of a young
fellow who wandered dejectedly into a camp where some thirty
fortunate miners were busy on their claims. He explained,
when they asked him, that he had been unable to locate a claim
where there was any gold, and that he was through. Where-
upon one of the miners made his proposition. "Boys," he said,
"I'll work an hour for that chap yonder if you will." The rest
agreed, and at the end of the hour they turned over to the
young man something like a hundred dollars in gold dust. They
then made up a list of tools and told the boy, "Now go and
buy these tools and come back here. We'll stake out a good
claim for you, and after that you'll paddle your own canoe!"

Not that the honest miner was any plaster saint, either.
Death was no stranger to him; he had seen plenty of it on his
journey to this new California, no matter how he came; he
met such matters with a rough humor, and thoroughgoing
sense of the practical. Frank Marryat, in *Mountains and Mole-
hills,* is authority for the frequently repeated yarn of the burial
service that turned into a miniature gold-rush before the serv-

ice was so much as read. The incident took place in the southern mines, somewhere near the banks of Carson Creek, where a miner died and his companions decided to give him the real thing in funerals:

A miner of the neighborhood, who had the reputation of having been a prominent and powerful preacher in the eastern states, was called upon to officiate; and he consented to do so. After assembling and taking "drinks all around," the party proceeded with becoming gravity to the grave, which had been dug at a distance of about a hundred yards from the camp. When the spot was reached and the body lowered, the minister commenced an extempore prayer, while the crowd reverently fell upon their knees. For a while, all went well; but the prayer was unnecessarily long and at last some of the congregation began, in an abstracted way, to finger the loose earth that had been thrown up from the grave. It proved to be thick with gold, and an excitement was immediately apparent in the kneeling crowd. Upon this the preacher stopped and inquiringly asked, "Boys, what's that?" took a view of the ground for himself and, as he did so, shouted "Gold! Gold!—and the richest kind of diggings! The congregation is dismissed!" The dead miner was taken from his auriferous grave to be buried elsewhere, while the funeral party, with the minister at their head, lost no time in prospecting and staking out new diggings!

Stories such as these might be multiplied a hundred times, yet none of them would reflect more than one aspect of the miner's life. For the real thing, the day-to-day story of the average man's labors in the gold country, the best source—like the best source for the facts about the journey to California— is in the diaries and journals kept by the men who were there. Many of these, good, poor, and indifferent, have been published, and the reader will have no trouble in finding several of them easily available in libraries. None of them, however, tells the simple, often unhappy story better than the diary of the same Hiram Pierce, whose record of the Isthmus crossing is so artlessly brilliant a picture of the hardships of that perilous voyage by land and sea. Here is the "honest miner" in the foot-hills with his friends, working, suffering discouragement, learning to cook, writing his letters home, thinking of his loved ones, solacing himself with the mail from "the States," setting it all down in plain language which shows his remarkable faculty for observing what went on around him and for coming to shrewd and sensible conclusions about men and events as he saw them.

Hiram Pierce and his little company had their first taste of mining in the American River up toward Auburn:

Arrived at the diggins. The Senery at the river is wild in the extreme. The water appears to have forced its way through a perfect Mtn. of Granite boulders of imence Size, 20 or 50 tons. There is I judge not more than 100 men at work in this place, averageing perhaps $10 per day. Prices high. Molasses $1 per bottle, 1½ pints. Vinegar the same. Mellons are brought up and sold for $2 to $5 a piece & small at that. Pork $5, flour 40cts a lb. Lumber $1.50 a sq. foot. Smith and myself made a tent and had a good night's Rest. The gold at this place seems difused through all the Earth but is verry fine.

Rose & got breckfast. At 11 attended preaching under a live oak by Rev. George Denham, a Congregational Minister from New Bedford.

Got breckfast & went to work. Made a small show. It looks rather Shady. All of us got much less than an ounce. It is verry much like work. In afternoon made a Sheet iron cradle.

All hands went to work. We gathered less than an ounce. Potatoes $1 a piece, onions the same. Axes, $8. Boots, coarse, $16.

At night the Wolves & Kiotas give us plenty of music.

Went out prospecting & find that every Stone & foot of Ground has been turned over. It is a most wild and romantic Sene. We bake pancakes, fry pork, drink Tea or Coffey & sleep on the Ground. It is verry warm during the day. The nights are pleasant & fine, no dew. The wolves stole some meat from a neighbor's tent, taking it from within a foot or two of his head. We got 2 small loaves of bread baked at a Mormon family that arrived overland. They charged $1 per loaf for baking & verry heavy hard bread at that. Barley for feeding horses is $1 per quart, cheese $2.50 per lb. The diggins look rather poor, verry few get over one ounce per day.

Continued work with the Cradles & gathered 2½ ounces, this being our best day.

Forepart of the day was cloudy & comparatively cool. We all continued digging, getting about an oz. All feeling verry tired. Men are coming & going. They try the different digins & run from place to place. I feel somelike the Rich Man, as though I would gladly warn my brethren & friends against comeing to this place of Torment.

Morning verry warm. I was verry much fatigued. Attended preaching; exelant meetings. Wrote home & sent a rough drawing of the diggins & one dollars worth of gold dust.

I felt verry tired. My back getting lame in consequence, as I think, of getting my feet wet & sleeping on the ground nights.

Still digging. Though my back is lame, I appear to be the nearest convalescent of anyone here of our party. Daniel Newcom has a verry sore hand caused by poison. Smith has a sort of felon on his hand caused by rubbing on the cradle, & Haskins hands & feet are sore from Scurvey & Sunburnt. My back is lame but I carry dirt & Haskins rocks the cradle. A great many are laid up about us, some with sore hands & feet caused by poison & some with disentary.

The reader will guess at the outcome. What with sore backs, bad hands, dysentery, and chills, the little company gave up the battle. Hiram, because he was in charge of affairs, had to go back to San Francisco with the rest and see to selling off company supplies and closing the books. This he did, at the same time taking medicine to cure his chills and fever, which improved. The business concluded, Hiram joined forces with another group, bound this time for the southern mines to find ground that had not been "turned over, every Stone." Their route took them through Stockton, then up across the Stanislaus and into fairly new country near the Tuolumne River, where they settled down to build cabins against the winter cold:

Rained last night, Comenced building a chimney. Provisions are very high. Pork, flour, Coffey, sugar & beans are $1 a lb. Candles $1 a piece. Saleratus, $8. The men are, many of them, getting no more than $2 or $3 a day.

The men went to work but I chose to clene up & remember the Sabeth, though they said they should charge me $8.

I had a chill today. Continued work on the house. The manner of

85

building was to cut the logs, get a pair of cattle & Hawl them to gether, lay them up, then chop large trees & split out boards, part of Oak & part of Pine, for the roof & door & floors, & for want of nails to put on the roof it was fixed by lashing on poles to hold the boards on. The peaks were closed with rawhides. We then put up berths & had quite a comfortable house.

Cool morning & a chill took hold of me & I was unfit for work during the day. The wild Indians came round our tent & stole two mules. They took one off a few rods & shot an arrow through him & cut out some Meat. The other they drove off. They were barefoot & go naked, notwithstanding the Snow is kneedeep where they come from. The Yankies are verry much enraged & will shoot them sooner than they would a Deer.

A frosty morning & a clear day. Worked on the house. I was taking medicine. Took 13 grains of calomel & followed it with Quinene.

Got our house done & fitted up my berth. Had no chill.

Rained all day. Tinkered for myself & made my cradle. Two men were attackted by 3 Grisley Bears just below us. One of them got into a tree & the other shot one of the bears. The man pursued him & in backing off he fell down & the bear comeing up he stuck the muzel of his Gun in his mouth, when the bear turned & left him.

I made the first begining to wash gold for myself. I could work but a few minutes at a time, on account of rain.

A cold frosty morning & the ground was frozen hard. The Sun does not shine on our house until 9 & then so far South that his rays are feeble, & it again disappears at ½ past 3 behind the Mountain. We made an attempt at washing but with verry poor success. I had the dum Ague. Prospects not verry bright.

A bright morning but clouded up & was cold. At 1 I was attackted by a severe Ague fit. My feet & legs are much subject to cramps. Took a stiff dose of pills & feel rather down.

Worked until 12, then had a chill followed as usual by fever. Got $4.

A fine warm day like summer. Spent the day reading and writing. We are located in a ravene some 10 rods wide, with lofty mountains on all Sides. The creek runs to the East. We can be said to be fairly in the Mts. The one in front of us is covered with those lofty pines of which Freemont speaks.

Christmas Day. I spent most of the day in diggin, though I got but $1. I allso mended my pants & took supper of our everyday fare, fried pork & hoecake.

It had begun to look as though the new attempt might be no more successful than the northern venture where so many men before them had turned over the ground. By the first week of January, Hiram was despondent:

Ten months since I left home & have not made a dollar but am in debt for my board & my Health seems insufficient for the task. After the opperation of the Phisic I felt some better. Oh the loneliness of this desolate region! No Meeting, no Society, nought but drinking & card-playing & hunting on the Sabbath. At noon I had a slight chill & severe headache. In the afternoon I felt sore & stiff.

Felt much better. Dug 3 hours & began to feel chilley. Got $2.50. Today 2 Indians called at our house, naked except a cotton Shirt that served as breech cloth on one & the other had a blanket verry curiously wrought of feathers.

A verry wintery morning. I tried digging 2 hours, but the ground verry full of water & I made nothing. Carried a letter to a sort of an express that takes them down to Stockton & San Francisco once a month at $4 & brings them up at $2.

A pleasant day. Dug $6. Last night called for my board bill & was charged $21 per week, 10 weeks $210 for pork & hoecake & done part of the cooking myself at that. Resolved to board my Self.

By February, the rest of the group gave up the struggle. Hiram stayed on with one man for company, but did no better:

A fine day. After breckfast worked hard & got $2.
Worked verry hard but with poor success.
Comenced work on my claim in the aroyer, but got verry little.
Dug a hole in my lot. A perfect failure.
A fine day. Made some cake in the morning. Wrote a letter home.
Worked in sinking a hole. Got $1. Paid for 1 lb dried Aples $1. Potatoes $1.
Saw a man pick up a piece of gold near our House worth $100. Got 8 letters from the family. Carrige on them, $11.

Things went on like that until March, when Hiram began to feel ill again:

87

Worked in forenoon. Got $8. At noon had a dum Ague. Felt weak
& headache.

Did not work. My ill health & water prevented. Fixed an auger.
One year to day since I left my happy home.

Worked but got little. Kept my bed most of the day.

A fine day. Dug $6.

Dug $2. Felt well.

A fine day. A caucus was held today by the miners to nominate can-
didates for the different offices to be voted for tomorrow. I have now
spent four months and one half in this place & worked hard, & been
diligent, yet lack $125 of paying my board from my earnings & live
some of the time as I would hardly ask a dog to live.

Hiram had one more fling at gold, down on the Merced
with a new partner. But the luck was no better. They found
gold, but not enough to leave anything over after living expenses were paid. His note is brief and to the point:

Worked again on the Bar & then concluded to abandon it & give it
up as a total loss. It is so full of immense Boulders that it is next to
impossible with our tools to get down to the ledge, & if we could get
there it must be richer than anything I have yet seen to pay.

Having abandoned the bar, Hiram and his partner spent a
day or two prospecting up the river, but turned up little:

Went to work & got but little. Became disheartened. Went up a creek
prospecting, got nothing, came back & talked of starting for Home.
Cooked some beans & washed. Howard's face as long as a Horse's head
& I with a sty on my eye. Mr Bixby died this p.m. in a fit. His leg &
foot mortified. I killed 2 tarantlers close to our tent as big as small
Chickens.

Whether it was the bad luck prospecting up that unnamed
creek, the stye in his eye, Mr. Bixby's horrid death or maybe
the "tarantlers" big as chickens, Hiram's talk of going home
blossomed into action the next day. From his dwindling cash
reserve he settled his board bill, paid his way down to San
Francisco and engaged passage for New York by way of the

88

Isthmus. His diary records the vicissitudes of the trip on which he suffered from a fever contracted on the Chagres River and as a result lived almost entirely on oranges between Jamaica and home. On January 8, 1851, his journal closes with a final entry:

Still weak & feeble with Chagres Fever. Joined my family with rejoicing.

One may suppose that the feeling was mutual. Hiram Pierce had had nearly three years of adventuring, had spent far more money than he had made, was ill with rheumatism and strange fevers, and no younger for his hardships. As the Californians put it, he had "seen the elephant." Yet he had come back; something many another Argonaut had not done. His family, at any rate, had reason enough to rejoice.

Hiram Pierce, to be sure, was a conservative and godly man; moreover he was a bit older than most of his companions and he had a family to draw him home again.

There were others who stayed, tens of thousands of them, not much luckier than he at making their fortunes, but more hopeful, perhaps, or less willing to go back to unromantic jobs. Some of them, without doubt, were rough customers, drinkers, brawlers, good-for-nothings. Very likely, too, some hitherto conservative young men were led to throw restraint to the winds now that they were far from home. The mines held enough of these to lend color to the wild tales of week-end carousing that have come down to us, the notion of the "miner's Saturday night" as one steady round of drinking, gambling, and visiting the euphemistically named "fandango houses" of the settlements. The fact remains that, in these first years at any rate, most of the Argonauts were not like that. Ninety-nine out of a hundred hoped for nothing better than to make their pile and take it home with them. Their minds and their hearts were in the East, with parents and sweethearts. Because they had always been decent, law-abiding citizens the ideas of law and order were ingrained in them. Wherefore the first thing they did was to come together, group by group and settlement by settlement, and put together some assortment of rules, by which their lives would be governed. They were Americans, and as such they believed in laws. Many of them had come to California as members of a "Company" which, as a matter of course, meant rules and regulations to govern the association. The principle of getting together and talking things over in a manner fair to all was one too deeply rooted to ignore. From one end of the mines to the other, acting independently because the spirit of fair play and respect for law was a part of them, groups of miners established what were to be the rules of the game of gold, the actual foundation of the principles of mining law which developed through the years in California.

It was natural that the first matter to receive attention was the question of rights in mining claims. The regulations differed slightly in different areas, but in principle they were all the same. At bottom they were made to protect all men's rights equally, to prevent any one from riding over the rights of his neighbor, to apportion the good luck—if there was any —as evenly as men could do it. Here, for instance, is a typical example of early miners' laws, reprinted for the first time from the single bluish-white sheet of paper on which they were drawn up in ink that is now faded and brown:

By Laws for Washington Flat

At a meeting of the miners upon Washington Flat, held April 6, 1850, Mr. H. D. Pierce was chosen Chairman and Mr. Thomas Day Secretary. The House being called to order, the Chairman stated the object of the meeting, which was to select an Alcalde and a Sheriff. Mr. J. P. Ward was elected by Ballot to the office of Alcalde and

Mr. J. Shores to the office of Sheriff. A motion was then made and carried that three men be chosen to draw up resolutions to regulate mining operations. Mr. J. F. Thompson, P. T. Williams and Mr. Thomas Day were chosen as such committee. Agreeable to which, the committee reported Saturday eve, April 13, the following resolutions which were adopted.

1st Resolved:
That each individual be entitled to sixteen feet upon the River extending from bank to bank.

2nd Resolved:
That no claim shall be forfeited unless left for three consecutive days without tools, unless prevented by sickness or winter.

3rd Resolved:
That any Company designing to turn the River shall give at least one week's "Public Notice" of their intentions in order to allow every person an opportunity of joining said Company. And said Company shall be entitled to all they improve.

4th Resolved:
That power to decide in questions of difficulties respecting claims or mining operations be vested in the Alcalde.

5th Resolved:
That these resolutions may be altered or amended by a vote of the majority of any Public Meeting duly notified.

Jas. F. Thompson,
Chairman of Committee

The reader will note that no attention is paid here to the ordinary matters of government any community would require. The Forty-Niners were not greatly concerned about such affairs. It was the law about gold mining that must first be clearly set down and understood. As for other things, an Alcalde had been well and duly elected; he could judge in any sort of case, even if he did bear the Spanish designation. And he had a Sheriff to enforce his decisions. Well and good. The community could take care of itself.

In general, the community did just that, often with Spartan

Jackson, Amador County, 1857

Jackson's first fame came from its use as a stage stop
and way station for teamsters hauling freight between the valley

towns and Mokelumne Hill. It later became the county seat and the site of two deep underground mines.

severity. Whippings were common, sometimes a thief was branded or had his ears cut off; Bayard Taylor records meeting a man whose sentence for stealing gold had been to receive one hundred lashes, have his head shaved and his ears cropped. Occasionally thieves were hanged. A killing, even in a drunken fight, meant the noose, and often without too much ceremony. Sometimes the Sheriff did his best to prevent such summary executions, but seldom with much success. The miners seemed to realize that in a new, sparsely populated country where such riches abounded justice must be swift and harsh. And the results came close to justifying the means. In those first years, there was relatively little crime. A man could leave his cabin for days or weeks, come back to it, and find everything as it was left. Men seemed to realize that the interests of one were the interests of all. Bound together in a common enterprise, they saw they had to stick together, reject the individual who refused to conform and do it severely enough so that the nonconformist would adjust himself for the common good or get out.

Sometimes, to be sure, administration of justice bordered on the comic. The typically American frontier humor was coming to its height, and the frontier was rough and enjoyed its roughness. There was, for example, the court of a firebrand Texan, Major R. C. Barry, who had settled in Sonora, Tuolumne County, and for his strength of character rather than for any attainments in the law was elected justice of the peace. The records of this strangest of all Justices are still preserved, scraps and odds and ends of paper upon which the redoubtable Major kept notes of the cases that came before him. Edna Buckbee, in *The Saga of Old Tuolumne,* reprints many of them, and a few samples are worth quoting. One, for instance, demonstrates how little the gentleman from Texas thought of any Mexican:

No. 60. This was a gambling scrape in which T. Smith the monte deeler shot and wounded Felipe Vega. After heering witnesses on both sides, I ajeudged Smith guilty of the shooting and fined him 10 dolars, and Vega guilty of attempting to steele 5 ounces.

I therefore fined him 100 dolars and Costs of Coort. Costs of Coort 3 ounces. R. C. Barry, Justice Peace. U. H. Brown, Constable.

The Major was something of a minor Solomon in his way, too, as is shown by his decision in a claim-jumping suit:

No. 500. Civil caze. This was a caze in which James Touer had jumped a peece of grun that the Wideawake Co. claimed as part of thear claim. Upon heering the evidense of all the witnesses on boath sides, and taking the caze under avisement, I came to the folowing conclusion that boath parties is in falt. I therefore decree that the grun be equally divided, and one haf be returned to James Touer and one haf to the Wideawake Co. and that each pay one haf the Costs of Coort share and share alik. Costs of Coort 6 ounces, and that each stand comited til each of them pays thear amount. R. C. Barry, Justice Peace. U. H. Brown, Constable.

It is clear that the "Costs of Coort" were well to the fore in Justice Barry's consideration. Indeed, the following decision makes this abundantly plain:

No. 516. This is a suite for Mule Steeling in which Jesus Ramirez is indited fur steeling one black mare Mule, branded O with a 5 in it from sheriff Work. George swares the Mule in question is hisn and I believe so. On hearing the caze I found Jesus Ramirez of feloaniusly and against the law made and privided and the dignity of the people of Sonora steeling the aforesade mare Mule sentensed him to pay the Costs of Coort 10 dolars, and fine him a 100 dolars more as a terrour to all evil dooers. Jesus Ramirez not having any munney to pay with I rooled that George Work shuld pay the Costs of Coort, as well as the fine, an in defalt of payment that the said one mare Mule be sold by the Constable John Luney or other officer of the Coort to meet the expenses of the Costs of the Coort, as also the payment of the fine aforesade. R. C. Barry, Justice Peace. John Luney, Constable.

It is hardly surprising that now and then some litigant of greater temerity than his fellows would complain of the sum-

93

mary style in which the fiery Major conducted his court. Such complaint was made regarding the high-handed manner in which Justice Barry had commandeered the stolen mare mule in order to make sure of his costs. The Major himself adds the postscript to the case.

H. P. Barber, the lawyer for George Work in solently told me there were no law fur me to rool so I told him that I did not care a damn for his book law, that I was the Law myself. He jawed back so I told him to shetup but he would not so I fined him 50 dolars and comited him to gaol fur 5 days fur contempt of Coort in bringing my roolings and disissions into disreputableness and as a warning to unrooly citizens not to contredict this Coort.

The Major was plainly a man who meant business, though it is also apparent that he judged his cases honestly and intelligently, as a man who relied upon his common sense and let the law books go hang. One more quotation will show that though the Major watched his costs he was also willing to mete out punishment which brought the court no profit:

No. 736. In this caze injun Bill was indited fur arsonizing a remada belonging to one John Brown by which he has lost all his furniture, bedding, tools, rifle, shotgun, pistol &c. Sentensed injun Bill to pay 32 dolars and pay for the remada and contents, in defalt to be comited to gaol 60 days and be floged 30 times on his bear back. Costs of Coort, 32 dolars, all of wich was pade by some one. R. C. Barry, Justice Peace. Uriah H. Brown, Constable.

Doubtless the question of the Constable's middle name has already troubled the reader. It would be pleasant to write here that Judge Barry's court sat in the late seventies, which would allow time enough for the Browns to have named their boy out of Dickens and for him to have grown to constabulary age. Unhappily, the cases cited are of the year 1851, not much more than a twelvemonth after the publication in England of *David Copperfield*. To be sure, there is always the possibility that Constable Brown adopted his name entire. Men did that often

94

enough in the mines, when they preferred to leave their pasts behind them. If our Brown was such an escapist there is the heart-warming possibility that his middle initial did, incredibly, stand for "Heep."

The fact that the miner took his law hard did not mean, however, that he was above a bit of gentle joshing when it came to rules and regulations for arranging his daily life. J. M. Hutchings, an Englishman who had his two years of sweating and freezing in the disappointing rivers of California, provided the joke of the year in 1853 when he suddenly conceived the notion of printing on the reverse side of a letter-sheet "The Miners' Ten Commandments" and circulating these throughout the mines. Decorated with a fine, robust border of sketches depicting the miner's life—including a large drawing of an elephant—this new decalogue made Hutchings' fortune. Hardly a cabin in the hills was without a copy tacked to the wall, for the flowery humor of Hutchings' Biblical periods suited precisely the temper of the Argonaut who knew only too well at first hand the wisdom of the author's admonitions. The full text is long and repetitive, but the highlights are worth recording:

The Miners' Ten Commandments

I

Thou shalt have no other claim than one.

II

Thou shalt not make unto thyself any false claim, nor any likeness to a mean man by jumping one.

III

Thou shalt not go prospecting before thy claim gives out. Neither shalt thou take thy money, nor thy gold dust, nor thy good name to the gaming-table in vain; for monte, twenty-one, roulette, faro, lasquenet and poker will prove to thee that the more thou puttest down the less thou shalt take up.

IV

Thou shalt not remember what thy friends do at home on the Sabbath day, lest that remembrance may not compare favorably with that thou doest here. Six days shalt thou dig or pick all that the body can stand under; but the other day is Sunday, yet thou washest all thy dirty shirts, all thy stockings, tap thy boots, mend thy clothing, chop thy whole week's firewood, make up and make thy bread and boil thy pork and beans, that thou wait not when thou returnest from thy long tom weary. For in six days' labor only, thou canst not work enough to wear out thy body in two years; but if thou workest hard on Sundays also, thou canst do it in six months.

V

Thou shalt not think more of thy gold, and how thou canst make it fastest, than of how thou wilt enjoy it after thou hast ridden roughshod over thy good old parents' precepts and examples, that thou mayest have nothing to reproach and sting thee when thou art left ALONE in the land where thy father's blessing and thy mother's love hath sent thee.

VI

Thou shalt not kill thy body by working in the rain, even though thou shalt make enough to buy physic and attendance therewith. Neither shalt thou destroy thyself by getting tight, nor stewed, nor high, nor corned, nor half-seas over, nor three sheets in the wind, by drinking smoothly down brandy slings, gin cocktails, whiskey punches, rum toddies, nor egg nogs; for while thou art swallowing down thy purse, and thy coat from off thy back, thou art burning the coat from off thy stomach.

VII

Thou shalt not grow discouraged, nor think of going home before thou hast made thy pile, because thou hast not struck a lead, nor found a rich crevice, lest in going home thou shalt leave four dollars a day and go to work, ashamed, at fifty cents and serve thee right.

VIII

Thou shalt not steal a pick or a shovel or a pan from thy fellow miner; nor take away his tools without his leave; nor borrow those he cannot spare; nor return them broken, nor trouble him to fetch them back again, nor talk with him while his water rent is running on, nor

remove his stake to enlarge thy claim, nor undermine his bank in following a lead, nor pan out gold from his riffle-box, nor wash the tailings from his sluice's mouth. Neither shalt thou pick out specimens from
the company's pan to put them in thy mouth, or in thy purse; nor cheat
thy partner of his share, nor steal from thy cabin-mate his gold dust;
for he will be sure to discover what thou hast done, and will straight-
way call his fellow miners together, and if the law hinder them not
they will hang thee, or give thee fifty lashes, or shave thy head and
brand thee with "R" upon thy cheek, to be known and read of all men,
Californians in particular.

IX

Thou shalt not tell any false tales about "good diggings in the mountains" to thy neighbor that thou mayest benefit a friend who hath mules
and provisions, tools and blankets he cannot sell, lest in deceiving thy
neighbor when he shall return with naught save his rifle he present
thee with the contents thereof, and, like a dog, thou shalt fall down
and die.

X

Thou shalt not commit unsuitable matrimony, nor covet single
blessedness, nor forget absent maidens, nor neglect thy first love; but
thou shalt consider how faithfully she awaiteth thy return; yea and
cover each epistle that thou sendest with kisses until she hath thyself.

And a new Commandment I give unto thee; if thou hast a wife and
little ones that thou lovest dearer than life, thou keep them continually
before thee to cheer and urge thee onward until thou canst say "I have
enough. I will return!" Then as thou journeyest toward thy home they
shall come forth to welcome thee and in the fullness of thy heart thou
shalt kneel together before thy Heavenly Father to thank him for thy
safe return. AMEN. So mote it be.

FORTY NINE

It is not hard to see why the "Commandments" sold more
than a hundred thousand copies in the first year after Hutchings introduced them to the mines. It is even easier to understand why their author forswore mining and stuck to publishing. He tried to repeat his success with a "Miners' Creed"
and a little later with a set of "Commandments for California
Wives," neither of which brought him any profit. But he had

97

made a tidy sum with his first venture, enough to let him found and publish for five years *Hutchings' California Magazine,* which later became a significant part of the state's literary life.

It must not be supposed that the honest miner of these earlier days had no fun at all.

He worked hard and long, and if he did better than ten dollars a day on the average he was a very lucky man. His costs were sky-high, even when it came to the barest essentials of living, and there was much that he could not buy at any price. He spent his Sundays washing and mending, baking the next week's bread, repairing his tools, industriously bringing his diary up to date, and conscientiously writing home. Sometimes he could get to a near-by settlement large enough to boast a church, or, if he preferred to let down a little after the week's labors, a saloon. But it took a little time for even the crude towns to grow, to acquire the trimmings wherewith the miner might decorate his week-ends, and in any event hundreds of camps were isolated, lost in the cañons and arroyos of the great California rivers. For a time, the miner made his own entertainment, and a man with a banjo or a fiddle was in demand for miles around. Down in San Francisco things were different. As early as 1849, the Philadelphia Minstrels had made an appearance at the Bella Union, and there were enough pianos and halls to play them in so that concerts were a popular form of entertainment. Stephen Massett had written "You're All the World to Me" and it was selling well, while by 1852 the Calvary Presbyterian Church had its organ installed and San Francisco's élite heard the "Stabat Mater," done for the first time in California. But the mines were content with fiddle or flute, banjo or guitar, and the miners sang because singing was a group affair, something that reminded them of home.

98

Many of their songs were straight reporting. The journey to California was fresh in the minds of all, and such tunes as "Crossing the Plains" and "Coming Round the Horn" were sung everywhere. One stanza of the latter is a good example of how well the Forty-Niner liked to recall the minutest details of his great experience:

> We lived like hogs penned up to fat,
> Our vessel was so small.
> We had a "duff" but once a month,
> And twice a day a squall.
> A meeting now and then was held
> Which kicked up quite a stink;
> The Captain damned us fore and aft
> And wished the box would sink.

The song, "The Fools of Forty-Nine" was another popular favorite; so was "The Ballad of the Happy Miner," and just to show that there was still hope, no matter how unlucky a man might have been, there was "There's a Good Pile Coming, Boys!" which no doubt helped many a weary gold-seeker pluck up courage. "Oh, Susannah!" must have come in for its share of choruses, of course; it was one song everybody knew. And there was the ironic number called "Hangtown Gals," in which the miner expressed his opinion of the ladies who thought themselves too good for him:

> Hangtown gals are plump and rosy,
> Hair in ringlets, mighty cozy;
> Painted cheeks and jossy bonnets,
> Touch 'em and they'll sting like hornets!

CHORUS

> Hangtown gals are lovely creatures
> Think they'll marry Mormon preachers;
> Heads thrown back to show their features,
> Ha, ha, ha! Hangtown gals!

99

Perhaps the most symbolic of them all was the song into
which the miner put the whole of his disillusionment with the
grand bonanza fairy-tale, the song whose title was the widely-
used phrase that meant a man had paid his money and, Barnum-
wise, been hoaxed—"Seeing the Elephant." Here again in one
of the verses the miner used his song to show what he thought
of the girl who considered the mere miner so far below her:

> I fell in love with a California girl
> Her eyes were gray, her hair did curl;
> Her nose turned up to get rid of her chin,
> Says she, "You're a miner, you can't come in!"

Not that all the singing had to do with California or the
mines. There were plenty of homesick men who liked to
revive memories of yesterday, and the fiddlers often enough
sawed away at "Joe Bowers," or "The Hog-Eye Man,"
"Wait for the Wagon," "Camptown Races," "Pop Goes the
Weasel," and other melodies brought along from the east.
But they were in California and it was the new country and
its occupations, its habits and its customs that were foremost
in all minds. Yankee-like, when men found things hard they
joked about them, made wryly humorous comments, produced
songs that expressed the full irony of their position. Wherefore, just as the enthusiastic, hopeful, rousing "Oh, Susannah!"
was the theme of Forty-Nine, so another briefer, sharper,
dryer little verse became the theme of the Fifties, when the
miners had seen the elephant, knew where they stood, and
had their own opinion of the new thousands that were crowding in. In four short lines the song showed the temper of the
changing times:

> Oh, what was your name in the States?
> Was it Thompson or Johnson or Bates?
> Did you murder your wife
> And fly for your life?
> Say, what was your name in the States?

The honest miner might affect to scorn "Hangtown gals," and perhaps he did. Not all Forty-Niners had left wives behind, however, or sweethearts either. As the foot-hill country settled down and the first camps began to take on the aspect of permanence, more than one Argonaut who had been lucky enough to salt away a bit of money wished that he might find a good wife in this lonesome California. Already their more fortunate fellows were bringing out families from the East. Schoolmarms were wooed and often won before they had begun to instruct the children they had come to teach. And the growing air of domesticity was tantalizing to the bachelor who had to sew and scrub and cook still, as he had done in the beginning. Then every one had had to tackle those tasks. Now, only a year or two later, a man felt awkward doing a woman's work. It was too bad that more young ladies from "the States" where there were so frequently not enough men to go round could not turn the circumstances to good account.

As a matter of fact, some did, making the risky trip all the way to California to try their luck at husband-hunting. At least one such enterprising maiden has left her story in an early Marysville newspaper through whose advertising columns she boldly set out to find the man she wanted. She must have had a sound sense of humor, that young lady of Forty-Nine, and there can be little doubt that any woman possessed of her spunk and spirit eventually got what she was after in the new country. Here is her advertisement, a curiously modern note echoing from the past:

A HUSBAND WANTED

BY A LADY WHO can wash, cook, scour, sew, milk, spin, weave, hoe, (can't plow), cut wood, make fires, feed the pigs, raise chickens, rock the cradle, (gold-rocker, I thank you, Sir!), saw a plank, drive nails, etc. These are a few of the solid branches; now for the ornamental. "Long time ago" she went as far as syntax, read Murray's Geography and through two rules in Pike's Grammar. Could find 6

states on the Atlas. Could read, and you can see she can write. Can—
no, *could*—paint roses, butterflies, ships, etc., but now she can paint
houses, whitewash fences, etc. Could once dance; can ride a horse,
donkey or oxen, besides a great many things too numerous to be named
here. Oh, I hear you ask, could she scold? No, she can't, you ———
——— good-for-nothing ———!

Now for her terms. Her age is none of your business. She is neither
handsome nor a fright, yet an *old* man need *not* apply, nor any who
have not a little more education than she has, and a great deal more
gold, for there must be $20,000 settled on her before she will bind
herself to perform all the above. Address to DOROTHY SCRAGGS,
with real name. P. O. Marysville.

Miss Scraggs was straightforward enough, and if her price
was high, doubtless she was worth it.

Not all women in the mines, however, valued themselves so
highly. The miner who could by no means afford a wife with
the extraordinary accomplishments of this young lady of
Marysville, nor perhaps any wife at all, was not entirely at a
loss for feminine companionship. At first the American miner
affected to scorn the Mexican "fandango halls" with which
the southern mines particularly were well supplied. When
there was music and he had the urge to dance he found himself a partner among his fellow miners. At such dances half
the men tied handkerchiefs about their upper arms, and these
were the ladies. It did well enough for the sake of sport. But
the prejudice against fandango halls soon broke down. Often
these were combined with gambling rooms; always they included a well-stocked bar. And as the miner began to pat-
ronize them more and more frequently, their number grew.
More Mexican girls, too, moved up into the camps, some of
them dancing partners and some a good deal more than that.
It was a girl of this undetermined status who caused the first
great scandal of the gold rush, the girl Juanita, first and only
woman hanged in the mines. The story of her taking-off—not
to mention its justifications—is in many ways the clearest re-

flection of the way in which the mines were changing, moving on into a period in which men would have to organize more strictly for law, order and justice, for defense of their property and themselves against the new and irresponsible element that was beginning to infest the golden hills.

Like most tales of the time, that of Juanita is full of contradictions and confusions brought about by those who have told her story without caring greatly about facts. There is even ground for questioning her name; in most re-tellings of the story she is Juanita, but there is some evidence that she may have been christened Josefa. Undoubtedly she was of Latin blood, probably Mexican, perhaps Spanish or Chilean. One narrator says positively that she was Peruvian, and he may be right.

Juanita lived in Downieville in the summer of 1851, occupying an adobe house with a Mexican named José. She may or may not have been properly married to him; most accounts speak of her as a "dance-hall girl," a euphemism in common acceptance. Downieville was a thriving mining community of some three thousand souls, sprawled along both banks of the North Fork of the Yuba River, its two portions connected by a bridge between Jersey Flat and Durgan's Flat. (This, by the way, explains why in some accounts the bridge is called Durgan's and in others the Jersey Bridge.) The town had its quota of saloons and dance halls, perhaps a few more than its share. And when a bang-up Fourth of July celebration was announced, miners came from up river and down to join in the doings. Liquor and oratory flowed in their just proportions, flags flew from every roof and window; it was a holiday worth shouting about and the Yuba miners made all the noise they pleased. There was one stabbing, but the offender was sentenced to a whipping and got it on the spot. Downieville liked its good time, but its citizens prided themselves on their respect for the rights of others.

Precisely where the Scotsman, Cannon, and his friend Lawson had been on that Fourth of July it is impossible to tell now. Doubtless they had done their best to celebrate the occasion along with the rest of the town. It is well established, however, that late in the evening, on their way home, the two managed to smash the door of the house in which lived Juanita and her Mexican lover. It may have been purposely done; there are those who claim that Cannon had been pursuing Juanita without success, and he may have conceived the drunken notion of breaking in on her, José or no José. Or the whole affair may have been an accident; there is at least one account which makes much of Cannon's good behavior and general peaceable demeanor as a well-known citizen of Downieville. Nevertheless the door was broken down. Cannon and his companion went on their way without doing further damage; their Fourth of July was over.

On the events of the next morning, accounts conflict again. One is to the effect that Cannon, headachy and remorseful, took Lawson with him to apologize for the broken door and to offer to have it fixed. Another says that Cannon and Lawson were passing the house, that the man José came out into the street and demanded payment for the damage, that Cannon denied any knowledge of it, and that the argument became sufficiently heated so that Lawson was compelled to caution the Mexican against any use of a deadly weapon. Whichever version you choose, Cannon and Lawson were at the door of Juanita's house on that morning of the fifth of July, and whatever the words that led to the act, Juanita snatched a knife from her dress and buried it in Cannon's breast.

It did not take long to gather a crowd, improvise a quick court, and condemn Juanita to hang. There was some debate about the verdict; a Dr. Aiken did his best to convince the miners that the girl was with child and should be spared; several others made speeches in her defense. But it was no use.

A temporary scaffold was run up on the river bank near the bridge, Juanita was permitted to speak long enough to repeat her story that Cannon had insulted her, and the executioner dropped the noose around her neck. One story declares that her hands were not tied, that she raised her long braids so the hangman might adjust the rope properly about her throat, and that she called *"Adiós, Señores!"* as the drop fell. Perhaps she did.

As to the justice or lack of it which prompted the action of the citizens of Downieville that day, discussion has been rife ever since. Not many years ago the people of the town did not like to be reminded that they had once hanged a woman. To-day they take pains to tell the visitor the story. It may be that the older men regarded the affair as did the editor of the Sonora *Union Democrat,* who wrote bitterly of the incident in his paper.

At Downieville [he said] was perpetrated the greatest possible crime against humanity, Christianity and civilization. A drunken gambler, with criminal audacity, had thrust himself into the presence of a Spanish woman of doubtful character. She was *enceinte;* enraged at his demeanor she seized a knife in a moment of passion, thrust it into his breast and killed him. The gambler was popular, as gamblers may be and as many are. The mob, in angry excitement, seized the poor, trembling, wretched woman, tried, convicted and hanged her; hanged her in spite of her situation, her entreaties, and the fact that she killed her assailant in defense of her person.

But it is apparent that to-day's citizens rather lean toward the account of the incident given by a correspondent signing himself "Veritas," in the San Francisco *Alta,* a few months after the affair. "Veritas" explained that he was weary of hearing the Juanita case misrepresented, particularly by a recent newspaper article, and proceeded to give his view.

It would be difficult [he wrote] to find in the annals of human wickedness an instance of a murder so unprovoked and so unjustifiable.

Murphy's, Calaveras County, California 1857

When John and Daniel Murphy came up to the gold country from Monterey in 1848, they hired Indians to work their diggings at this spot. By the

end of the year, those laborers had washed out the incredible
sum of a million and a half dollars for Daniel and John.

The excitement that the affair created was great; but in the speedy trial that followed, scarcely a dozen persons out of the thousands who witnessed it could see the slightest injustice. It was true that, for the defence, it was stated by "her physician" that she was pregnant; but at the consultation that followed, it was declared by competent professional men that "there was no reason to believe pregnancy existed." The people did not "by vote order" Dr. Aiken to leave town because he declared the woman to be *enceinte,* but because they believed his object was to screen her from justice.

The victim in this instance was not the first nor the second who had been stabbed by the same female. He was a man who had by his good conduct and peaceable demeanor made hosts of friends, by whom his untimely fate is deplored. It is disingenuous and unfair to speak of Scotsmen having been on the jury, &c. The trial and execution of the murderess were the acts of Americans, who are generally too magnanimous to admit of any favoritism in the administration of justice.... I have lived long enough in Downieville to know that its inhabitants are not the bloodthirsty, diabolical monsters they have been represented; on the contrary they have heretofore been too mild in their punishment of offenders; and in the case before us, nothing induced them to pursue the course they did but retributive justice.

To-day's reader may take his choice. Whatever the right of it, Downieville did hang a woman. That act, just or unjust, may serve as a line drawn between the early and innocent days when gold mining was a game—a hard, exhausting, often unlucky one but still a game, played among friends—and the dawning of the second phase of California's gold rush. It was not that the "honest miner" disappeared. It was simply that there came to be fewer of him in proportion to the men who came to see what they could pick up by their wits rather than with their hands and backs. And for a few feverish years the story of the mines is the story of the early-day bad men and the struggle to put them down.

4.

"Scoundrels from Nowhere"

AS the 1850's advanced, and rush camps continued to develop where fresh strikes were made, the mines rapidly took on their new complexion.

It was not a very pleasant one. There were fewer of the decent and honest Californians who had grown up in the quiet land of plenty and had taken their fling at the gold in the creeks more for the fun of it than anything else. The Forty-Niners had pushed them aside anyway. Most of them had gone back to their ranches, into business or banking, had moved down into the new cities around the Valley and the Bay where excitement might be less but profits more certain. Now, however, the Forty-Niner was being elbowed out of the way in his turn. Men were pouring into California from everywhere. Any one who stopped to think saw what was happening, though not every one interpreted it in the same way. Indeed, two well-informed men of the period ascribed the new, turbulent, lawless spirit to almost opposite causes.

One was a shrewd, dry Scotsman named Hugo Reid, long a California rancher and trader and married into one of the old Spanish families. His letter to a friend, preserved in Susanna Bryant Dakin's *A Scotch Paisano,* makes clear his views. He writes:

Don't go to the mines on any account. They are loaded to the muzzle with vagabonds from every quarter of the globe, scoundrels from nowhere, rascals from Oregon, pickpockets from New York, accomplished gentlemen from Europe, interlopers from Lima and Chile, Mexican thieves, gamblers of no particular spot, and assassins manufactured in Hell for the express purpose of converting highways and byways into theaters of blood!

That was putting it frankly; Hugo Reid knew what he thought and liked to say it openly and plainly. But it was not all of the story. Many a bad character in the mines had been a bad character before he ever saw California; but there was another side to the matter, and the Editor of the San Francisco *Alta* saw that. One day the news of a particularly bold robbery and murder put him into the frame of mind to say what he thought:

Men come to California in the hope of speedily becoming rich. Bright visions of big lumps of gold and large quantities of them, to be gathered without any severe labor, haunt them night and day before they reach here. Here they hope to find a land where the inevitable law of God that "man shall earn his bread by the sweat of his brow," has been repealed, or at least for a time suspended. They come here with this hope, and it takes but a few short weeks to dispel it. They are disappointed; their impatient desire for the attainment of speedy wealth seems to have no prospect of gratification. Temptations are about them on every hand. They drink and they gamble. They associate with men who, in their Eastern homes, would be shunned by them as the worst of their kind. They forget the admonitions of their mothers and sisters, given them at parting. They forget the purity of their early youth, the hopes of their riper manhood. They sink lower and lower, until they become thieves, robbers and desperadoes.

Doubtless there was something in that, too. The new lawlessness was partly due to the influx of bad types from the rest of the world—ex-convicts from the Sydney prisons, shady characters from the East, reckless adventurers from anywhere and everywhere. Some of it was the result, as the *Alta* editor suggested, of disappointment; the young man who came to California to get rich and did not get rich lawfully, turned to crime if he lacked the strength of character to take hard work and discouragement in his stride. Over and above these things, there was the harsh treatment given the "foreigner" by the American miners who resented the Mexican and the Chileño especially because of their dark skins. The taxes cooked up by these new Californians and imposed upon the Mexicans and others of their color were bad enough. But more than once it did not stop at taxes. Mexicans were beaten, driven off their claims, robbed and often enough murdered on the slightest pretext or none at all. It was not surprising that many of them took to the road to revenge themselves upon the Americans who had refused to let them have their equal chance.

Those who had time to scan the San Francisco newspapers on the morning of Saturday, July 30, 1853, saw at first very little to excite them.

True, there were more strikes on the water-front and the labor unrest seemed to be spreading. Firemen and coal-passers were demanding higher pay, and they had actually found the effrontery to organize into associations and parade by torchlight. This had stimulated carpenters, bricklayers, plasterers, and blacksmiths to ask raises on their own account, which was extremely disturbing to men who believed in sound American principles.

But there was always some fracas or other with labor. It was pleasanter to note that the clipper-ship, *Wings of the Morning,* had beat her way successfully round the Horn with a large consignment of choice liquors and fine Havana cigars. On the night before, Miss Leach had sung *Oh, Araby! Dear Araby!* so fetchingly at Meiggs's Music Hall that she was compelled to render several encores, and down at the American Theater audiences were offered a double bill—*The Rivals,* and a shorter playlet, *Actress of Padua,* in which Mrs. Sinclair, according to the *Herald's* drama critic, had "full scope for the portrayal of the passions dominant in the female breast." The city council was exercised over the annual problem of whether to renew its contract with the State Marine Hospital, build a hospital of its own, or try boarding public patients with private physicians. Down near Mariposa there had been a minor dance-hall shooting; nothing of much account, so the correspondent hinted, but merely a fight over "one of the ladies."

There was one mildly interesting story on the second page. It was headed, "Capture & Death of Joaquin, the Bandit."

That little item, scarcely a hundred and fifty words long, chronicled the end of a man whose career later became the theme for dozens of stories, articles, plays, and even a motion-picture—the bandit Joaquin Murieta. Publicized, glorified, exaggerated into a curious combination of horrid monster and chivalrous gentleman, Joaquin Murieta has come down to us to-day in the guise of as fantastic a Robin Hood as sentimental human nature ever invented. Hardly a town along the Mother Lode is without its cavern, cellar, or tunnel, in or through which Murieta dodged the law. From one end of the foot-hills to the other the legend runs: Murieta once held up a store here; Murieta killed a man on that hill; Murieta and his lieutenant, the frightful Three Fingered Jack, slaughtered seven Chinamen in those woods. More, those who tell the tales repeat them solemnly as truth. The fiction and the few facts have become so closely interwoven that no one questions either. Yet it is possible to trace, at least fairly closely, the development of the Murieta legend. And when this is done it becomes apparent that, philosophically at least, there were two Murietas. One was the Mexican who had turned outlaw and killer and was making sufficient nuisance of himself, in company with others like him—including several also named Joaquin—so that a company of State Rangers was formed to drive him and his friends out of the hills or otherwise get rid of them. The other Murieta was a creature born full-panoplied from the roving imagination of a half-breed editor named John R. Ridge. Naturally it is the latter Murieta that has become the legend. When legends are a-building, facts are awkward and hampering affairs.

The *Herald* reporter confined himself at least fairly well to facts. He wrote:

The famous bandit, Joaquin, whose name is associated with a hundred deeds of blood, has at last been captured. The Company of State Rangers under the command of Harry Love, have been diligent in their search for the robber and his band ever since their organization. We apprised our readers some time since that they had received information that Joaquin was lurking in the wilds of Tulare Valley, whither they accordingly directed their search. It is reported that they have encountered the robber-chief himself at the head of his band at a place called Panoche Pass. A desperate fight ensued—the robbers, well mounted, attempted to fly, but being closely pursued by the Rangers, they kept up a running fight until Joaquin and one of his lieutenants were killed; two others were taken prisoners, and three managed to make their escape. Several of their horses fell into the hands of the rangers. The victors, finding further pursuit of the fugitives useless, cut off the head of Joaquin and placed it in spirits, to be brought to the settlements as proof that the veritable robber himself had been killed.

That was the entire story. The *Alta's* account was substantially the same, excepting that its conscientious correspondent added a postscript in which he made the point that during the "engagement" the Rangers had been commanded not by Captain Harry Love, their rightful head, but by Captain "Burns." As it turned out, the name should have been "Byrnes," but otherwise the addendum was accurate. Just why Captain Love was not in the field at the moment of the fight was never properly explained.

Who and what, then, was Murieta? The plain truth is that nobody knows very much about him. Between the years 1850 and 1853 the peace of the gold region was troubled by various outlaws, some of them certainly Mexican, several of them rejoicing in the name of Joaquin—among them Joaquin Carrillo, Joaquin Valenzuela, and Joaquin Murieta.

For two years, these men with groups of lawless hangers-on, had ranged the country stealing cattle, robbing settlements, holding up travelers, killing whenever it seemed to them necessary, often wantonly, which gave color to the notion that revenge might be involved as well as gain. Then the State grew tired of it all. Perhaps the pressure that was brought to bear on Governor Bigler and his legislature was the result of aroused public sentiment. Perhaps it was specific pressure, brought by persons interested in profit through upholding the law; there is at least fair ground for suspecting that the latter was the case. Whichever it was, early in May, 1853, an act was passed authorizing one Harry Love to form a company of State Rangers whose duty it would be to scour the hills and capture or kill the bandits who were causing all the trouble. It is interesting to note that this Act did not specify Joaquin Murieta. It defined as the purpose of the Rangers the capture of "the five Joaquins," fixed the pay of each Ranger at the not inconsiderable sum of $150 per month, and set the period of their authority at three months. To this incentive was added a reward of one thousand dollars to be paid by Governor Bigler himself. Aside from the fact that such an Act was ridiculous on the face of it—a legislature can hardly outlaw with the stroke of a pen five men who have been convicted of nothing—the whole affair smelled of skullduggery somewhere. Only Harry Love was authorized to do the job. Only Harry Love and his company could collect the reward. His task was to get Joaquin Murieta, Joaquin Carrillo, or anyway some Joaquin. It was odd that no one thought to raise a question at the time. Even for that day, to any one who thought twice it must have looked suspiciously like a set-up made to order for Captain Love.

Very likely it was the reputation of Joaquin Murieta that made anything seem logical that would lead to his capture. For Murieta was the most talked about among all the bandit Joaquins. Maybe his name was easier to remember. Maybe he was in fact the most dangerous of the lot. It was fairly well established that Three-Fingered Jack, his right-hand man, was a villain of the deepest dye. In fact, Jack (whose real name was said to have been Manuel Garcia) had been known throughout California ever since he and several companions had committed two peculiarly atrocious murders shortly after the Bear Flag incident half a dozen years earlier. Whatever the reason, it was Joaquin Murieta whose name had gone abroad, and no matter what theft, robbery, or murder was committed—perhaps by Joaquin Carrillo, Joaquin Valenzuela or another—it was Murieta who had done the job. There was no doubt that he was an outlaw, and if perhaps he hadn't committed all the crimes ascribed to him—even if he was now and then accused of killings occurring simultaneously at places a hundred miles apart—well, he was bad enough and he'd better be caught. Anyhow, some one had better be caught.

It was with this background that Captain Love and his Rangers rode out to perform their duty in the latter part of

May, 1853. And it was with these things in mind—many people thought a few months later—that Captain Love and his men began to wonder, toward the end of July, just where they were getting. They had ridden furiously up and down the hills, used up more than two-thirds of their authorized time at $150 per month per man, and so far had nothing to show. There was a reward, too, and they were no nearer that. In their eyes a Mexican was a Mexican, and no Mexican was any good. There was no point in admitting failure. Clearly the thing to do was to announce success. But the Governor might or might not pay the reward merely on say-so, while a bandit's head and a set of affidavits were actual evidence. Wherefore a head, duly (though not very well) preserved in spirits, was brought to the Governor. Along with it, in another jar, was a mutilated hand declared to be that of Three-Fingered Jack. The reward was collected and so was the pay. Better yet, a few months later a generous legislature, stimulated by some one unspecified, decided that one thousand dollars was nothing like enough for such an achievement, and voted an additional five thousand dollars to Captain Harry Love.

It did not take long for the whisper of shenanigans to get round. Less than a month after the capture and beheading were announced, the editor of the *Alta* was giving voice openly to what so many others were hinting. On August 23, 1853, he printed his story.

It affords some amusement to our citizens [he wrote] to read the various accounts of the capture and decapitation of "the notorious Joaquin Murieta." The humbug is so transparent that it is surprising any sensible person can be imposed upon by the statements of the affair which have appeared in the prints. A few weeks ago a party of native Californians and Sonorians started for the Tulare Valley for the expressed and avowed purpose of running mustangs. Three of the party have returned and report that they were attacked by a party of Americans, and that the balance of their party, four in number, had been killed; that Joaquin Valenzuela, one of them, was killed as he was endeavoring to escape, and that his head was cut off by his captors and held as a trophy. It is too well known that Joaquin Murieta was not the person killed by Captain Harry Love's party at the Panoche Pass. The head recently exhibited in Stockton bears no resemblance to that individual, and this is positively asserted by those who have seen the real Murieta and the spurious head.

But the *Alta's* editor was not content to let it go at that. He had his own ideas about Captain Love and his crowd and was willing to express those too. He continued, rather testily:

All the accounts wind up by recommending the continuing of Love's company in service. All right. The term of service was about expiring, and although I will not say that interested parties have gotten up this Joaquin expedition, yet such expeditions can generally be traced to have an origin with a few speculators.

Moreover, this enterprising newspaper man was determined to have his say on the whole matter of this situation of too many Joaquins. He went on:

At the time of the murder of General Bean at Mission San Gabriel, Murieta was strongly suspected of the crime, and efforts were made to arrest him but he managed to escape. Since then, every murder and robbery in the country has been attributed to "Joaquin." Sometimes it is Joaquin Carrillo that has committed all these crimes; then it is Joaquin Murieta, then Joaquin something else, but always *Joaquin!* The very act of the legislature authorizing a Company to capture "the five Joaquins" was in itself a farce, and these names were inserted in order to kill the bill.

Plainly, the stand of the *Alta* was that the entire business was a humbug, and that Captain Love and his men had got themselves a Mexican head—Valenzuela's perhaps, or another's—arranged for affidavits that it was Murieta's head, since Murieta was best known and his capture would reflect the greatest credit on them, collected their reward and their pay and called it a day.

So much for what happened at the time, the facts as far

as they can be verified by contemporary records. The "Head of Joaquin" was shown in different museums for many years, though it was never completely accepted as the head of Murieta and was constantly the subject of debate. There were arguments also as to Joaquin himself, where he had come from, which crimes he had actually committed, whether he had gone back to Mexico, if the head-in-spirits was not his. Quite naturally none of them came to anything. As for the public, it believed what it chose. The story had got beyond proof anyway. Before long it had begun to grow into a legend.

Just what form the legend might have taken if left to itself is impossible to say now. Because something happened to give it definite shape. Two stories were written about Joaquin Murieta. And from them has stemmed practically everything that has been written or told about him since.

In the autumn of 1859, the California *Police Gazette* brought out in serial form *The Life of Joaquin Murieta, the Brigand Chief of California.* The author, whoever he was, did not sign his story, though he might have done so with credit since it was an immensely readable tale. As for its relation to the facts, that was something else. Done in the flowing "literary" style of its time, it included details of Joaquin's youth in Mexico, quoted conversations Joaquin was supposed to have had with his men in the privacy of their hideouts, and any number of equally obvious fictions. It was unquestionably a work of the imagination for the most part, a dime-novel terror tale, written better than most of its kind but sheer yarn-spinning nevertheless. Indeed, there was no effort made in it to establish any basis of authenticity whatever, other than the declaration by the author that this was the true story of Joaquin Murieta, his life and character, told without ornament. Since this sort of mock-serious assurance was a literary convention of the day, even in the most fantastic fictions, very little reliance can be put upon it. For that matter the internal evidence is plain; throughout, the story gives itself away as pure invention, on its own grounds merely a piece of out-and-out imaginative writing aimed at the type of reader who would be likely to see the periodical in which it appeared, the reader who would be pleased with the yarn for its own sake and perfectly satisfied not to inquire too closely into its truth. It would be interesting to know whether the unknown author expected his tale to be taken as fact, excepting by those who uncritically swallowed whole any story that achieved the dignity of print. It would be even more interesting to know what that anonymous fictioneer would think if he could see his frank imaginings accepted as fact by the scholars of to-day. That is to say, if the imaginings were really his. They may not have been. They may have been lifted wholesale from a half-Cherokee poet, politician, and editor, John Rollin Ridge.

John R. Ridge, well known in the California of his time, also wrote a story of the life of Joaquin. Moreover, he published it five years before the *Police Gazette* tale. Unfortunately, it had little circulation at the time. Authorities have wondered why copies of that 1854 edition were so scarce, since the book was published in San Francisco and should have had a wide reading, at least in California. The answer appears in a letter from John Ridge to a friend in the East. In that letter, written late in 1854 and now preserved in the records of the Cherokee Nation, Ridge declares flatly that his San Francisco publishers decamped with the profits, failing properly to circulate the book they had set up, and that this dishonesty had discouraged him to the point of wishing to leave California. He did not leave, but many years later, in 1871, issued a "third edition" of his story of Murieta, in its preface declaring that "a spurious edition had been foisted upon unsuspecting publishers" since his original one had appeared, and adding that this spurious edition had made fictitious additions to his own "true" tale. Perhaps his new publishers felt that they had better be cautious. At any rate, it appears that they considered the "spurious" edition to be the second, wherefore the 1871 printing was called the third.

In any event, both the Ridge story and that of the unknown *Police Gazette* author are essentially the same. There is one notable discrepancy; the unknown *Police Gazette* author calls Joaquin's wife "Carmela," and kills her off at the very beginning of his tale, while Ridge says her name was "Rosita" and concludes with the florid statement (one wonders where he got his information) that she returned to her native Mexico, "silently and sadly to work out the slow task of a life forever blighted to her, under the roof of the parents of her dead lover." Mr. Walter Noble Burns, author of a twentieth-century book about Murieta, meets this difficulty by calling the girl "Rosita Carmen," which is a pleasant and harmless compromise. In any event, the significant thing about the early accounts and those derived from them in recent years is the interpretation of Joaquin Murieta as a wronged man, persecuted by the American miners, forced to see his wife raped and his brother hanged, himself tied to a tree and whipped for a fault he had not committed, in short driven to his way of life by gross injustice. Whether or not these things happened to Murieta, they parallel things that did happen to many a Mexican. Whatever Murieta did or did not do—and there is no way, now, to disentangle fact from fiction—he and many another like him may well have been forced to an extralegal way of life by the brutal treatment that Americans in general accorded all foreigners, but especially Mexicans, who presumed to think they had any rights in California's gold.

As for the rest of the legend, it follows the traditional Robin Hood pattern too closely to need repeating here. Murieta was gallant to the ladies, true to his word; he robbed and killed those who had money, but gave to the poor. He could control with a mere syllable that frightful monster, Three-Fingered Jack, who loved to slit Chinamen's throats. He would shoot down his own men if they dared to disobey him. In every particular he was the typical folk-hero of all countries and ages. As has always been the case with such heroes' names, Joaquin's has lived. The *Police Gazette* version of his story has turned up in some odd places, translated into many languages. (It is always that version, by the way, and not Ridge's.) One edition was brought out in Santiago, Chile, the text translated from the French. In it, of course, Joaquin is a Chileño. Dramatists have had their way with Joaquin, too; one going so far as to concoct a love-affair between the bandit and the fiery dancer, Lola Montez. Unfortunately such a romance is hardly likely. Lola reached San Francisco in late May, 1853, by which time Captain Love's reward-hunting Rangers were on the trail. She was so well received in the City that it was early July before she got even as far as Sacramento, and mid-July before she appeared in Marysville. By July 25th, some one, Murieta or another, had been beheaded down in Panoche Pass in the Tulare Valley a hundred or two miles away, and all the Joaquins were lying low. As for the movie version, it is a frank enough fiction, based on Walter Noble Burns' tale, which in turn is drawn from Ridge, the *Police Gazette* of 1859, and perhaps from the paper-back that appeared in 1865 in DeWitt's 15-cent series.

To be sure, there is no reason why Murieta should not be fictionized, made into as black a villain or as shining a hero as happens to suit the temperament of the fictioneer or the temper of the time. To be embalmed in novels and plays is the ultimate fate of all folk-heroes, and good swashbuckling material they make, too. But it is as well to distinguish the truths, as far as they may be ascertained, from the inventions; and in the case of Murieta it happens that the known facts are few and the inventions many. It may seem too bad to remind the

Sonora, 1853

Sonora was one of the widest-open towns of them all in a
wide open era. Founded by Mexicans and originally known as

Sonorian Camp, it was one of the first to conclude that only
Americans had the God-given right to mine for gold and that
Mexicans most certainly were not Americans.

citizens of Hornitos and Angels Camp, of Columbia and Sonora and Coulterville and a hundred other towns that remain from the gold days, that the tunnels and caves, the cellars and stone ruins and box-cañons to which they point so proudly as Murieta's hideaways may never have seen Murieta or any Joaquin. To the reader, such captiousness with a first-class legend may appear no more than wilful contrariness, deliberate destruction of a pretty dream to no purpose. But the chances are no harm is done. There is no record that fairy-tales commonly dissolve when faced with a mere truth. The beds that George Washington slept in, the writing-desks at which the Marquis de Lafayette carried on his interminable correspondence—the law of probabilities has never operated to lessen their number. Nor will any amount of sniping destroy or even damage the Murieta Legend. Dark and daring, his eyes flashing fire, his knife ever ready for a gringo's ribs or purse, his horsemanship superb and his aim unerring, Joaquin Murieta will ride down the years as California's most romantic bandit. His cattle-thievery forgotten, his cold-blooded murders (if indeed he committed them) conveniently ignored, he remains the perfect gold-rush manifestation of man's age-old compulsion to make a hero out of the best materials available, because The Hero is a creature men need.

Down by the Bay, the city of San Francisco was beginning to have its difficulties with such groups as the Hounds, who boldly used the words "Law and Order" to cover up their depredations and were not satisfied with burning out the Chileños and Chinese but brazenly demanded toll, much in the manner of the twentieth-century racketeer, from the solid business men of the town. Sacramento likewise was troubled with lawlessness, as were the other new-made cities and towns of those early years.

At first, the gamblers, ex-convicts, and others looking for ways to live by their wits were not anxious to risk the discomforts of the raw mining camps. But before long they realized that, after all, the source of the gold might be the best place to go after it, and they began to move up into the foot-hill country. Legitimate—if somewhat grasping—business men had already made fortunes by selling miners the luxuries they craved at prices no one but the miner would pay; the Argonaut had become accustomed to exploitation, perhaps even gloried in it a trifle. It was something to be able to pay the price asked and no argument about it. And there was always more gold.

Psychologically, then, everything was set for the Age of Disorder to succeed the Age of Innocence. Towns such as Sonora, Columbia, Angels Camp, Placerville, Nevada City, and many more had their three dozen bars apiece, at least some of them equipped with fine mahogany and shining plate-glass mirrors in the best city style. They had their gambling-houses, their dance halls—the last very often Mexican—their sporting element which loved its bull-and-bear fights and encouraged such other expressions of the manly spirit of swagger as the limitations of a gold camp permitted. Gold was still plentiful in the gulches and the new-fangled quartz-mining was beginning to show results. The framework was ready for such predatory individuals as had found the city competition too stiff and were seeking easier pickings. All they had to do was to step into the picture. They stepped, and by the thousands. For a season the "honest miner" seemed to exist only as prey for the robber, the dishonest saloon-keeper, the dance-hall girl, and the professional gambler. Quite particularly the gambler.

Bret Harte, among others, did his bit to glorify the gambler of the gold-rush days. As a matter of fact, he was a glamorous enough figure without fictional trimmings. His work was not heavy; his hands bore no callouses from pick or shovel; his dress was of the finest broadcloth. He possessed *savoir-faire,* adaptability, a kind of individual charm which has since become more familiar as salesmanship. He was no tough; indeed, it was far more likely that his manners at least approximated those of the proper gentleman. Many were in no way dishonest; practitioners of an exact science, they relied upon their mathematical understanding to bring them the profits they were content to keep within decent limits. The reader will remember the gambler, Cannon, stabbed in Downieville by Juanita, and will recall that there were plenty to testify to his qualities as a first-class citizen. But there were all kinds, good and bad. And whether they were honest or crooked, they had two things in common. They had to be men who could inspire confidence—temporarily, at least—in the breast of the miner who wanted to take chances with his gold-dust. And they had to be males. Gambling was a man's affair.

Yet there was in those early days one notable exception to that rule. In the booming, high-flying camp that called itself Nevada City there flourished in 1854 and 1855 a woman gambler whose establishment became famous throughout the mines. Her game was *vingt-et-un,* and she dealt it herself. Her gaming-rooms were the last word in respectability; her private life—for those two years—was beyond reproach. She paid her losses with a smile; she was not fussy about cigar smoke or the fumes of alcohol, though she would permit no bad language and no fighting. She was, in short, unique, a marvel well worth journeying many miles to see, even if it meant the trip back again with pockets lighter by the number of ounces of dust the traveler had taken with him.

Eleanore Dumont came from nowhere at all. One day nobody had heard of her; the next she had alighted, a trifle dusty, from the Sacramento stage, and Nevada City was in a buzz about her. By this time the mining towns were sufficiently accustomed to women so that a new arrival caused no great stir, provided she fell into one of the usual categories. A new dance-hall girl was one thing; a wife brought out from the East by some successful miner was another. Even a school-teacher or a young lady coming to wed a fellow-townsman was a fairly commonplace occurrence. But this Eleanore Dumont could not be placed. Plump and dark, about twenty-five years old and eminently self-possessed, she conducted herself with reserve, indicated that she was French, dressed well and spent most of her first week decorously in her hotel room or sitting in the parlor reserved for ladies. She was a puzzle to Nevada City, which understood most things.

However, she was not a puzzle for long. Within ten days the town learned why she was there. Their enlightenment came in the form of an invitation for those who were so inclined to attend a gala opening of Madame Dumont's new gambling house, where there would be free champagne for all and the opportunity to risk their dust on the belief that they could assemble a handful of cards so that their pips would total closer to twenty-one than the cards Madame Dumont held.

It was natural that the gala opening should be well attended. After all, a woman gambler was something out of the ordinary. For that matter, unattached women of any kind were in themselves rare enough so that the chance to talk to one was not lightly to be ignored. The miners for miles around got out their best clothes, brushed their boots, and came in droves. Madame Dumont charmed them, dealt twenty-one like a veteran, chatted prettily with every one, yet permitted no familiarities. No one went to the pains to estimate the lady's take on that first night, but it was agreed that the opening had been a tremendous success.

The true measure of Madame Dumont's genius lies in the fact that she was able to continue in business. The respectable

123

citizens of the town were outraged of course. Men running
gambling-houses were bad enough, though it was impossible
to do anything about them; but a woman——! The morning
after her opening the odds were five to one around town that
Madame Dumont would not run her game a week. Yet she
stayed, dealt the cards every night, chaffed the losers, and
good-humoredly paid the winners, and managed somehow to
give offense to no one. The most captious critics could find
nothing in Madame's place to complain of, excepting the obvious fact that a lady would not be running a card game.
Since Madame had not claimed to be a lady, there was no
argument. On the other hand, Madame Dumont's was never
stuffy. With the magnificent talent of the Frenchwoman for
managing any kind of commercial enterprise in a businesslike
fashion, yet with just the right degree of friendliness, Madame
kept her clientèle happy, allowed her patrons just enough rope
but never too much, made every man-jack of them feel that it
was a privilege to lose the week's painful siftings across the
table of a woman endowed with such superior gifts as a hostess. Before the week was out it was quite clear that Madame's
success was no mere matter of novelty; she was in Nevada
City to stay.

One of the curious things about Madame Dumont is that she
was able to plan her enterprise so well up to a point, yet unable to see in advance that her very success was bound to carry
the seeds of failure. Wherever she came from——and no one has
yet solved the mystery——she had learned to understand men
in general and the California miner in particular. One writer
who has touched upon her career suggests that she must have
spent a long time observing the habits of the miner, perhaps
in San Francisco where the better heeled went to spend the
money they had made in the hills. Certainly she knew how to
handle men, was thoroughly familiar with the game she dealt,
had learned to drink wisely and to roll her own cigarettes with

deftness and charm. Yet, for all her shrewdness, one thing had not occurred to her. The game of twenty-one is self-limiting; one dealer can not play against more than half a dozen at a time. Almost immediately, Madame Dumont found herself up against this difficulty. A hundred or two miners might crowd her place of business and buy drinks. But if they were unable to get near the table all evening they would not come back very often. There was only one thing to do. She must take in a partner. And since women of her own talents were not to be found on every bush, the partner had to be a man. Her choice was a young but capable gambler named Dave Tobin.

Tobin knew his business; Madame Dumont was a good enough judge of character to make sure of that. And for a time the establishment prospered very well under joint direction. Keno and chuck-a-luck games were added, and two more assistants were hired to conduct faro and poker tables. Madame herself dealt only her favorite twenty-one, and her table became the goal of the few who had large sums to risk, either because they had brought full pokes with them or because they had been lucky at poker or faro. It seemed that nothing could stand in the way of Madame's success. Perhaps she would have made her pile and retired if her partner had not had notions of his own.

The trouble was that young Tobin had ambitions. He was well able to understand his importance in Madame's scheme of things. Without him, or another equally able, Madame would have to come down again to a single table, reducing her take to what could be risked by a dozen or two players an evening. Plainly his importance justified a much larger share in the profits than his initial arrangement provided. He took his proposition to Madame Dumont.

There is no way now to tell whether Madame Dumont's success had gone to her head, whether she believed she could manage the thousand-and-one details of a place the size hers had come to be and still maintain the personal contact so necessary to her business, or whether she simply resented the idea of sharing any more of her profits. Whatever her reasons, she told Tobin flatly that he could expect no more than he was getting. Like a good gambler Tobin called her bluff, took out his share in cash, and departed for New York where he opened a highly successful and reasonably famous gambling-house of his own. Madame Dumont stayed on. Apparently things were going to work out well enough without Tobin.

But something was happening to Nevada City. The river gravels were thinning out, and so were the dry diggings in that area. Quartz mines were beginning to develop, but they had not yet shown the values that would shortly astonish Californians. And in this period of transition, Madame Dumont grew restless. Her scheme of catching Nevada City at its peak and skimming the cream of its prosperity had worked just as she thought it would. Maybe the best thing to do would be to operate the same way on other camps. Like the typical miner, Madame was beginning to think in terms of the greener grass in the next field. Like the miner, too, Madame translated hope into action. Early in 1856 she closed her place and moved on. She did not know it, but it was the beginning of the end.

The record of her next twenty years is no more than a piecing together of odds and ends of rumor and report. She found very soon that the mushroom gold-camps were a different matter from Nevada City with its stable population, its attraction as a county seat. More and more toughs were flooding the hills, and none of them was anxious to see a woman cutting in on his chances for profit. Madame Dumont was fading, too; night life was not easy on a woman, and it was always necessary to drink a little, sometimes more than was wise. The plump, vivacious little Frenchwoman grew older and stouter, sharper of eye, harder of countenance. New camps did not give her the deference she considered her due; it became constantly more and more difficult to keep "the boys" in their places. Gradually, without realizing it, she was losing her youth, her freshness, the very qualities that had made her unique. Her nickname was the last straw. Some one, with the Californian talent for hitting off a personality in a word or two, noticed the darkening line of Latin down on her upper lip and christened her with the name by which she was thereafter known. "Madame Moustache," he called her. It is hard to believe that she could have escaped hearing it whispered.

The name followed her, too, in her increasingly wide travels. She turned up in the boisterous camp of Pioche, in Nevada, in the late 1850's. Legend places her in Idaho, in Wyoming where she operated in the construction camps of the Union Pacific in the railroad-building era, in the Black Hills, and later down in Deadwood. In 1877 she was in Eureka, Nevada, where her establishment included various entertainment other than the *vingt-et-un* game with which she had so modestly begun. But the day of the boom-camp was dying. The West was growing orderly, settled, calm; there was some of the old life still in the cattle-towns, but Madame Moustache was a creature of the mining camps at heart. And in the end it was one of the last of the mining camps that called her. On the morning of September 9, 1879, the Sacramento *Union* carried three brief lines that must have stirred the memories of at least a few old-timers. "Bodie: September 8," the dateline ran: "A woman named Eleanore Dumont was found dead to-day about one mile out of town, having committed suicide. She was well known throughout the mining camps." That was all; she left no explanatory note, told no one what she planned to do. The citizens buried her quietly and forgot her. Her only obituary appeared a year later in the official *History of Nevada County, California*, in which the historian printed a brief sketch of her career as far as he knew it, closing with the single sentence, "Let her many good qualities invoke leniency in criticising her failings."

Even crime must have its pioneers; some one has to be first with the new dodge, the untried trick, the theft more daring than any before it.

One of the most interesting things about the early 1850's, with its rising crime-curve, its increasing proportion of brawlers, gamblers, thimble-riggers, thieves, and cutthroats in the mines, is that there was one point at which such hard cases stopped. Though the old decencies were breaking down under pressure, though individuals were robbed and sometimes murdered, the shipments of gold proceeding from the foothills down to the cities were pretty generally left alone. The record is plain; in the larger sense, the gold was safe. No one has risked an estimate on the number of miles the stages covered in those first years, nor how much treasure they carried. But stages and gold got through. Murieta was dead, his head in a bottle in a side-show—if it was his head. Such marauders as Rattlesnake Dick and a dozen others had been pursued, caught, and disposed of. But neither they nor anybody else had tried to hold up a stage. It just wasn't done.

As a matter of fact, no one tried that trick until the summer of 1856. In July of that year a one-time doctor turned robber came to the conclusion that he and his gang of small-time stick-up men would try something really big for a change. So deciding, the doctor-bandit made himself a pioneer, though he knew or cared nothing about that. On August 12th the shocking head-lines spread the news. Tom Bell and his crowd had stopped the stage running from Camptonville to Marysville, with a shipment of a hundred thousand dollars in gold. California had seen its first organized stage hold-up.

Tom Bell had already got himself into the news on several occasions.

He had come to California after the Mexican War in which he served with Colonel Cheatham's Tennessee Volunteers in the capacity of hospital attaché. There is no record of where he had received his medical degree or how he acquitted himself in Mexico. His true name was Thomas Hodges, and somewhere he had acquired a badly broken nose, "dented in at the bridge level with his face," which a historian of the period mildly notes gave him a "somewhat repulsive appearance." In California, he had tried mining and gambling—here the Doctor is the authority on himself—and, finding that neither pursuit made him rich, took to grand larceny. It was during his term in State's Prison that he made friends with one Bill Gristy, also known as Bill White, who escaped with him and helped him build up his gang. As for the name by which Doctor Hodges was known, he had chosen to call himself "Tom Bell" because there was already a petty cattle-thief by that name operating in the gold country. He had learned something about the law, and if a duplicate pseudonym would confuse its myrmidons he was in favor of it.

For nearly a year, Tom Bell and Bill Gristy tried their hands at various forms of crime, building up an organization of as tough characters as had ever come together in the mines. Every time any of them robbed any one the victim was told that it was "Tom Bell" who had singled him out. Splitting up into small groups, the gang worked the foot-hills from Auburn north, running off cattle, breaking into stores, occasionally holding up a lone traveler and relieving him of whatever cash he had. Often two robberies were committed almost simultaneously, half a hundred miles apart, in each case "Tom Bell" being the robber reported. And for a time the scheme did confuse the law badly. No sooner did a sheriff get his men on the trail of Tom Bell up in Shasta County than word came that Bell had just been seen at the Mountaineer House, between Folsom and Auburn on the Sacramento road. The Mountaineer House was known to be a rendezvous of shady characters; its owner, Jack Phillips, a "Sydney duck" was suspected of aiding in all kinds of crooked work. But by the time peace officers called to make inquiries, Mr. Phillips would be standing innocently behind his bar drawing beer for the stage-driver and passengers who had stopped for a breather before tackling the hills. Nevertheless, in spite of his care, reports on Tom Bell began to filter through. Slowly the picture of the man took shape. He had a badly broken nose; that was something. He was a tall man, broad shouldered and wiry in build. His hair was long and yellow, hanging to his shoulders, and his whiskers were trimmed so that the sandy moustache came around his mouth to join the goatee of the same hue. He was of a quick and sanguine temperament, fearless in a fight. All this helped. Particularly it aided the officers in distinguishing between the right Tom Bell and the wrong one.

Yet the depredations went on. Teamsters were stopped, robbed, and told to roll along. Apparently any victim would do; in the spring of 1856 the gang held up a vegetable peddler near Rabbit Creek. The next day a driver named Dutch John who was hauling a load of beer from Volcano most appropriately to Drytown, was halted by five men who told him they were "taking contributions." One of them offered the additional information that the contributions were for Tom Bell's gang and added that the driver had better be quick about forking over. Dutch John offered them all he had—thirty dollars and a twenty-five cent piece. The robbers gave him back the two bits and told him to buy himself a drink with it.

The newspapers picked up all of this, of course, and they became more and more bitter about the failure of the law to catch up with Tom Bell. "Doubtless," wrote the editor of the

Sacramento *Union,* sarcastically, "this man is now emulous of the reputation of Joaquin, and is striving for the character of the dashing highwayman!" He added, in the proper editorial manner, that it was time something was done. As he put it, grandly: "It is incumbent upon our authorities to take immediate steps in the premises."

It was shortly after this that Mr. Farmer, proprietor of the Mountain Springs house near Amador City, had the adventure of his life. After he had retired for the evening he was awakened by the sound of horses and a loud knocking at the door. Prudently he put his head out of the window and inquired what was wanted. The men below explained that they had lost the road and that they wanted to get to Ione. No such slim excuse could fool the astute Mr. Farmer. "The road," he replied, "is not far off. I reckon you can find it!" The leader then asked Mr. Farmer if he would let them in and give them something to eat and drink. The Amador *Sentinel* reported his reply, a classic for Yankee brevity and firmness. "No," said Mr. Farmer, "rather think I won't!" and slammed down the window. It was not until he got his copy of the weekly paper the following Saturday that he found out what he had done. He had refused help to four members of the Mokelumne Hill delegation to the Democratic Convention, lost on their way down to Sacramento.

The first few months of 1856 witnessed continuing robberies by the gang, but the officers were also learning more about Tom Bell.

They discovered, for instance, why it was that so many travelers who paused for refreshment at the Western Exchange Hotel on the road to Nevada City were robbed so soon after they left. The proprietress of the inn, Mrs. Hood, was in the pay of Bell, and some anonymous investigator for the law had noted the manner in which members of the Bell gang made themselves known to her and to the bartenders. It was a simple enough trick—a bullet with a hole bored through it, hung on a knotted string. When the customer pulled out that oddity with his money as he paid for his drink or his dinner, then the bartender or Mrs. Hood knew he was one of Bell's men and "spotted" for him the wayfarers who carried sizable amounts of money. The police, too, had learned of the association between Bell and Gristy, and they were watching Mrs. Hood's inn and the Mountaineer House. Sooner or later, Gristy or Bell himself would stop at one place or the other and that would be that. Perhaps Bell got wind of how the chase was narrowing down. Perhaps it was merely that he felt the time had come to do something dramatic. At any rate, he now laid his plans for a really big haul, nothing less than a stage and its treasure-box.

On the morning of August 11th, the regular stage pulled out of Camptonville on the long road to Marysville.

John Gear was driving as usual, and there was a full load of passengers. Up beside Gear sat a man named Dobson, messenger for Langton's Express, his rifle handy beside him. There was a good reason for extra care on this trip; stowed beneath the seat was a strong box in which was one of the largest shipments of gold that Langton's had carried for months. A good part of it belonged to Mr. Rideout, gold-dust dealer of Camptonville, who was accompanying his shipment. He was not on the stage, however. He had decided to go by horseback instead. This decision was to save his gold for him, but he could not know that. All that occupied his mind when he rode out of town was that it would be a good idea in such dry weather to keep a few minutes ahead of the stage and the dust it would kick up.

Not far out of Marysville, the road forked, one branch taking the high side of the small cañon made by Dry Creek, the other following the lower side.

It was about half past four in the afternoon when Mr. Rideout came to the fork. He had had a hot day's ride, and the trees and brush on the old road led him to choose it rather than the new one the stage would follow. It was a bit longer, but there was no hurry now. In a few minutes he would be in Marysville, the stage would have come along after him, and his gold would be safely checked in at the express office and locked in the safe. Jogging slowly under the overhanging branches, Mr. Rideout was enjoying the grateful coolness when three men rode out from behind some brush, pointed pistols at his head and told him curtly to dismount.

Mr. Rideout was not armed, and he had the good sense to obey. The robbers frisked him, found that he had neither money nor pistol, and told him disgustedly to cross over on foot to the lower road. What they might want with his horse Mr. Rideout did not know, but he was both angry and embarrassed. Any moment now the stage would be along, and he would have to step out and ask for a ride, looking like a fool. He had no way of knowing that his unexpected appearance on that old road had spoiled as good a plan as a smart highwayman had ever worked out. A few minutes earlier, Mr. Rideout's choice of the old road would have made no difference. The three men who cut across the ravine to intercept him would have had time to tie the horse, see Mr. Rideout well down the road, get back to their three companions and carry out the original plan for the hold-up. Six mounted men, three on each side of the road, would have stopped John Gear and his stage, and in such circumstances six are almost as good as sixty. But Mr. Rideout hadn't been earlier. And as he scrambled up the far bank to reach the road and stop the stage he could hear coming, it was three men, not six, that spurred out into the main route ahead of him, shouting at Gear to stop his horses. As Mr. Rideout paused to take in this new development, he could hear the other three crashing down the bank

Downieville, California

By 1852, Downieville had a population of five thousand
hell-raising miners, more than its share of saloons and dance

halls, and was the site of the first hanging of a woman in California. The two portions of the town were connected by a bridge across the North Fork of the Yuba River.

behind him, trying desperately to join their companions in time.

No one can say now what might have happened if there had been no Mr. Rideout at the forks of the Marysville road at the wrong moment. If Tom Bell and his five men had ridden out according to the original scheme, three on each side, guns leveled, it might have been a different matter. Dobson, the messenger, was a courageous man, but no one can shoot in two directions at once. But Mr. Rideout had come along. Three of the band had ridden over to cut him off, and the attack could be made from one side of the stage only. With things as they were, Dobson didn't think twice. He raised his rifle and fired, tumbling one of the bandits from his horse, at the same time shouting to John Gear to drive on.

In such encounters it is always surprising to note how quickly things happen. By the time Mr. Rideout got up the bank, the fight was over. Forty shots altogether had been exchanged, including those fired by armed passengers inside the stage. Two of the bandits had drawn back into the brush, taking their wounded companion with them, and as Gear whipped up his horses Mr. Rideout saw that his own animal had followed him down the ravine and up the bank on the other side. Automatically, he swung into the saddle and raced after the stage. As he drew abreast, Gear shouted to him to ride on into Marysville and spread the news. Dobson was wounded and others might be. The quicker Mr. Rideout could make it, the better. Mr. Rideout was delighted to oblige.

Nearly two decades later, a historian describing the event wrote seriously that by the time the stage got to town a procession had formed, headed by a brass band, and was starting out to meet it. However this may have been—and it was quick work if it happened—the band had no reason to play happy music. Dobson was wounded in the arm. John Campbell, a passenger, had been creased along the forehead by a glancing shot that had just missed his eye. Another man was shot through both legs. The stage itself was punctured in a dozen places. And Mrs. Tilghman, wife of a barber in Marysville, had been instantly killed by a bullet through the head. Next day, the Marysville *Express* printed a full account of the hold-up, but in spite of the tragic results the editor was unable to resist one small joke at the end of his story. One of the passengers, he wrote, had told him that at the first shot one white man and four Chinese had abruptly left the stage, headed back toward Camptonville. They had not, he said, been seen since.

They caught Tom Bell, though it was a long chase. They caught him by the time-honored method of first catching one or two of his men.

By great good luck, one of the men they nabbed was Bill Gristy, Tom's first lieutenant and with Tom the founder of the whole Bell organization. Perhaps they did not call it the "third degree'" in those days, but that is immaterial. The process was the same; they got Gristy and they softened him up. By next morning he was confessing everything, including some things that hadn't happened. More important, he had agreed to lead the officers to the new hideout that Tom had picked until the hold-up of the Camptonville stage had blown over. So did the Mexican they had captured with Gristy. That was how it came about that two separate parties of irate citizens, one guided by Gristy, the other by the Mexican, happened to meet near Firebaugh's Ferry, at the junction of the long slough which then connected the San Joaquin River with the Tulare Lakes.

Tom's idea had been that no one would think to look for him so far south of his usual stamping-grounds. About six miles above Firebaugh's Ferry, he and some of his men had simply taken over a disused ranch, brought down the buxom

Mrs. Elizabeth Hood and her children to manage the place, and gone out on a foray for cattle to last the gang through the winter. When one posse, under Judge Belt of Knight's Ferry, found the ranch through the Mexican's guidance, Sheriff Mulford and his men were already in possession, led to the rendezvous by Gristy. The Sheriff had not found Tom Bell. Mrs. Hood and her young daughters had been packed off to Stockton, and two elderly men who did odd jobs for Bell had been retained to cut wood and take care of the chores for the Sheriff, who was sitting tight and hoping that Bell would come back and walk into his trap.

For a week the two groups of citizens joined forces and posted guards to notify them of Bell's approach, if he came. Tired of waiting at last, they finally dispersed, Sheriff Mulford taking the Stockton road, Judge Belt and his crowd heading back for Knight's Ferry. It was disappointing to come so close, but there it was. Doubtless Bell had been warned and would stay as far as possible from the ranch where he had hoped to be safe. That might have been the end of the adventure, too, but for the fact that one man, Robert Price of Sonora, decided to ford the river a little higher up, thus saving himself a mile or two of riding.

Curiously enough, Tom Bell's chances once more turned on the accident of a lone rider on an unexpected road. For as Mr. Price crossed the river and rode up the far bank he caught a glimpse of a mounted man in a clump of willows. It was plain that the man, whoever he was, did not care to be seen. He sat his horse without moving. Mr. Price could see him out of the corner of his eye as he rode past.

Afterward Mr. Price admitted that he did not know just what had made him suspicious. He had not seen enough of the man to know what he looked like. It was just that in so lonely a spot a stranger had kept so quiet. But he decided that he should tell Judge Belt. There was another ford a little way south and west; he could cross the river again and catch up with the posse.

The Judge was interested. The lone stranger might be an innocent traveler; if he was, then no harm was done. But he and his men agreed that they should at least go back with Mr. Price and investigate. Why Tom Bell's sharp ears did not detect the sound of horses coming down the trail is something that can not be explained now. Perhaps he did, but felt sure that it was nothing to do with him. At any rate, when he looked up it was too late. Judge Belt, Mr. Price and another of the group were within twenty yards of him, rifles aimed at his breast. Bell made no move except to drop his gun as he was told and raise his hands above his head. "I believe," said the Judge, "that you are the man we have been looking for." Bell looked coolly at him for a moment and then said, "Very probably." That was enough. "Tie him up!" said the Judge.

Back at Firebaugh's they asked Bell a few questions. He admitted that he was Tom Bell? Yes, he was. He had tried to rob the Camptonville stage? Yes, he had made the attempt. Had he anything else to say for himself? Well, Bell said, he would like to make a full confession. Since they were going to hang him, he would feel better if they allowed him to do this.

The Judge and his men decided against it. A rider had been sent after Sheriff Mulford to tell him of the capture. When the Sheriff came back he would doubtless insist on taking the prisoner to jail and trying him according to the law. That did not suit them. Bell and his gang had not stopped to think about the law when they fired on the stage. Mrs. Tilghman, the barber's wife, had been given no chance; a bullet—it might just as well have been Bell's—had killed her in that battle. No, it was a little late to be talking about confessions. They knew all they needed to know.

Tom was told the verdict and asked for time to write two

137

letters, one to his mother and one to Mrs. Hood. They gave him permission and allowed him also to read aloud the epistle to his mother. It ran:

Dear Mother:—

As I am about to make my exit to another country, I take this opportunity to write you a few lines. Probably you will never hear from me again. If not, I hope we may meet where parting is no more.

In my prodigal career in this country, I have always recollected your fond admonitions, and if I had lived up to them probably I would not have been in my present condition; but, dear Mother, though my fate has been a cruel one, yet I have no one to blame but myself. Give my respects to all my old and youthful friends. Tell them to beware of bad associations, and never to enter into any gambling saloons, for that has been my ruin.

If my old Grandmother is living, remember me to her. With these remarks I bid you farewell forever.

Your only boy,

Tom

By the time Bell had finished it was four o'clock in the afternoon. One of the party asked him if he was ready, and Tom said he was, adding that now his life was worth nothing to him. He was told that he might have a drink of whisky if he wished, and he said he would like that. They asked him again if he had anything to say about others concerned with him in his career of crime, and he replied that he had no revelations to make; he would be gratified, however, to drink to the health of the party present and hoped that no personal prejudice had induced them to execute him. He then added a few rambling remarks about his past, saying that his first crime followed upon his ruin at gambling and that it had been the theft of eleven mules from a Mexican near Mariposa. Mexicans, he explained, had always seemed to him natural enemies. If circumstances had not made it necessary, he would never have robbed any good American of so much as one cent.

It is hard to believe that Tom Bell could have thought such

an argument would soften the hearts of his executioners. It is likely that he didn't really think so, that he was just talking. For all his calm demeanor, the knowledge that a rope was awaiting him must have struck coldly at his heart. Even a minute or two more of life was something. They wouldn't walk him out to that tall sycamore as long as he told them anything that kept them listening. But apparently they had heard enough. Two men took him, one at each elbow, and turned him toward the door. Between the cabin and the tree, he said desperately that he was only twenty-six years old. The information did not seem to interest anybody. As they settled the noose around his neck, he got hold of himself and began to pray in a low, controlled tone of voice. He was still praying when they walked away with the other end of the rope.

Ten minutes later, Sheriff Mulford and his Stockton men rode into the camp, just too late for the ceremonies.

It was a newspaper editor who had the last word to say on Tom Bell and the kind of violence he represented, the lawlessness which had aroused citizens at last to the necessity of strong and speedy action. As he had done so often before, the Editor of the *Alta* summed up the ideas of his fellow-scribes on the subject of bad men and their bad actions. Having printed in his paper the letter Tom wrote to his mother, he went on to drive home his moral. Gambling, drinking, laziness, bad company—these were at the bottom of it all, he said, and continued:

The confessions of many other robbers who have been captured and executed are but the reiterations of this story. Tom Bell, in his last words, adds his testimony to the same effect. Will not this be a warning to our young men? Will it not restrain them from indulgence in the evil courses which have been the cause of the existence of so many amateur robbers and desperadoes in California? From all we can gather, this man Bell, who has recently met with an ignominious fate, was one of liberal education and good family; one who, probably, on his departure from his home, left with high hopes and good determinations, and a mother's blessing on him. How many mothers are there yet to be doomed to like disappointment, to like sorrow, from like causes?

The fate of the desperado in California is becoming a certain one. The people are aroused to the necessity of self-protection, and although robbers may at first elude their vigilance, their careers will be as suddenly and as unexpectedly ended as that of Tom Bell. Let Tom Bell's admonition be a warning to all who, to-day, are treading in the path which led him to the gallows!

Neither Bell's nor the Editor's warning was properly heeded, of course. There were robberies and killings yet to come—many of them. But the arm of the law was growing stronger and public sentiment was with it. Maybe it was all very well for yesterday's hugger-mugger mining camp to conduct life loosely. But now California was getting somewhere. The early camps were changing fast. Many had faded out completely as the placers were exhausted. Fires, too, had swept the board-and-canvas settlements, but in those that had some chance of long life solid red brick and iron had begun to replace the flimsy construction that Shirley, for instance, had seen and recorded at Rich Bar. The stage-lines were developing fast, and there were banking offices and comfortable hotels now in towns that had been no more than a huddle of plank shacks a year or two before. The mines were growing up; that was it. And men became conscious that they would have to live up to their new stature.

5.

The Concord was a Lady

LIKE everything else in California, transportation moved ahead in giant leaps, compressing the development of years into months because of the need men had to communicate with each other and with their homes.

The United States Mail arrived on the scene early; Washington sent out its agent, one William Van Voorhees, in February of 1849. Mr. Van Voorhees could have had very little idea of what he was getting into. Perhaps, if he had glimpsed a little of the frontier country in Ohio or Kentucky, he was in some degree prepared. If, on the other hand, he had come straight from Washington, the raw newness and hurry of this crude land must have shocked him beyond measure. There is no record of what he thought when he learned that the mails must be entrusted to strange, wild, bearded fellows carrying knives and pistols, riding whatever sort of beast happened to be available. Yet there was nothing to do but fall in with the custom of the country, and Mr. Van Voorhees was a conscientious man. Letters began to find their way into the foot-hills by California-style post.

Alexander Todd was typical of those early carriers. At first, they charged whatever the traffic would bear—as much as half an ounce of dust per letter if the going was hard and no competitor wanted to tackle the job. Todd came down to four dollars a letter, but he was able to do this only because he had made an investment; moreover, he had to keep his rates at least this high because he had that investment to protect. His investment was a boat, in which he navigated the sloughs and free reaches of the San Joaquin River. A rowboat it was, and even a rowboat can carry a good-sized bundle of mail. Nor were letters all of it. Todd did not row his own boat. There were always miners going to and from the foot-hills; very well, then, they might as well earn their transportation. Todd let them earn it rowing, and charged them sixteen dollars a head "tax" as well. With a power-plant that cost nothing and paid the upkeep and amortization to boot, Todd's letter service at four dollars per missive did very well indeed. Gold-dust, of course, had to be more carefully carried; it required watching and such matters. Todd boosted his rates commensurately for valuables. As for a carrier of the United States Mail conducting a profitable business on the side, that was something about which Uncle Sam had very little to say. There was no use in trying to establish a set of postal rules and rates unless you could find men to abide by them. And here, in this curious Western country, you couldn't find men to do the job at all unless you gave them a chance to do it profitably.

Yet Todd and others like him—such men as Bill Ballou and

A. T. Dowd, who was the first to find the Calaveras Big Trees and was called a liar for his pains, and "Snowshoe" Thompson who traveled on skis for his trek over the higher, snow-covered ridges into Nevada—these and dozens of others took on the work, perhaps because fortune had not smiled upon their mining ventures, perhaps because they liked the freedom and the challenge of it. It was a challenge, all the way and all the time. There were wild animals to watch for, there were trails to break, there were floods in the winter and there were dust and heat in the summer, and always there were Indians, not to mention renegade miners who might take a chance even at the mail sacks if they thought they could make something at it. But they kept going, these amateur mailmen, these miners' messengers, and they were the first pathfinders in the gold-lined wilderness.

On their heels came the wagons, forcing the widening of the trails into roads, making it imperative to construct at least rough highways over which they might jolt their loads of lumber and liquor for the fast-growing towns in the mountains. The Sacramento and the San Joaquin, even the Yuba and the American rivers for short distances, carried all the heaviest traffic for many years. But gold was where a man found it, and not always convenient to a river bank. Wherefore, since the rivers were where they were, roads had to be cut.

Those old roads, hundreds of miles of them, represent one of the major engineering accomplishments of early mining days in California. Built with the commonest tools, hacked and hewed out of the earth and rock with little more than pick and shovel, they swept along the gulches, sliced deep into the mountain sides, leaped rivers and creeks on high, perilous bridges, keeping pace with the gold and the men. Sometimes groups of miners came together to put in so many hours of work a day for the good of all, to dig and blast and fell trees for corduroy where the red earth grew soft and the road sank in wet weather. Often a company or an individual would build a stretch of highway, grade and surface it with whatever rough-broken rock could be had, and try to make it pay for itself in tolls. One way or another, the job was done; the wagons, the mule-teams, the horsemen and pack-trains rolled over the new trails.

With this change, mail-rates dropped; the task was easier, except when delivery had to be made to remote settlements in the higher hills, to towns too thinly scattered to make a solid job of road-building worth while. Other haulage grew cheaper, too, and with the lowering of transport costs the mining camps could afford new luxuries. The principles of supply and demand began to function on an ever grander scale; as long as the gold held out, there was no limit to what men would want nor to what merchants would supply. A man might work all day in the burning sun, neglect to shave, get along through the week on salt pork, beans, and soggy biscuit. But if he felt like oysters and champagne on a Saturday night, if he insisted on the best Havana cigars and the finest liquors the States could furnish—and could pay for them—then somebody would get these things to him, no matter what. The mule-trains lengthened, the wagons rumbled more and more closely in each other's tracks. Season upon season, the roads improved, widened, dug themselves more securely into the cliffs, wound more suavely down cañon and arroyo. Men began to say to one another that it was no trick at all any more to get up into the hills.

All of this had been a matter of no more than a year or so. Forty-Eight had seen the great discovery. Forty-Nine had brought the new Californians, thousands upon thousands, to wash their gold, break their trails, expand these into roads, and begin to enjoy the luxuries their highways brought them.

Now the curtain was ready to rise on the most colorful era of all, the thirty years in which the stage-driver ruled the road and his glistening, magnificent vehicle was the most splendid sight upon it. That vehicle was the Concord coach, the epoch-making Yankee creation of Messrs. Abbott, Downing & Company, in their enormous four-acre plant at Concord, New Hampshire.

The Concord was a lady.

The point to remember is that the stage-coach of those days was by no means the dingy, worn-out, lifeless thing of the museums to-day. So shrewdly put together that its weight of some 2,500 pounds was utterly disguised, the Concord coach through sheer perfection of design was trim and tidy as a ship. Proud and glorious in delicate straw-colored running gear and body of English vermilion, her doors painted with miniature landscapes—often by a noted artist of the time, one John Burgum—her scrollwork, infinite in its variety, executed in colors by Charles T. B. Knowlton, she took the road as the clipper took the seas, a lady and no two ways about it.

When Abbott, Downing & Company had begun to manufacture Concords in 1813, they had taken over the egg-shaped body that Europe made the custom. But New England workmen, never tired of puttering to improve even the best, had brought about subtle modifications in the principle. The Concord coach emerged from their tinkering a new kind of vehicle. The egg was wider, more commodious, containing ample space—well upholstered as it needed to be—for nine passengers. Outside there was room for ten more. Front and rear were the "boots" which held baggage, mail, and express chests, when the last were not directly under the care of the driver and stowed under the driver's box. The frame was of stout New England ash, decking and wall-panels were of poplar. All metal—and the whole was so cleverly joined that

145

very little of it was necessary—was the best Norwegian iron. Wheel spokes were ash, too, and spokes, hub, and rim were so carefully selected, so thoroughly seasoned and so brilliantly fitted that Concord wheels stood up as no wheels anywhere had ever done before

But the heart and soul of the Concord was the thoroughbrace, that inspired device which made her what she was, gave her the strength and elasticity to ride the rough new roads, to give gracefully when play was needed, to recover as gracefully and go on.

These thoroughbraces were simply two lengths of manifold heavy leather straps from which the body of the coach was suspended so that it might rock fore and aft, cradling road-shock. Most people have thought of thoroughbraces as a plan to make the passengers more comfortable, but their job was far more significant than this. Few writers on the subject of the Concord coach have seen the importance of this second function as clearly as the Bannings, whose *Six Horses* is one of the classic works on Western stages and staging. They write:

Thoroughbraces performed a vital duty far beyond the province of any steel springs. It was a function of such importance to the Western staging world that we may hazard the contention that an empire, as well as the body of its coach, once rocked and perhaps depended upon thoroughbraces.

Without them there could have been no stage to meet a crying need. Without them, any vehicle carrying the loads that had to be carried, maintaining such speed as the edicts of staging demanded, would have been efficient only as a killer of horses. For thoroughbraces, while they served the purpose of springs to an adequate extent, had the prime function of acting as shock-absorbers for the benefit of the team. By the thoroughbraces, violent jerks upon the traces due to obstructions in the road were automatically assuaged and generally eliminated. It was the force of inertia—the forward lunge and the upward lurch of the rocking body—that freed the wheels promptly from impediment, and thus averted each shock before it came upon the animals.

There, in half a dozen sentences, is the real story of the thoroughbrace and of the Concord coach that made it possible for horses to last through the grueling task of carrying the coach up hill and down, over the rocks and through the potholes of a day before Macadam.

This, of course, was of the utmost significance in the rapid development and growth of the mining country and so of the whole of California. But it is one of those happy joinings of circumstance that make it possible, without stretching the facts too far, to say that California came into the Union on wheels.

The first Concord stage-coach reached San Francisco on June 24, 1850. But more were on the way in the bellies of the ships which were rounding the Horn in steady procession that year. By early autumn there were two competing stage-lines operating between San Francisco and the state capital at San José. Because they were fierce rivals, Hall & Crandall's stage and that of Ackley & Maurison left at the same times and from the same places daily—the down stage from the San Francisco Plaza at eight o'clock in the morning and the up stage from San José at seven. As far as their advertisements went, Ackley & Maurison stressed speed while Hall & Crandall bore down on safety. In the *Pacific News*, the former firm told readers that its line was "furnished with the best stages and horses the country could produce, and carries passengers through the whole distance—60 miles—in about six hours." Hall & Crandall did not ignore the time element in their solicitations, but made the point that the passenger would get there: "The great advantage this line possesses over all others, is that the Stages were bought expressly for the road, and with a particular attention to *safety*, while the drivers, who have served a long apprenticeship from New England to Mexico, make the *quickest* time and *never meet with accidents*, which are so likely to occur with the *old-fashioned* stage

Nevada City, Nevada County

By 1850, there were enough miners working the rich gravels of Deer Creek so that they felt something ought to be done about organizing the camp. They met, elected an alcalde, and officially

named their town Nevada, at least ten years before the
state of Nevada was separated from Utah Territory and
baptized.

coaches." The reasoning is a trifle muddled here, to be sure; like advertising men in every age, Hall & Crandall's copywriter wanted to get everything in—safety, speed, the experience of its drivers, and by all means a slap at its rival's coaches, though there could not have been much difference in Concords which arrived in California within a month or two of each other. Perhaps, however, it was the item of safety which persuaded California's first Governor, Peter Burnett, to choose the Hall & Crandall line when he had the biggest news of the year to carry to San José.

California had been admitted to the Union; that was the story. San Francisco had had its day and night of jubilation but San José was yet to be informed, and Peter Burnett was clearly the man to do the job. He elected to go by Crandall's stage with Jared Crandall, "the prince of drivers," on the box. Afterward, Governor Burnett admitted that there was nothing lacking in Hall & Crandall's speed. "After passing over the sandy road to the mission," he wrote, "there was some of the most rapid driving that I have ever witnessed. . . . The people flocked to the road to see what caused our fast driving and loud shouting, and without slackening our speed in the slightest degree, we took off our hats, waved them round our heads, and shouted at the tops of our voice, 'California is admitted to the Union!'" Ackley & Maurison's driver did his best; there were times when the horses were almost neck and neck; but Crandall, "a most excellent man . . . a cool, kind, but determined and skillful driver," won out; and the Governor was the first to bring the great story to his seat of government.

Yet, dramatic though this was, a fine flourish in the proper California style, it was when the enterprise of the stage-owners and the courage and dash of their drivers began to extend the lines into the hills that the Concord took its place as a prime factor in the development of the country. There was no lost time. By the spring of 1851 there were a dozen busy stage-lines in operation, covering roads that a year before had seen nothing faster than mule-teams and lumbering wagons. When California's first Concord, resplendent in gold scrolls, damask curtains at its windows, rolled around the San Francisco Plaza on June 25, 1850, the gold mines of the foot-hills, a hundred and twenty-five miles away, entered upon their era of growth. With the stage-coach to tie it together, to knit it into a coherent whole, the Mother Lode country came into being as an entity for the first time. Slim, strong and lovely, proud and trim, the Concord was a lady, and, as a lady may, she lent men the strength to come of age.

Jim Birch had come out to California in Forty-nine, bound from his home in Providence, Rhode Island, to see what he could turn up in the new El Dorado. A youngster still—he was twenty-one in that year—he nevertheless belonged to the aristocracy of the road; in his own New England he had been a stage-driver. With him came another young man, Frank Stevens, a fellow whip of his own age who had also heard the call of gold. Those two young men were to build California's first great staging empire.

Stevens seems to have been less imaginative, more conservative than his friend. At any rate, he could have seen no great opportunity for men of his profession to make much of a living in this higgledy-piggledy California to which he had come. Nor did he try the mines; evidently he listened to those who were only too willing to tell the new-comer how hard it was to pick up or wash out a profit in the hills. He had a little money and this he promptly invested in a rickety wooden hotel in Sacramento City, down by the wharves along the river bank. At least, where men came in and out of town so frequently and in such numbers, there should be a chance for a merchant dealing in rooms and board. Not that Stevens was a dull fellow entirely; it was merely that he liked to play it safe. Certainly he had a genuine flair for selling his potential customers the right thing at the right moment; his hotel sign was proof of that. It read: "Rest for the Weary and Storage for Trunks."

Jim Birch, however, was another breed of cat. Restless, dynamic, quick in thought and action, he believed in getting about, seeing the country, keeping on the move. Moreover, he was a staging man by temperament; transport was in his blood. His friend Stevens could stick at renting rooms if he wanted to. He, Jim Birch, was going to follow his own trade. If Alec Todd could carry letters from place to place at four dollars each, surely Jim Birch, who had had experience, could carry people, and at a good deal more than four dollars. He thought it over. One morning in the autumn of 1849, he appeared in front of his friend's hotel with a rancho wagon to which were hitched four fidgety mustangs. Upright on the seat, as straight and proud as though he were sitting on the box of one of his far-away Rhode Island stage-line's Concords, he gave the call that marked the beginning of the Birch Lines: "All aboard for Mormon Island and the Forks of the American River! All aboard!"

By the next year, Birch had saved enough to invest in the new Concords that were coming into the state so fast. By 1851 he had extended his original route and added two more in order to compete with the other lines that were springing up. Sacramento had mushroomed, and at stage-time even the wide road by the docks was jammed with sweating horses and stages, hub to hub and four abreast. Each line had its runners who threaded through the crowds of passengers, seizing blanket-rolls and carpet-bags, steering their customers to the stage, stowing their baggage and darting off for the next victim. The early morning air was filled with their cries: "This way, sir, *this* way for Shasta! Shasta and Tehama right here!

Baxter & Munroe for Shasta and the north!" "Nevada this way! Here! Nevada City line!" And "Right here, sir, for Stockton. Birch stages connect for Sonora and the Southern Mines!" Jim Birch was in the business he liked, the business he was meant for. In that year, too, his friend Stevens had joined in the race to provide the new kind of transportation, and founded the Pioneer Line from Sacramento to Hangtown, the very line which old Jared Crandall, a dozen years later, would extend across the ten-thousand-foot granite walls of the Sierra and on toward Salt Lake City. This was something like it for both New England boys. They had the feel of the reins in their hands again, the sway and swing of the Concord coach beneath them. Better yet, they had the whole of a new land to explore and exploit. This was the life! Let the grubbers dig and shovel and freeze in the mountain streams. Birch and Stevens would get their share of the gold anyway, and by doing the thing they loved. *"All* aboard!"

The point about Birch was that he was not only a driver but a business man, an American with the characteristic nineteenth-century tendency to organize, develop, and coördinate whatever he got his hands on. What he saw all around him in California irritated him by its inefficiency. Here were dozens of stage-lines cutting each other's throats, dividing the business at rates that left a bare margin of profit for anybody. It was an expensive matter to import Concords all the way from New Hampshire, not to mention the fine horse-flesh that had to be bought too. Worse, a traveler never knew exactly what fare he might have to pay, nor just how he was to be routed. With lines battling for business, a man might have to go round Robin Hood's barn to get from Sacramento to Sonora, for example, when by a sensible system of organization he might go almost as straight as an arrow. Jim Birch thought about these things, talked to Stevens, and saved his money. On New Year's Day, 1854, the story was out. There had been an amalgamation. Horses, men and equipment of more than three-quarters of the state's stage-lines had been merged into one far-flung transport system, the California Stage Company. Its officials were staging men who knew every angle of the business, and before long they would be responsible for carrying passengers a daily distance of some fifteen hundred miles, inside the state of California. And Birch and Stevens, barely twenty-five years old, were running the show. James E. Birch was President, and Frank Stevens was Vice-President.

The Company was the largest staging firm in the world, too, with stock assessed at a million dollars. Where were you bound? Northward to Marysville, over to Bidwell's Bar, Charley's Rancho, Forbestown, Dry Creek, Long Bar? East to Ophir, Auburn, Yankee Jim's, Iowa Hill, Secret Diggings, Half-Way House, and Rattlesnake Bar? South to Mokelumne Hill and Angels Camp, Murphy's, Columbia, Shaw's Flat, and Sonora? The California Stage Company would carry you. And Jim Birch had made it. Californians did not grudge him his success, his mansion in Swansea, Massachusetts, tales of which came back to the West, his commuting by sea between New England and the Pacific Coast. He had put California on wheels.

James Birch might have gone much farther. In his head were grand plans for an overland mail and passenger service with way stations and relays of fresh horses across the deserts and mountains of the Southwest. He might have beaten Butterfield at his own game—that same Butterfield who was later to be the giant of giants in Western staging. He might have wrested from Butterfield the fat mail-contracts handed over to him by President Buchanan, partly because the President knew him and partly because there was New York money behind him. At the least, it would have been a battle of the Titans.

But Birch never had a chance to make the fight. On the

night of September 12, 1857, the side-wheeler, *Central America,* was caught in a storm south of Hatteras. Her seams had spread, and there was time only to transfer women and children to a sailing vessel that stood by until her own gear was too crippled to allow her to do more. Birch, on his way home in the palatial liner, made one valiant bid for life by manufacturing a kind of raft out of wreckage. But it was no use; weakened by the strain, he was forced to loosen his grip and was swept into the sea. He had just time to give to George Dawson, a mulatto seaman, a large silver cup he carried with him. Later, Dawson and a single white survivor on the raft were picked up by one man in a drifting life-boat, and the three managed to keep alive for nine days, using the silver cup to bail out the boat and to catch rain-water to slake their thirst. More than four hundred miles from where the *Central America* had sunk, the three men were at last picked up and brought to New York. The silver cup went to Birch's widow and Frank, her small son, for whom Birch had been bringing it home. There was no doubt about where it belonged. Engraved on its side was the inscription ordered by John Andrews, one of the California Stage Company's agents: "From John to Frank."

The ensuing ten years saw a fantastic multiplication of stage-lines tracing their paths through the deserts and mountains of the new West.

Among the owners whose names were to grow suddenly famous, then fade and be almost lost to memory, were such men as Ben Holladay, Chorpenning, Hockaday, Crandall, and a dozen others. Most noted of all was that Butterfield who was so close to the Buchanan administration and who might have found himself engaged with an adversary worthy of his steel had Jim Birch lived to fight him. Butterfield held the mail contracts that gave him his bread and butter and more than a little jam, and though he eventually gave in to Wells, Fargo, it was only when he had so consolidated his forces that he was able to make the great express company pay him a fine round sum to take over. But Butterfield and the company that succeeded him traveled the Southern Route, and that long and arduous roundabout journey called for government spending on a scale that was upsetting to some people, chiefly to the supporters of the far shorter Central Route by way of Salt Lake. Whether the scandal that was being whipped up in Washington would have actually resulted in a change is a matter for speculation now. For although reform was in the wind and retrenchment was forcing the political insiders to take it more easily with Uncle Sam's mail-money, the Salt Lake route did not look like much. There was sectional jealousy. There were whispers that the line from Salt Lake westward didn't even run stages, that the mail was packed out of town in a decrepit Concord that was cached out of sight as soon as possible while the mail was transferred to mule-train. What the Central Route needed was some dramatic method of advertising to the country that it was the ideal way for the mail to come. Perhaps, if this could be done, the Congress could be roused to the need for a mail subsidy that would justify a really good stage-line from Salt Lake to the Pacific, not to mention a telegraph system—in fact, maybe some day even a railroad.

That dramatic advertisement came sooner than any one expected. It came through the most glamorous bit of Western history of them all, the Overland Pony Express.

The Pony was the idea of three men, William H. Russell, Alexander Majors, and William B. Waddell. Russell had the plan; Majors had the money, made through years of hard work and successful government contracts for his wagon-trains; Waddell had the name. Together they made the plan a fact. On April 3, 1860, the first westbound pony left St.

Joseph, Missouri. Ten days and seventy-five ponies later, the letters in the St. Joe pouch arrived in San Francisco to the accompaniment of bonfires and bands. One newspaper reported the event in the humorous style then in fashion, concluding: "The greatest excitement prevailed, after which the various parties participating in the celebration adjourned, pleased with themselves and the rest of mankind and the Pony Express in particular. All took a drink at their own expense." Sixteen days later, on April 29, the first round trip was completed at the California end, the mail-bags carrying the interesting news of Butterfield's sellout to Wells, Fargo & Company. The Overland Pony Express was a fact, even if it was not a profitable fact as far as Russell, Majors & Waddell were concerned.

The dramatic quality of the pony's dash across the far western mountains and plains has often obscured the unhappy truth behind it. True, the Overland Pony Express brought about the very thing it was intended to accomplish. It focused the eyes of the country on the shorter Northern Route. More important, it foreshadowed the transcontinental railroad; indeed, there are historians who feel that it was the pony, and the pony alone, that made a reluctant Congress move at length in the direction of faster and better communication with the Pacific and so paved the way for Judah and Big Four to get their railroad through. However that may have been, the pony's contribution was enormously significant. But it was also enormously costly. Even at prices ranging from $5 as far down as $1 per half-ounce, the letters that riders could carry in their double pouches did not add up to a tenth of the cost of maintaining the route. By the time the Overland Pony Express had been in operation just eighteen months, the telegraph wires were joined and messages began clicking over them. All in all, the pony had earned $101,000 in cash. But the outgo had been something over a million dollars. Alexander Majors paid the difference, though it left him bankrupt. The Pony Express was dead.

Yet it had lent color and grace and drama to the saga of the West. It had brought California forward another tremendous step. It had added a whole private legendry of its own to the growing Western story. It had developed men like the famous "Pony Bob" Haslam who rode the section over the Carson deserts, dodging Indians while he slipped from one pony to the next, covering on one historic occasion no less than three hundred and eighty-four miles with only nine hours' rest. William Cody, long before he became known as "Buffalo Bill," rode Pony Express; if the story is to be credited, so did "Wild Bill" Hickok; so did any number of other lesser lights. And there is no question that they were a hardy, heroic crew. Across prairie and desert and mountain, through flood and sand and snow, two thousand miles in ten days and the schedule must stand—that was a job that took men. Wherefore the glamour of the Pony that has lasted to this day. Californians had scarcely time to grow accustomed to the thunder of his hoofs before he was gone from the scene, vanished like the "belated fragment of storm" that Mark Twain called him. But those hoofs struck sparks from the imagination, the kind of electric fire to which the Californian invariably responded. What if the Pony did lose a million dollars? What if his day was over before it had much more than begun? For a year and a half he had flared like a comet in the western sky. A year and a half is long enough in California history. The Central Overland Pony Express lived briefly and died in a welter of confusion and debt; but the Pony and his rider will live romantically and gloriously as long as the Old West is remembered anywhere.

Romance and glory, however, were not the Pony's alone. The stage came before and remained for many a year after the Pony's way-stations had crumbled to dust. The Concord was a lady, but in proper fashion a man was in command. That man was the driver, by all odds the most romantic figure in California's transportation in any age.

Small boys and big men looked up to the stage-driver while he looked down on them from the strategic height of the Concord's driving seat. Whip-stock in hand, elbows squared, fingers sensitive to the least tug of the lines between them, the Concord driver knew pride in his profession and showed it. Six horses, four wheels and a brake—with this equipment the California Jehu would engage to get his passengers anywhere. Up and down the precipitous grades, around hair-pin turns or straight across a broad mountain meadow, the Concord rolled and rattled in its cloud of red dust, keeping to schedule, carrying men, mail and treasure, a living part of its day and time. Now and then its driver drank too much; swaggering was his specialty; often he swore like a trooper. Sometimes he died in line of duty, always he risked death a dozen times a week. But he brought the stage in on time, and he brought it in with a flourish. There was, for instance, Mr. Henry Monk.

"Hank" Monk deserves a reasonable degree of fame in his own right. As one of the Central Overland drivers, he had been holding down the section across the Sierra from the Nevada side into Placerville ever since Crandall had opened it in 1857. Winter or summer, Hank Monk never failed; his passengers and his mail got through. True, if the stories are to be believed, Monk was not above having his good time when the circumstances were suitable. There is a tale that once he drank so much that he became confused and gave whiskey to his horses and watered himself, in this way accidentally becoming sober enough to handle a drunken team. Yet, after a lifetime of driving, Monk was able to boast with truth that in twenty years of negotiating the dangerous Sierra passes he had never injured a passenger. He was clever; he knew how to get the utmost out of his horses, how to coax his rolling wheels within inches of the abyss. But he was cool and careful, too; like the rest of his clan who were able to stay in the profession, he had to be. And the mere fact that he was one of the best known among a hundred other top-notch drivers in California is warrant enough that Hank was outstanding in his field.

Yet his fame does not rest on his achievements but upon as pointless an anecdote as was ever remembered for three-quarters of a century. Because Horace Greeley happened to take Hank Monk's stage for the last leg of his serio-comic overland journey, because Mark Twain and a dozen or two other journalists happened to fictionize one incident of that rapid ride into Placerville, the name of Hank Monk has come down the years, a symbol of all stage-drivers and all stage-driving in the days when California was the rough and tough frontier.

Greeley had been advising young men to "Go West!" quite a while before he made up his mind, in the spring of 1859, to have a look at the country he had been boosting.

Even by New York standards, he was hardly an old man when he started. But by the time he clambered aboard Hank Monk's stage he felt a good deal more than his forty-eight years. In the two weeks it had taken him to get from Leavenworth to Denver he had slept occasionally in a tent but more often in the wagon or under it. Once a herd of buffalo had frightened the mules, and in the crash that followed the runaway, Greeley acquired a wrenched leg. Moreover, the accommodations in Denver were hardly of the best; his efforts to make up for his weeks of lost sleep were put to naught by the sounds of revelry from the bar-room of his hotel and by the fact that his bunk boasted neither mattress nor pillow. From Fort Laramie, the worried editor had been compelled to ride perched on top of sixteen mail-sacks, with the result that when the leaders of the team doubled back crossing a swollen river, not only the sacks but Greeley were pitched into the water. Worse yet, he was soaked again before he reached Salt Lake City; his stage tipped over in the depths of the Sweetwater and his precious trunk was swept away in the flood. Wherefore, when he made his way to the top of Hank Monk's stage and perceived the violent inclines and declivities ahead it is not surprising that he was apprehensive.

He might have been wiser to confine his expression of nervousness to the pages of his written record, where he set down very plainly how he felt. "Our driver was skillful," he wrote, "but had he met a wagon suddenly on rounding one of the sharp points or projections we were constantly passing, a fearful crash was unavoidable. Had his horses seen fit to run away ... he could not have held them, and we might have been pitched headlong down a precipice of a thousand feet. Yet at this breakneck rate we were driven not less than four hours or forty miles, changing horses every ten or fifteen, and raising a cloud of dust through which it was difficult at times to see anything."

Unhappily, Greeley was not content to think his thoughts and let it go at that. If a stage could tip over on the level prairies, if a man could be dumped into rivers near the Mormon settlements, what might not happen in a country like this, where granite and pines seemed to take a bitter pleasure in trying to reach the sky itself, only to change direction and dive toward sea-level whenever the fancy seized them? It did not occur to him that his driver, Mr. Monk, had been covering this route successfully, day in and day out, for at least a year. It did not strike him, either, that just perhaps a stage-driver might not relish being told by an inky editor how to handle his team. Instead, he "yelled at Hank Monk and begged him to go easier," and paved the way for the reply that got a laugh at Greeley's expense over half the civilized globe: "Keep your seat, Horace. I'll get you there on time!"

It is on the wings of this anecdote that Hank Monk's name has been wafted to notoriety, made so famous that every one who thinks of staging in early California thinks immediately of Hank and Horace and of that bouncing, rattling trip to Placerville recorded by Mark Twain and his fellow-journalists of the period. Stage-coach—Hank Monk—Horace Greeley; the progression is inevitable in the mind of the reader who has ever heard the yarn. Oddly enough, however, the sequel to the story is forgotten, duly set down though it was in the columns of the California press some years later. The incident related in that sequel may or may not have basis in fact; for that matter, the original yarn may have been no more than an invention. But because it is plausible, in the light of Greeley's tragic end, it is worth repeating here.

A dozen years after his fearful ride with Hank Monk, Greeley was his party's candidate for the Presidency of the United States. Monk noted his one-time acquaintance's elevation in politics and it occurred to him that it might be a good idea to write him a letter, recall old times, and hint that in the event Mr. Greeley was elected President he might find a job for one who was less able than he had been to pursue his strenuous career—perhaps a minor postmastership or something of the sort. Hank carried out his idea, and the newspapers published Mr. Greeley's reply. When he wrote it, Greeley may have begun to suspect that the country was not for him; perhaps he was already near the edge of that final insanity into which his loss of the election and his wife's sudden death so tragically plunged him. At any rate, if the *Pioneer* is to be believed, this is what he wrote Hank Monk:

"I would rather see you ten thousand fathoms in hell than give you even a crust of bread. For you are the only man who ever had it in his power to put me in a ridiculous light before the American people, and you villainously exercised that power."

Poor Horace! If he did indeed write those two sentences, it is quite clear why he was a successful editor but a failure as a candidate for high public office.

Hank Monk, though famous, was only one of a long line of whips whose names were spoken with respect when drivers met to talk their shop. Al Grinnell, Charlie Crowell, Jared Crandall, and "Coon Hollow Charlie," Ned Blair, Curly Dan, John Shine, who was once held up by Black Bart though it was nearly ten years before he learned who had stopped him that day on Funk Hill, Reason McConnell, David Taylor, J. J. Crowder, John Sickles—the list is endless. They drove for the Pioneer, for Birch & Stevens, for Butterfield and Chorpenning and Langton and at last, most of them, for Wells, Fargo. Good men all they were. That is, all but one—Charlie Parkhurst. Not that there was any weakness about Parkhurst, who was as courageous, as skilful, as resourceful, and as hardboiled generally as any driver in the Sierra. But there was a very good reason why the term "good man" doesn't apply. Charlie Parkhurst was a woman, though it was more than fifty years before any one discovered that fantastic fact.

So far, no one has learned Charlie Parkhurst's true name. There is a story that she ran away, as a small girl, from a New England orphanage, dressed in boy's clothes and simply stuck to the style thereafter. However that may be, she turned up at the stables of one Ebenezer Balch in Worcester, Massachusetts, looking for a job and Ebenezer took her on, saying that he would make a man of her. Charlie must have laughed to herself but she said nothing, then or later. She simply pitched in and did the work of two boys, washing carriages, cleaning out the stables, watching the drivers, learning all there was to know about horses. When Mr. Balch moved to Providence, Rhode Island, and set up as an innkeeper, he took Charlie with him and taught her to drive. She took to

View Of The Plaza, Marysville, California

Marysville owed its sudden growth not to gold, but to
its location at the head of navigation at the junction of
the Feather and Yuba Rivers and to a sharp real estate promoter.

To thousands of miners in the northern camps, Marysville was The City. In fact, in 1853, only Sacramento and San Francisco were larger.

it like a duck to water, and it was not long before the best customers used to call for Charlie. She had the knack, that was the size of it, and there were few who could come up to her way with horses or her style.

Only once in her New England career did Charlie ever have to call for help, and she must have raged inwardly when she had to ask the man beside her to handle the lead reins. Cold was what did it, so the story goes, a long wait in the snow for a coach-load coming back from a dance. With Charlie's hands frozen to stiff lumps, the horses were simply too much for her.

There is no record that it ever happened again. Her fame grew, and coaching men knew the name of Charlie Parkhurst from one end of New England to the other. It was not strange that when Birch and Stevens had their California lines established they should have sent for Charlie. And in California her reputation increased. There is a story of her coolness on one occasion when she was driving across a bridge over the swollen Tuolumne River and felt the structure begin to shiver and go down. Charlie's reflexes were in perfect working order. She laid on the whip like a bullwhacker, and the astonished team leaped as it had never leaped before. Horses, coach, and passengers made the other shore just in time to see the bridge go crashing down behind them.

Twice Charlie was held up by highwaymen, and the first time she had had to comply with the grim command, "Throw down the box!" from an armed robber who knew she had no weapon.

"I wasn't thinking of this," so Charlie is supposed to have said. "But the next time you try it I'll be ready for you!"

The next time it was no lone bandit who stopped the stage, but a gang of road-agents. It made no difference to Charlie. She was ready, just as she had promised. Before the leader realized that he had picked a Tartar, Charlie had fired point-blank at his breast, whipped up her horses, and was out of sight around the next bend. A searching party found the body of the robber in a tunnel near the scene of the hold-up. After that, ambitious highwaymen left her alone.

Altogether Charlie Parkhurst drove stage for nearly twenty years in California, and the Bannings, in *Six Horses,* list her as being among the "select whips" of the entire gold region. But the life was a hard one, and in her sixties old Charlie decided to quit the road. She settled on the Moss Ranch, half a dozen miles from Watsonville where life was quieter and the climate more equable. Late in 1879 she died, alone and unattended. Her body was found by friends who had dropped in to call, and for the first time since she had run away from that dour New England orphanage somebody besides herself knew that Charlie Parkhurst was a woman. A nine days' wonder, this story was printed in newspapers from California to Charlie's native New England, investigated, authenticated, as strange a tale as ever came out of the mines.

Stories of the stage and its drivers could be spun endlessly, but a gentleman named J. Ross Browne, a mining engineer with a taste for literary expression, said the last and the best word. Writing in the fair and flowery style of the Seventies, Browne took a dozen pages in a book about the new West to set down his impressions of the men who drove the Sierra roads. Unlike Greeley, Browne understood the genius of these knights of the reins and was willing to give them all the credit that was coming to them. Was he writing, perhaps, of Charlie Parkhurst, or another Charles? One can not be sure. But his appreciation will do for the whole clan of Charlies:

Imagine yourself [he wrote] seated in front of the stage, by the side of the gallant old whipster, Charlie, who knows every foot of the way, and upon whom you can implicitly rely for the safety of your life and limbs. Holding the reins with a firm hand, and casting a penetrating eye ahead, he cracks his whip, and away go the horses with inspiring velocity—six magnificent chestnuts, superbly adorned with flowing manes and tails. The stillness of the night is pleasantly broken by their measured tread, and the rattle of the wheels over the gravel echoes through the wild rifts and openings of the canyon like a voice from the civilized world telling of human enterprise. Down and still down we plunge into the gloomy depths of the abyss; the ghostly forms of the trees looming up on our left; to the right, rising far beyond the range of vision, the towering heights of the Sierra; and ever and anon yawning gulfs in front and bottomless pits of darkness still threatening. ...And you, my good friend, crossing the Sierra of California once or twice in a lifetime, imagine you have done great things. You boast of your qualities as a traveler; you have passed unscathed through the piercing night air; have scarcely shuddered at the narrow bridges or winced at the fearful precipices.... But think of Charlie! He has crossed the mountains a thousand times; crossed when the roads were at their worst; by night and by day; in storm and gloom and darkness; through snow and sleet and rain, and burning suns and dust; back and forth; subject to the risk of different teams and different stages; his life balanced on the temper of a horse or the strength of a screw.... All hail to thee, Old Charlie!... that same Old Charlie, all over the roads!

It is possible that Mr. Browne was a student of De Quincey; there are turns of phrase here, a degree of fondness for the use of the semicolon, even whole sentences which suggest that he had at least read *The English Mail*. But what of that? Browne's testimonial comes from the heart. He rode with the Charlies who drove California's Concords, and he knew their worth.

It would be the perfect conclusion to this chapter if one could only quote the average passenger in the stage-coaches of early days and find him—or her—as enthusiastic as Mr. Browne.

Unhappily very few were as sympathetic, as well aware of the difficulties of the road, as ready to make allowances as Mr. Browne showed himself. In general, the passenger in the Concord traveled because he had to, resented the jolting and jounc-

ing fiercely, considered the discomforts an outrage to his—
and again, her—sense of what was fitting and proper. That
the driver was performing miracles every moment did not
occur to the stage-coach passenger, and if he had thought
about it he would likely have dismissed the idea as sentimental
and quite unworthy of a pioneer. It was a driver's job to handle his horses and there it was. But a body certainly had a
right to expect better of the stage companies. If it was the
fault of the roads, why weren't they fixed? And why did the
stages have to travel at the death-defying speed of ten miles
an hour? Passengers did not choose to remember, at such moments, that when the driver did occasionally find it necessary
to slow down to a walk they were the first to complain of the
snail's pace at which they were being transported.

Wherefore the journals of the day are full of bitter comment on the wretchedly uncomfortable conditions under which
Californians were compelled to go from place to place. Women
in particular noted the unpleasantness of it all, reported in
their diaries and letters the accidents they had heard about
(but very seldom saw), made it plain that the cramped interior of a stage-coach was far from being as elegant as it
seemed. It must have been a woman, indeed, who set down
these anonymous verses in which the lovely Concord, performing a task that no vehicle on earth could have accomplished
as gracefully or as efficiently, is robbed of its last shred of
romance at the point of a quatrain:

> Creeping through the valley, crawling o'er the hill;
> Splashing through the branches, rumbling by the mill;
> Putting nervous gentlemen in a towering rage.
> What is so provoking as riding in a stage?
>
> Spinsters fair and forty, maids of youthful charms,
> Suddenly are cast into their neighbors' arms;
> Children shoot like squirrels, darting through a cage—
> Isn't it delightful, riding in a stage?

Feet are interlacing, heads severely bumped,
Friend and foe together get their noses thumped;
Dresses act as carpets—listen to the sage:
"Life is but a journey taken in a stage!"

Not that women were the only complainants. They merely put their objections more delicately. The male passenger had his troubles, too, and in the male manner he was even less reticent about airing them. Maids of youthful charms being cast into their neighbors' arms didn't bother the masculine traveler; what made him angry was chiefly the notion that he wasn't getting his money's worth. He didn't like the crowding either, to be sure; but, as the song, "The California Stage Company" shows, it was the sense of being cheated that irritated him most:

There's no respect for youth or age
On board the California stage,
But pull and haul about the seats
As bedbugs do about the sheets.

You're crowded in with Chinamen
As fattening hogs are in a pen;
And what will more a man provoke
Than musty plug tobacco smoke?

The dust is deep in summer time,
The mountains very hard to climb;
And drivers often stop and yell,
"Get out, all hands, and push uphill!"

They promise when your fare you pay,
"You'll have to walk but half the way."
Then add aside, with cunning laugh,
"You'll have to push the other half!"

CHORUS

They started as a thieving line
In eighteen hundred forty-nine;
All opposition they defy,
The people must root hog or die!

166

Thus the public's response to the prodigious feats of Birch and Stevens, of the Wells, Fargo Express and the United States Mail, of the Hank Monks and Crowders and Crandalls, and all the Charlies who drove the Concord over the raw, new roads, meeting emergencies every moment of the day or night, taking Californians where they had to go and delivering them, if weary, at least sound in wind and limb. A marvelous performance? Not a bit of it. A rascally monopoly, no less!

Doubtless there was truth on both sides. But in the end one truth remains. It was the Concord that opened up the mines, that brought them into touch with the growing, thriving towns in the great Valley and with San Francisco down by the Bay. It was the stage-driver, more than any one else, who enabled the miner in the hills to cease being a solitary creature, bewhiskered and lonesome, dependent upon bacon, beans and home-made biscuit and perhaps a six-months-old newspaper for his moments of relaxation, and to become once more a citizen of the world. The stage brought him his luxuries, the fine wines and barreled oysters and Havana cigars that helped make life worth living again, the mail and the news that linked him once more with home, the entertainment which did more than anything else to justify the long hours of digging, washing, and rocking that gold-mining meant. Most especially the entertainment.

6.

Shakespeare ... Song and Dance

FROM the beginning, the miner in California required to be amused in his off hours, and in one way or another he managed to do something about it.

The saloon came first; wherever men are gathered together in large numbers with hard work to do in the daytime, the beneficent escape-qualities of alcohol are in demand for the evening hours. The mining towns had hotels almost immediately; but the fact was that the hotels grew up around the bars that were their forerunners. With the bars went two other forms of amusement, gambling and women. The pattern is inflexible, general, historic, not peculiar to the California gold rush.

In California, however, the Mexican influence slanted the

development. And it was the Mexican influence that was responsible for the "fandango hall," so frequently mentioned in the records of the time.

The fandango hall was a good many things. One drank and one danced, at least. When there were not enough girls to serve as partners, miners danced with each other; with liquor and music at hand the urge was irresistible. Outwardly, moreover, the fandango hall was a remarkably orderly place, at any rate in the earlier hours of the evening. Propriety, after all, was in the blood and bones of most of the men who had come to California to get rich. Whatever may have been the private morals of the Mexican girls who were drafted in numbers to meet the miners' natural insistence on a good time after a week of toil, they handled themselves in public with restraint and what passed for modesty. One woman who came out to California as an infant in 1851 set down thirty years later her childhood recollection of one such place of amusement. Naturally her youthful memories were conditioned by her innocence, yet if there had been rowdyism it should have been impressed upon her mind, innocent or not. She recalls nothing of the sort, but has a vivid memory of slipping away from her house in the evenings and stationing herself outside the door of a fandango hall in Columbia, spending hours in rapt contemplation of what little she could see beyond the edge of a screen, listening to the music of a harp and violin and watching the dancers glide by and disappear to the genteel rhythms of the waltz.

There were, of course, the Juanitas who caused trouble now and then; the reader will remember the dramatic hanging of the girl in Downieville. On record, too, is a vivid and shocking account of two Mexican girls from a dance hall meeting in the public street at the chilly hour of five in the morning and fighting it out—no doubt over some miner whose poke was fuller than most—with shawls wrapped around their left

arms and daggers in their free hands. They slashed and
stabbed each other so severely that both died before the sun
was up. But the reader will also recall that Juanita, who knifed
the gambler, Cannon, did so because he had drunkenly insulted her. By her code, public impropriety was not per-
missible. Gentility and refinement were the watchwords; as in
the gambling parlors of Madame Moustache, let all be done
with decency. Witness this advertisement from a Marysville
newspaper in which the proprietress of a place of entertainment carefully stresses the matter of liquid refreshment, at
the same time making it clear enough that there was more to
do in her house than just drink:

SEÑORA JUANA RIBERO begs to inform the hombres in the
"Queen City" that she has taken and fitted up in magnificent style
THE NEW RETREAT in D Street, with the choicest liquors, wines,
etc. that can be purchased for either love or money in Calif., to which
she calls the attention of the citizens in general.

Having led off with this splendid claim, however, the Señora
delicately assures the reader of her advertisement that wines
and liquors are not, after all, quite the whole story. The place-
ment of the italics, an innocent maneuver with type if ever
there was one, does the trick in the final sentence of the announcement:

The whole establishment will be conducted by the above lady.

There was prejudice against the Mexican element, however,
and as time went on there were more thousands who wanted
to dance and drink of a Saturday night. What Yankee specu-
lator thought up the idea of importing girls from Germany
the record does not show. Some one did—perhaps several such
bright minds. For newspaper editors began suddenly to grow
indignant about this new scheme. More wives were coming
into the mines; that was the reason for the editorial fulmina-

tions. After all, the way to keep subscriptions was to please the womenfolk, and a high moral tone was what the ladies liked. The editor of the *Alta* seems to have hit precisely the right note of outraged respectability combined with sensationalism in his piece shrewdly headed "PEONAGE! DANCE GIRLS!":

It may hardly seem credible that a system of peonage of Anglo-Saxon flesh and blood is rife in California. The system of importing females from Germany, by contract, has been carried on with great profit to one or two parties in this city. Young girls are bought up, sent out here in ships, and have to serve a term of years to their master —no matter what labor may be required.

In our city and throughout the interior, dance houses are supplied with women to act as partners to visitors, and this is the allotted work of the white peons we speak of. As a class, they are hardy, healthy-looking girls, from sixteen to twenty-five years of age, of strongly marked Teutonic cast of features, blessed with stout limbs and brawny hands; being evidently selected from the agricultural districts. These girls receive shelter, food, raiment and a gratuity of three hundred guilders, or about $240 per annum. They are hired out by the contractor to the various dance houses at the rate of $4 per night, up to 12 o'clock, and $7 if retained until morning. Five generally is the complement necessary to carry on the dance, and the party is usually dressed in a calico uniform, josey and skirt. Their duties consist in waltzing or dancing with any man who may chance to drop in. The visitor approaches his partner, and without interchange of compliments, the girl used to the business resigns herself to him with all the submission of a well-trained animal; the music strikes up a lively air, and off they rush in the giddy whirl. After a race of five minutes, the music ceases, and each girl marches her partner to the bar where he "treats." This duty performed, she is ready to repeat the same course with any one present. During her labors she holds no converse—it being a part of the business to avoid familiarity or even acquaintance-ship, as such manifestations ofttimes promote difficulties, personal encounters, etc., from jealousy.

These dance girls are orderly, for the "boss" well knows his success depends upon the quiet he can maintain. In all their actions, one sees the boorish stolidity of the uneducated German, though, doubtless, the life they lead is pleasant to them, as not one of the two hundred and odd bondwomen have ever attempted to violate their contract. To an American, their appearance is not engaging. They are not over neat; blue eyes, listless and unanimated, blonde hair, and teeth unfamiliar with dentifrice, predominate, and so stereotypic are they, that one will answer for the whole.

We are informed—and if it is true, it reflects greatly to their credit— that, as a class, they are virtuous; though how the fact can be reconciled with their employment we are at a loss to know. Notions of propriety forbid that a female who can be fondled and clasped by every comer, be he drunk or sober, uncouth or comely, can be chaste; yet such a miracle may exist.

This *corps de dance* is divided into phalanxes, who do service alternately in the city and country, by which system the purveyor is enabled to give each of his customers, once or twice a year, new faces as a change in attraction. They are, ideally speaking, the *Bayaderes* of California; they enter upon their labors conscious that they have a duty to fulfill. They have rendered dancing epidemic. Everybody dances in California, reveling in the intricate steps and whirls of the polka, the mazourka, varsovienne; and straight fours, hoe-down, shuffles, freeze-outs and Jarsey reels are obsolete. Germany and France, mistresses of the dance, hold dominion. *Vive la bagatelle!*

Despite his sniffy references to the unattractiveness of the girls, the editor of the *Alta* seems rather to have enjoyed describing what went on in a California dance hall; his left-handed compliments in the matter of the young ladies' virtue suggests a certain relish for his self-assumed task. Nevertheless, the note of honest indignation had to be injected somewhere, and he took care of it nicely in his last paragraph. "Socially speaking," he writes—perhaps realizing that his momentary lapse into French might have sounded frivolous— "these dance halls are a moral pestilence and should be abolished." He could not have felt very sanguine about it, for he concludes pessimistically, "We fear that all the arguments we could bring to bear in support of this doctrine would fall unheeded on the ears of those who should act therein." Unquestionably he was right.

If a man did not like to drink or dance, he was still at no loss for week-end amusement.

For instance, he could watch a bull-and-bear fight, make his bets, spend happy hours debating in advance the relative chances of the furious grizzly, captured especially for the purpose, and the fighting bull of Spain which the advertising posters assured him had been imported by way of Mexico particularly for its ferocity and its instinctive knowledge of how to attack and defeat a bear of the California Sierra. That the bear was nine times out of ten a mangy, ailing specimen, remarkable chiefly for its obvious anxiety to find an exit from the ring and leave bull and audience far behind, or that the bull had never been nearer Spain or Mexico than the confines of a rancho down in the San Joaquin Valley did not disturb the miner on pleasure bent. There was always the off-chance that the bear might make a stand, that the bull might be goaded into rushing its opponent, in which case there would undoubtedly be blood shed and bets paid. And the entrepreneurs of these contests knew quite well that such an off-chance was enough. Their posters were extravagant, their claims couched in the kind of language that Barnum was employing with such success in the East and in Europe. Though editors vied with each other to condemn the brutality of such exhibitions, though itinerant preachers spoke at length on the vileness of men who could enjoy so foul a spectacle, bull-and-bear fights had their day, drew thousands of miners who crowded around the improvised plank arenas in the hope that a real battle would be staged.

Once, so the story runs, a true grizzly, bolder than most, did make a stand, faced the oncoming bull, and broke its neck with a single well aimed blow. The fight, to which everybody had been looking forward for a week, was over in the half-minute it had taken the bull to make up its mind to charge.

Brief as it was, it had been a fight; but the fact did the managers of the enterprise no good. An angry crowd of miners, expecting more for their money, stormed the box-office and ran the promoters out of town. Another time, in the Southern Mines, a bull had caught the bear broadside on, and though bruin's weight had been too great for his enemy to toss him, he had been gored to a bloody mass with no chance to make a battle of it. The crowd hadn't liked that show either; revolted, the miners tore ring and grandstand to pieces, advised the showman to remove his property, alive and dead, and descended on the town's fourteen saloons for a two-day celebration of their high-mindedness.

It was neither the brutality of such shows, however, nor their essential fakery that put an end to them. The new roads and the stage-coach were beginning to bring into the mines the same kinds of entertainment that city people were getting, down by the Bay. Companies of first-rate actors were seizing their opportunity to go on tour through the camps where the money was. Singers, dancers, touring stock-companies, even circuses were making their way into the hills, and the crudity of the bull-and-bear fight was outdated in short order. The final blow was delivered by an anonymous newspaper wit who set down in four short sentences the story of a Nevada City exhibition. His yarn, completely in the tradition of California humor, serves excellently as an epitaph for this form of amusement:

Yesterday's hugely advertised bull-and-bear fight proved a distinct disappointment to our citizens. So anxious was the bear to get away that he made straight for the plank walls of the arena, which he clawed frantically in his attempt to scale them. The animal might have got over, but for the presence of mind of Dr. Kendall, who beat it back with a heavy cane as fast as it got its paws within reach. As all know, Dr. Kendall is a heavily bearded man, and in the midst of the affray the bear looked up, saw his antagonist for the first time, muttered "Et tu Brute!" and gave up.

174

After that, even the wildest claims, set in the largest type, could hardly have sold a bull-and-bear fight to the smart Argonaut.

Sophistication has its advantages, and in the middle Fifties the California miner must frequently have reflected upon the rapidity with which the civilizing process had taken place in his foot-hills.

The day of the "lonely miner," so widely celebrated in his time, had passed. True, there were still plenty of outposts, many a tiny settlement out of reach of the softening influences of a theater, a barber-shop or a Chinese laundry. Off in the hills were groups of cabins huddled into camps which were lucky to have one bar, and a general store to serve as post-office, boarding-place and wagon stop. Up the river cañons and dry arroyos it was still possible to find a single shack or tent, inhabited by a solitary who preferred to pursue his hunt for gold in his own way. But this kind of thing was the exception. The camps where the mines really amounted to something had burgeoned into towns; some were quite touchy about it, and insisted on being called cities. Columbia, for instance, had made its enormously rich deposits furnish its people with almost everything a real city could boast. In a few short years the town had burned down twice, yet had sprung up again, replacing wood and canvas with fine brick buildings decorated with ironwork balconies and protected against the dishonest by tall iron doors and shutters. Columbia had two theaters, seventeen dry-goods and produce stores, four hotels and half a dozen boarding-houses, two barber-shops, three drug-stores and twice as many laundries, a general assortment of carpenter shops, banks, tobacconists, wagon-makers, doctors, and lawyers. It had even a printing shop, a brewery, a daguerreotype studio, and a Chinatown.

Such luxury was demonstrably good evidence of the advan-

175

Placerville, El Dorado County, California, 1856
Dry Diggin's was the original name of Placerville when
it was established in 1848 by miners who found Coloma too

crowded. At it grew in size and violence, it was renamed
Hangtown. By 1856, self-conscious civic leaders,
seeking respectability, changed the name to Placerville.

tages of sophistication. Yet the disadvantages were apparent also. Columbia had an exceptional equipment of saloons, gambling houses, and fandango halls, sometimes separately run, more often in combination. And one such complete amusement palace helped to prove, as late as 1855, that men do not become civilized all at once, that the business of growing up, in towns no less than in individuals, is marked by cycles of development, by loops and spirals which advance upon to-morrow but now and then parallel a more primitive yesterday.

The particular place of resort which underlines this point for Columbia's benefit was known as "Martha's Saloon." A newspaper editor of the time, in language moderate but clear, defined both saloon and Martha beyond need of further detail. He wrote, simply: "The house was one of bad repute, as was its proprietress." No doubt there were in prosperous little Columbia other houses and other owners whose repute was no better. But Martha will live in mining-camp history because in her bar, almost in the center of a town which prided itself on its culture and refinement, there took place a quarrel which set off the most shocking, most utterly horrifying show of mob violence in all California's gold-rush years.

Martha's Saloon stood at the corner of Main and Jackson Streets, conveniently close to the flow of traffic as a successful saloon should be. Its bar opened hospitably on the bias, covering both approaches with a fine impartiality. Behind the bar proper was a back room in which poker players might enjoy relative quiet, and from this back room opened the private apartments occupied by Martha and her new husband, John S. Barclay. They had not been married long. Martha had visited in Chinese Camp, twenty miles away, met young Barclay who did a thriving business there as a gambler, fallen in love with him and persuaded him that together they might do much better at their trades than either could hope to do separately, especially since Columbia was booming on a scale that Chinese

Camp could hardly hope to equal. Barclay saw the force of
her argument, married her, and the two returned to Columbia,
made over the back room, added some more tables for the
poker players, and prepared to welcome the extra profits
which should accrue from two experienced people operating
where but one had been before.

Perhaps Martha's arguments would have been justified; the
saloon under double management might have increased its
profits, and the marriage might have proved a long and happy
one, as marriages are apt to do when love and money are
pleasantly combined. There is no way now to tell. For the
newly enlarged enterprise had been under way only a few
weeks when, at four fifteen on the afternoon of October 10,
1855, Mr. John Huron Smith walked into Martha's Saloon
and demanded a drink.

Mr. John H. Smith was drunk. Evidently he had been
drunk before in Columbia, since the editor of the *Gazette*,
acting as correspondent for the San Francisco *News*, though
he did his best to give Mr. Smith a good character in reporting
the happenings of that dreadful day, let slip the fact that
Columbians were aware of their fellow-citizen's weakness. He
described him as "much esteemed ... and, when not under the
influence of liquor, a peaceable and friendly man." But on this
Wednesday afternoon Mr. John Huron Smith was under the
influence—so much so that he carelessly knocked a pitcher from
the bar and broke it.

A pitcher, whole or broken, is hardly worth a man's life.
But when one party to an argument is drunk and disputatious
and the other is profane and abusive, anything is enough to
precipitate a first-rate row. The evidence was that Martha
swore at John Huron Smith, and Martha's repute was bad
enough so that it may be assumed her vocabulary was good.
The evidence, further, was that Mr. Smith lost his head to
the extent of seizing Martha and pushing her into a chair,

177

and, worse, slapping her when she let go an expletive of un-
usual force and pungency. At that moment Martha's new husband entered from the back room, drew his pistol, and shot
John Smith dead.

Under almost any other circumstances a man who caught
another in the very act of shoving his wife into a chair and
slapping her might have shot the aggressor and been ap-
plauded for his act. A few days later, the San Francisco
News made the point, commenting editorially: "We venture
the belief that it would be dangerous to strike any respectable
lady in the presence of a husband that possessed a spark of
manhood." Unfortunately Martha was not respectable. As
for Barclay, the papers reported that he had been "much
esteemed" in Chinese Camp, which was all very well in its
way. But he was in Columbia now. He was a gambler. He
was the consort of a woman whose house enjoyed a bad reputation. Even though the town marshal immediately hustled
him off to jail, the citizens of Columbia were far from satisfied. Smith—when he was not under the influence of liquor—
had been a "peaceable and friendly man." Dead, he was no
longer drunk. As the evening wore on, the murmurs grew
louder; Columbians felt more and more friendly toward the
late John Huron Smith, less and less peaceable about the
manner of his sudden taking-off.

The whole affair might have ended with a night of mutter-
ing and threats, a morning of wiser counsel. But the late Mr.
Smith had had one especially good friend in J. W. Coffroth,
recently elected State Senator and very fond of oratory. Here
was a golden opportunity for a rabble-rouser to exercise his
talent, and Coffroth was not one to miss it. He was popular,
widely known, and exceptionally able as an extemporaneous
speaker. It was no time at all before he had a crowd around
him and was well launched into a speech.

He began by saying that he was a man who favored the

178

idea of justice taking its course. As he warmed to his work, however, it was quickly apparent that he was also a man who knew an exception to a rule when he saw one. The man Smith had been a respected and beloved fellow-townsman; that was something to remember. He was, further, a citizen of exceptional merits and unusually fine qualities; he, J. W. Coffroth, would be glad to enumerate these. Having done this at some length, he made it clear to the men of Columbia that he knew them to be people of good judgment, men who understood what justice was and who would be ready and willing to see that justice was done in any case that might come before them. In this particular case, he continued, though all should be done according to legal procedure, there could be no harm in expediting matters a bit. Indeed, the facts here demanded expedition. For that matter, immediate action in itself was hardly enough. It was as plain as the three thousand noses on the three thousand faces before him that this was a question of speedy vengeance overtaking the perpetrator of what was nothing less than foul and cold-blooded murder. He, Senator Coffroth, had been elected to make laws, true; but this was an occasion on which he had no hesitation in saying that the law should be laid aside. He closed by hoping that the men of Columbia agreed with him.

They agreed to the extent of disarming the town marshal and breaking open the jail with sledges and crowbars. The record contains one pathetic touch here. Writes the local reporter: "As the door was sprung from its hinges, the frightened prisoner leapt out and attempted to run, but was seized."

Events then moved with dreadful swiftness. There was no room in the center of town for so large a mob, and Barclay was marched out on the Gold Springs road half a mile or so to a point where the great flume of the Tuolumne Water Company crossed a level clearing on its forty-foot stilts. Here a ring was formed and by torch-light a jury of twelve men was appointed to serve under the direction of John Heckendorn, local editor, who was called the judge. The prisoner was allowed a defender, a young lawyer named Oxley. Prosecutor was the man who incited the crowd to this performance, the man who had already demanded vengeance, who had urged that the law be set aside—J. W. Coffroth.

Barclay must have seen then that he had no chance. Coffroth had the crowd where he wanted it. When Oxley, sticking manfully to his guns, called for the mob to disperse, insisted that his man be given a proper trial, that at least the citizens of Columbia should think it over until to-morrow, he was shouted down with cries of "Enough! No! Hang him!" When Coffroth spoke, the mob quieted as if by magic, except when they roared approval of such ringing quotations as "An eye for an eye!" Oxley tried again, asking for fair and square justice, sparring desperately for time, but the mob would not listen. As a matter of form, the jury was ordered to "retire and consult." Coffroth, the political idol of his Columbia friends, had won his fight to hang the man who had shot his friend.

There was one more effort made to preserve the dignity of the law. When it was plain that the town constabulary could do nothing, some one had sent for Sheriff Stewart, who arrived at this moment, strode through the crowd, laid his hand on the shoulder of the prisoner, and demanded that he be turned over in the name of the law. It was a brave gesture, but it came to nothing. Stewart was overborne by the mob, and a few hotheads, fearing that their man might escape them after all, hustled him to a spot directly beneath the flume, hastily knotted a rope, slipped the noose over the prisoner's head and tossed the other end over the flume high above. The sheriff made one more try, fought off the men holding him, seized a knife and rushed toward the prisoner in an attempt to cut the rope from his neck. But it was no use.

Stewart was knocked unconscious, disarmed, and made fast, and a dozen yelling men on the other end of the rope jerked Barclay into the air.

Even that half-mad mob must have shuddered then, as the light of the torches revealed the frightful error that had been made. In the disorganized rush with which proceedings had been carried through, no one had thought to pinion Barclay, and now, high above the heads of the crowd, the wretched man reached upward, seized the rope over his head in a desperate grip and hung there with the frantic strength lent by the fear of death.

What followed is best recorded quickly. First, those on the other end of the rope drew the victim up and let him down suddenly several times, in hopes of breaking his hold. Barclay's grasp still held. Then half a dozen of the mob swarmed up the supports of the flume, crawled along it to the rope and shook it violently, but without success. One of them, according to the reporter who wrote the story, shouted hysterically, "Let go, you damned fool, let go!" Still Barclay clung fast. It was a miner with a pistol who put an end to the ghastly drama by hammering with his weapon at the victim's wrists and fingers until the blood spurted, the bones cracked and his grip was finally loosened, his broken hands falling at his sides. For the edification of its readers, the *Gazette* pursued the story to its very end: "Drawing up his legs, the prisoner gave a few convulsive kicks and then hung straight in the red glare of torches and bonfires which cast a horrid flush upon the scene."

The newspaper repercussions were loud and, fortunately, effective. For the Barclay affair had shocked even the extremists. Men who had been indifferent to the processes of lynch law suddenly saw what one editor pointed out the following week, that if this kind of thing went on no man could be sure of justice. The reaction was salutary. There were other cases, later, in which the miners took the law into their own hands; but their number steadily decreased. Moreover, the administration of justice by the courts improved rapidly, and with the growing assurance of regularized punishment for minor and major crimes the foot-hill towns swung solidly toward law and order. After all, too, there were beginning to be other and saner outlets for the miner's energy. Wives and children were no longer any rarity in the hills; a man had his home to look out for, his family to support, his membership in a fire company to occupy him with one regular meeting a week and whatever impromptu shindig might arise in celebration of a blaze well and truly extinguished. The saloons and gambling-houses did not suffer too much from the new moderation; there were plenty of men still on the loose, and the Californian had always been and always would be a hard drinker and a willing gambler. But as the camps grew to villages and then to towns there were dozens of fresh preoccupations to anchor the miner to respectability. He was growing a little older, for one thing. He had his lodge, his church; there were taxes to pay and problems to be settled in town council. In brief, the logical course of events was turning him inexorably from an adventurer into a citizen. And as he became less the rover and more the man of substance, his taste in amusement underwent a metamorphosis. The theater had always possessed an enormous pull for the miner, even in his wildest days. When he went down to San Francisco he saw the shows. Shakespeare or song and dance, it didn't much matter; the glamour of the stage was there. Now the Concord coach was making it possible for the best San Francisco talent to get up into the mines, and the miner responded nobly. Perhaps it is not going too far to say that, symbolically at least, it was the Booths, the Chapmans, Lola Montez, Lotta Crabtree and their fellow-Thespians by the hundreds who stripped the red shirt from

182

the miner's back and replaced it with the sober broadcloth of the solid burgher who knew good entertainment when he saw it and liked it when he could get it.

The change took time. In the early Fifties even the elder Booth found the gold country none too hospitable to his favorite tragic rôles. Constance Rourke, in her *Troupers of the Gold Coast,* suggests that Booth was ahead of his time where the mines were concerned; that when tragedy stalked the hills every day and suicides were commonplace, when so many men were eaten up with remorse for their folly in pursuing the golden will-o'-the-wisp, Booth, in such somber plays as his favorite, "The Iron Chest," hit too close to home. It is a plausible idea. Even young Edwin Booth, genius as he was, had many failures in his mining-camp tours; in one brief season, for example, his company had the ill luck to be dogged by fires in town after town, so many, in fact, that when the bedraggled troupe came to Downieville, deep in its cañon of the Yuba, the members found that their presence was considered a jinx. Invited to leave, they took the hint, broken in morale and bogged down in debt.

But the more lightly conceived sorts of theatrical entertainment unfailingly drew the crowds. When the Chapmans came along—the greatly talented Caroline and her brother William—the miners saw what the theater could really mean to them. The Chapmans' tour of the southern mines in the winter of 1852-1853 was a triumphal procession. They played *She Stoops to Conquer* when they happened to feel like it, offered shrewd and witty burlesques when they thought it better to lighten the mood even more, always maintained the extravagant tempo of mining-camp life itself, sensed almost magically what their audiences wanted. The camps received them with open arms, flung gold and silver at them, mobbed the small ramshackle theaters wherever they played.

The mines had been discovered by the theater, and the miners showed that they could and would reward with fantastic generosity the players who gave them what they wanted. Now the stage was set for the entrance of the two women of the theater whose names, more than any others, are associated with California's gold-rush days—one beyond her youth but still glamorous because of her exciting past, the other no more than a child but the greatest gold-camp favorite of them all—Lola Montez, Countess of Landsfeldt, and Lotta Crabtree, the airy, fairy, singing, dancing, miners' darling.

It was inevitable that Lola Montez should come to California.

Her dancing was ordinary, her talents as an actress were no more than fair. But Lola was lovely. Lola was notorious. Gossips the world over had heard her story, knew that she was no Spaniard but an Irish girl, Eliza Gilbert from Limerick, who had eloped with an army officer at fifteen, quarreled with her husband and left him, picked up a little knowledge of the dance and blossomed suddenly in London as Lola Montez, the new sensation. Those who did not know all this had at least heard the tale of her two years as mistress of the doting Ludwig of Bavaria, of the revolution she had caused, of her flight back to England, her second marriage, and the consequent trial for bigamy due to her neglect to do anything about her first. Her beauty had saved her in London courts. Bigamist though she was, nothing came of the trial but a thumping sensation and columns upon columns of publicity in *The Times*. The publicity so impressed New Yorkers that hundreds of them filed through her hotel suite when she arrived in America, solemnly shaking the hand that had been caressed by mad Ludwig and paying a dollar a head for the privilege. New Yorkers also thronged to see her in the "Spider

Dance" she had made famous. The spiders were merely contraptions of rubber and whalebone, and Lola's dancing, spiders aside, was no better than that of a hundred less advertised coryphées. But there was the aura of delicious scandal about Lola. She was graceful and she was beautiful, and this was enough.

Now, ripely handsome at thirty-five, she was in California, which was quite in the proper course of things. San Francisco welcomed her royally; as a reporter put it, she was "seen, admired, sung, courted and gone mad over," which was no more than she expected. Moreover, she married yet again, this time a dashing Irishman, a San-Franciscan-about-town who was also a newspaper owner and noted wit, one Patrick Purdy Hull. Lola said that she had married him because he could tell a story better than any one she had ever known, and Californians liked her for her boldness. Nevertheless, there was an undercurrent of skepticism in her reception. Some observers failed to be carried away by Lola's beauty and the glamour that hung around her, and retained their critical senses sufficiently to note that her performances were really nothing to get excited about. The versatile Chapmans made fun of her dances and dramatics in a whole series of uproarious farces such as *Who's Got the Countess?* At least a portion of the fourth estate was out-and-out acid about the public fuss that was being made over this celebrity. The Shasta *Courier,* for instance, in its story of the wedding, said: "It affords us the most exquisite happiness to inform our readers that Mr. Hull is connected with California press. Of course, he has immortalized himself. This is certainly a very great country."

But for a short while Lola triumphed. She played to capacity houses in San Francisco for nearly three weeks; people laughed at the Chapmans' shrewd burlesques of her dances, but they went to see her because she was Lola. And she had the good judgment not to wait for the reaction. By the first

185

week of July, 1853, she was ready for her tour into the back country.

At first, Sacramento did very well by Lola. Her initial performance was mobbed. Next day, two companies of volunteer firemen serenaded her, and she made a speech at the newly founded Swiss Rifle Club. That night there was a little difficulty. Some irreverent miners laughed during one of her dances, and Lola stalked furiously from the stage, declaring she would not return. In the end she consented to finish the program, but cut her performance so short that half the audience jammed the box-office and demanded its money back. Afterward a group gathered under her hotel window, beating tin pans and uttering catcalls. But Lola had a talent for pulling the fat out of the fire. Next evening, she made a pretty little speech in the theater, in which she explained that the demonstration the night before had been the work of "enemies who had followed her from Europe," referred neatly to the well-known gallantry of the California miner, and concluded by asking the audience shyly if she should go on with her dances. The audience rose to the occasion as she knew it would, and the response was sufficient to carry her through the rest of the week's engagements. It looked as though her tour might be a success.

It was not a success. In fact, it was not a tour. Marysville, next town on the itinerary, was frankly bored. Worse, on the first evening there, she and her husband quarreled violently. A story got about that Lola had thrown him downstairs and then pitched all his baggage out of the hotel window into the street. Californians liked their ladies spirited, but this was going too far. At Lola's third performance the house was almost empty. It was clear that the projected tour of the mining camps had to be abandoned. Four days later, Alonzo Delano, the well-loved "Old Block" who wrote humorous pieces, drew extravagant pictures of the mines, and did straight newspaper work for a living, reported the arrival of Lola in Grass Valley. "She is taking the hearts of our people by her affability and good nature," he wrote, little dreaming that Lola Montez was to become a resident of Grass Valley for almost two years.

Considering the degree in which Lola's name is woven into the story of California's gold days, there is surprisingly little known about her life in Grass Valley. That she was weary of equivocal receptions, of being reminded that her beauty exceeded her talent, there can be no doubt. Certainly she was willing enough to settle down and rusticate for a time. For Lola made the Grass Valley life her own. She bought a house, which still stands, though remodeled and changed in appearance since her time. She planted a garden and tended it—not as a pose but seriously, working the soil herself, dressing in old clothes for the job, transplanting native cacti to a corner which was her especial pride and joy. Very likely she was dramatizing herself in her new surroundings; Lola was temperamentally enough of an actress to fancy herself living the part of a retired and famous beauty, deliberately and dramatically leaving the world. At least she played the part with sufficient conviction. Perhaps it was her thorough rendering of the rôle that made the women of the town friendly to her. In nine cases out of ten, an actress with Lola's reputation for worldliness would have been driven out of town by the determinedly respectable miners' wives. But Lola's was the tenth case. The good ladies of Grass Valley must have sensed that she was not out to disturb the peace or the piety of their village; they seemed to take a kind of perverse pride in the presence in their midst of an ex-King's ex-mistress. When Lola made a brief trip down to San Francisco and it was learned that she had gone to take care of the legal formalities attendant upon getting rid of her husband Mr. Hull, the Grass Valley women were not disturbed; indeed, they may well have reflected that Lola's trial for bigamy had simply taught her to be careful. Even when she braved the wrath of the local minister, the general tone was one of approval. He had spoken in his pulpit of the dancer's presence in the town, suggesting that so notorious a character could not but have a deleterious influence upon the community, and Lola answered by costuming herself for the *tarantelle,* knocking at his door, and performing her dance then and there, when the unfortunate man came to see what was wanted. The story goes that she was almost immediately ashamed of her display of temper, and sent a large contribution to the church. That may have been another reason why no one seemed to object to her living in town, not even the minister, thereafter.

It is as a hostess, as leader of her *salon,* that Lola appears to have exercised her talents chiefly during her Grass Valley period. Her little house was filled with touring actors and actresses, with singers and musicians, wits and writers, painters and poets and every sort of artist. Lola danced for them sometimes, supplied them amply with potables, encouraged their hilarity, and begged them to come again. They came, bringing others, Ole Bull among them, and the two half-legendary nephews of Victor Hugo who were said to have come to California to try their luck in the mines. The extraordinary Stephen Massett, singer, composer, lecturer, and humorist, was a visitor at Lola's house; so were dozens and hundreds of lesser lights. They told stories and listened to them, sang and danced and played, fed Lola's curious collection of parrots, bears, and monkeys, went riding romantically along the mountain trails. Once Lola was reported to have fallen from her horse on such an excursion; the press noted that "she escaped unharmed, but was in great danger for a short time," which seems a fair statement of the case. Now and then an editor would print a story about her miniature menagerie. It was Alonzo Delano who put about the rumor that Lola had been bitten by a pet bear-cub, telling the tale rather lamely in shoddy verse:

> When Lola came to feed her bear
> With comfits sweet and sugar rare,
> Bruin ran out in haste to meet her,
> Seized her hand because 'twas sweeter!

But otherwise Lola was not much in the news. She had retired for a season, and that was that. Two stories about her did get into circulation, however, and because both have had a long and lusty life they they are worth mentioning here. Neither seems to have had any sensible foundation whatever.

One is the persistent tradition that when a local editor printed some inaccurate item about her, Lola appeared in his office armed with a horsewhip and gave him the hiding of his life. The odd thing about that tale is that it followed her wherever she went, turning up in different places and in different guises. In Sacramento, report has it that she gave the offending editor his choice of two pills in a little box, one poisoned and one plain. In Australia, the editor in the story did not get his lashing; his wife arrived in the nick of time and, being larger and stronger than Lola, tore the whip from her hand. In Marysville, dueling-pistols were offered the unhappy journalist; doubtless if the story were pursued far enough it would appear that one was loaded with ball and the other merely wadded.

The other yarn is even more fantastic. Lola was on a secret mission, no less. Financed by "powerful interests" unspecified, she was at the bottom of a plot to separate California from the Union and make it an independent monarchy with herself as Queen. Just what was to be accomplished by this, aside from the pleasant elevation of Lola to a throne, is never explained.

The curious thing, altogether, is that out of half a dozen

189

Columbia Southern Mines, California
Nearly ninety million dollars in gold came out of the mines
around Columbia. Its population, at its peak, has been estimated

at anywhere from 15,000 to 30,000. Miners from all over the southern mines were attracted to its hundred and fifty gambling places, thirty saloons, and fandango halls.

weeks of public performance—for all her dancing and acting
in the West tots up to no more than this—there should have
grown so considerable, even if indefinite, a legend of Lola
Montez in California. She came, acted briefly, spent a quiet
two years in Grass Valley in the foot-hills, and went away.
That was all. Yet her name has become a part of the gold-
rush background, no one quite knows why. And because it
has, it may be appropriate here to follow her to the end.

In the summer of 1855 she suddenly decided to go back to
the stage, left Grass Valley and sailed for Australia. The tour
was unsuccessful. A year later she came back, visited Grass
Valley long enough to sell her house while her effects were
being auctioned off in the city, gave five farewell performances
in San Francisco, danced her "Spider Dance" for the last time
in California and made her last curtain speech. On Thanksgiving Day, 1856, she sailed for New York on the *Orizaba,*
which was carrying an assortment of excited young men bound
for Nicaragua to join the filibustering expedition of William
Walker whose gray eyes were fixed on Destiny. A year or so
later she visited Paris and came back to America with a series
of lectures on such topics as "Beautiful Women," "Heroines
of History," and "Wits and Women of Paris." Concurrently
with her lecturing, a New York publisher tried to stimulate
some extra business by bringing out a little book, *The Arts of
Beauty: Or Secrets of the Ladies' Toilet,* purported to have
been written by "Madame Lola Montez." Perhaps it was
Lola's own, without benefit of ghost, though the involved references to Greek and Latin poets make it seem likely that
some hack pedant was hired to do the job. Occasional copies
may be found even to-day, though the Beauty Secrets are
thoroughly outdated now, and even the added chapters, "Hints
to Gentlemen," and "Fifty Rules for Fascinating," have lost
the punch the author worked so hard to put into them.

But Lola's day was past. Her lectures were tepidly received, and her money and good health ran out together. A little less than five years after she had said good-by to Grass Valley, she died penniless in New York and was buried in Greenwood Cemetery. Her headstone bore her dates and her maiden name, Eliza Gilbert. Out of a muddled sense of propriety, some one had ordered the stonecutter to add the prefix, "Mrs." Perhaps he thought of it himself.

Yet, indirectly, Lola Montez did contribute her bit to the theater of her day in the mining towns of California. For if there had been no Lola in Grass Valley at the right time there might have been no Lotta Crabtree to dance for the miners' delight. It was Lola who discovered the child, who petted her, made much of her, set her on an anvil in a blacksmith's shop in the mountain camp of Rough and Ready so that the crowd might watch the mite dance and hear her sing. It was Lola who had little Lotta in and out of her house, taught her the simple tricks of the profession, saw that the visitors who thronged her *salon* had an opportunity to watch her perform. In short, it was Lola Montez who made it certain that Lotta Crabtree had her chance to become the pet of the mines, the toast of the miners, and for more than half a century California's favorite daughter.

John Crabtree, a Lancashire lad come to the New World to seek his fortune, may have been a very pleasant sort but he was no business man.

In Nassau Street, in New York, his dusty, down-at-heel second-hand bookstore was a charming spot in which to chat with his cronies and spin out long dreams of growing rich to-morrow. The trouble was that customers stayed away. It was not surprising that when the miracle of gold in California burst on the country, John Crabtree's dreaming should have taken a westward turn.

Characteristically, John postponed doing anything about his visions. It was 1852 before he roused himself to action, posting off to California on the Rosinante of his grand illusion, perfectly certain that in El Dorado everything would come out all right. He left at home his energetic, practical little wife, Mary Ann. An upholsterer by trade and always in work, Mary Ann could easily take care of their five-year-old daughter, little Lotta, until he should send for them, which he would do the very moment he got his first sackful of gold dust together.

By the spring of 1853, Mary Ann Crabtree and the child were on their way across the Isthmus to join John. He had found no gold; as Mrs. Crabtree succinctly said later, "He never got any." But he had prospects. They would see when they got there.

John was not in San Francisco when his wife and child arrived. Fortunately they had friends in the bustling, lively city who took them in and made much of them. John was "somewhere in the mountains," that was all they knew. But he had promised to write soon, and in the meantime mother and daughter might as well see the city the whole world was talking about.

In her *Troupers of the Gold Coast,* Constance Rourke suggests that this brief stay in San Francisco may have implanted in Mary Ann Crabtree's prim mind the unwilling respect for the theater and its people that was to bear fruit later. Certainly there was every opportuniy in that dazzling, kaleidoscopic year for Mrs. Crabtree to see the theatrical world at its best. San Francisco was rich; it could buy the best, and it did. Dr. Robinson's *Seeing the Elephant,* a kind of *Hellzapoppin* of its day, had done its work to promote a feeling of rapport between audience and players. Maguire's Jenny Lind Theater, named for the famous singer (who never came to California in her life, legend to the contrary notwithstanding), had been packed night after night with crowds who came to

MORGAN HILL LIBRARY
660 W. Main Ave.
Morgan Hill, CA 95037
(408) 779-3197

Customer ID: **********2062

Title: Anybody's gold : the story of Califo
ID: B06809ZLA
Due: 05/29/09

Total items: 1
5/8/2009 11:37 AM

Use our CATALOG at
www.santaclaracountylib.org/catalog/
or TELECIRC at 800-471-0991

MORGAN HILL LIBRARY
660 W. Main Ave.
Morgan Hill, CA 95037
(408) 779-3196

Customer ID: ***********2025

Title: Anybody home? : the story of Cello
ID: B0980957V
Due: 05/29/09

Total items: 1
5/8/2009 11:37 AM

Use our CATALOG at
www.santaclaracountylib.org/catalog
or TELECIRC at 800-471-0991

see James Stark in Shakespeare and the old English comedies in which he excelled. French and Italian troupes did opera; there were dozens of smaller houses in which the miner might take his choice of farces, burlesques, or straight song and dance turns. There had been fires, but the theaters grew up again magically out of the ashes. And now, in 1853, there were the Bakers, Mrs. Judah, Junius Booth, Kate Hayes, Catherine Sinclair, and the incomparable, irrepressible Chapmans. Mary Ann Crabtree found herself in the middle of an exciting, disturbing, dramatic whirlpool like nothing she had ever seen before. It would be strange if she had not been interested, impressed, maybe inclined to wonder if the talent for mimicry she herself possessed, and which was beginning to be so evident in tiny Lotta, might not be turned to account.

If she had such ideas, however, they had to be at least temporarily suppressed. A letter came from John Crabtree. So far, ill luck had pursued him; he was a trifle vague about details. But now he had a magnificent idea. He was vague about that, too, but it was clear that he thought he had something. Mary Ann and Lotta were to join him immediately in the mining town of Grass Valley.

If Mrs. Crabtree was disappointed when she learned her husband's brilliant scheme, there was little she could do about it. He had found no gold, not yet. But he had a wonderful new prospect in which something was bound to develop. While he worked this out, she was to run a boarding-house in Grass Valley; that was the nub of his plan. Whatever might turn up in John's hole in the ground, there were all kinds of people in fast-growing Grass Valley who had to be housed and fed. Mary Ann was still a practical woman and used to hard work. At least she could make a living for herself and Lotta. And of course John's new mine just might pan out. She could not know that within a month the notorious Lola, Countess of Landsfeldt, would take it into her capricious head to settle in

Grass Valley, much less that this glamorous woman would buy a house only a stone's throw from her own.

The friendship that sprang up between the rigidly conventional Mary Ann Crabtree and Lola, the magnificently flamboyant woman of the world, is one of those curious paradoxes that defy explanation. The fact remains that Mrs. Crabtree liked Lola, defended her when at first the women of the town were inclined against her, trusted her sufficiently to allow six-year-old Lotta to spend whole days with the dancer. And when Lola taught the child bits from plays, songs, and fragments of dance routines, Mary Ann Crabtree did not mind. Lotta was quick to learn; such things pleased her and kept her out of mischief, gave her a chance to use some of the abounding energy with which she was blessed. Mary Ann, too, may have taken pleasure in Lotta's evident talent; she may have called to mind the gay, laughing show-folk she had seen down in San Francisco, and secretly hoped that her own baby might one day have the excitement and thrill of making an audience laugh or weep according to her whim. At any rate, she made no objection when Lola urged her little protégée to sing or dance for the stream of theatrical guests that flowed in and out of the Montez house so constantly. Even when Lola praised the child extravagantly, declared that she should go to Paris to study, that she would be a great actress when she grew up, Mary Ann Crabtree entered no demurrer. A mother is bound to relish kind words about her offspring, no matter if she knows privately that they are hardly justified; but Mrs. Crabtree was beginning to feel deep in her heart that the famous Lola was not so far wrong. Certainly when the merry, black-eyed little Lotta did a few steps of a Spanish dance or a Highland fling for Lola's guests there was more than a perfunctory response. Perhaps the child did have more than ordinary talent. Mary Ann Crabtree began to believe that this was true.

She might never have had a chance to find out but for a new

194

notion of her husband's which seemed at the time like a disaster. In the summer of 1854 the Crabtrees had had a second child, a boy this time. Hard upon the heels of the baby's arrival, John heard about some fresh, incredibly rich fields that had been opened higher in the hills. Nothing would do but that the Crabtrees should move on, bag and baggage, to the raw camp of Rabbit Creek. There, surely, was the fortune they had been waiting for. Mary Ann packed up and moved with her husband. She had no choice.

There was gold in Rabbit Creek, but not for John Crabtree. What little he made he spent looking for greener fields; he was not a man to stick to anything, as his wife was finding out. By the spring of 1855, Mary Ann was running a boarding-house again. But the seed planted in her mind so long ago had begun to grow. Lotta had shown that her liking for dance steps and songs was no mere passing fancy. A young Italian whose difficult name was anglicized to Mart Taylor had come to Rabbit Creek and had been so taken with Lotta that he had taught her new jigs and tunes. The child had performed a few times at miners' affairs and had been enthusiastically received. How far Mrs. Crabtree had planned ahead she alone knew. At least she had begun to see that her Lotta just might be the means by which both of them could become independent of John Crabtree's vagaries. For when the Montez took the trouble to ride over the hills into Rabbit Creek to say that she was tired of country life, that she had arranged a tour to Australia and wanted Lotta to come with her, Mrs. Crabtree refused. She wished Lola luck, but Lotta would stay where she was. When Lola rode away down the mountain Mary Ann may have wondered whether she was right. Such a chance for her daughter could hardly come again. She could not know that another chance, and a better one, was even then in the making. That miracle became plain when Dr. Robinson, now one of San Francisco's most influential producers, arrived in

Rabbit Creek with the child actress, Sue Robinson, in his company and demanded to see little Lotta Crabtree, about whom he had heard so much as he came through the mining towns.

Dr. Robinson might have engaged Lotta then and there. She performed well, she was enormously attractive with her reddish hair, her black sparkling eyes, her gay, infectious smile. She had been well trained by Lola and Mart Taylor; better still, she understood and liked her audiences and knew how to make them like her. Best of all, though she was almost eight years old, she looked much younger. There was an enormous vogue that year for children on the stage. Lotta was precisely the merry, appealing type to take advantage of this, and Dr. Robinson must have realized it. But almost at once a difficulty arose. Mart Taylor had the best hall in Rabbit Creek, but when he quoted his price Dr. Robinson thought it too much and decided to put on his performance in a dance hall across the way. Taylor, his ire aroused, made up his mind that he would show the Doctor what was what. He announced a show of his own on the same night, with Lotta Crabtree as his star. The San Francisco impresario might give his Sue Robinson the spotlight if he liked. Taylor would prove to him that the local child wonder would draw the local crowd.

Again it must have been a hard decision for Mrs. Crabtree to make. She knew the San Francisco producer's importance. He had been visibly impressed by Lotta's ability, her engaging ways. But it was Taylor who had taught the child, who had given her the chance at the smaller performances which had brought her to the great Dr. Robinson's attention. Mary Ann decided to stick with the man who had helped her daughter first. In a passion of haste she whipped together a green jacket, breeches and tall hat, while Taylor manufactured a pair of comic brogans and whittled out a shillalah. When the Irish costume was done, Mary Ann feverishly sewed together a simple white costume for the sweetly innocent number which would provide the contrast that good showmanship called for. By evening Lotta was ready, as excited as her mother and her teacher but perfectly at home because she knew everybody in the theater. Constance Rourke, who has understood Lotta better than any one, tells the story of that first real performance:

> She always had a way of laughing when she danced, hard enough to achieve by design when every breath counts, but natural for her. She seemed tireless, a tiny bubbling fountain of fun and quick life. On the rough stage with candles for footlights in the midst of smoke and shadows she danced again and again; every other number was forgotten, even Taylor's dancing and singing. Then she appeared in her white dress with a round neck and puffed sleeves, and sang a plaintive, innocent ballad, looking like a pretty little red-haired doll.
>
> The smoke-laden room was shaken with excitement. Money rained upon the stage; quarters, half-dollars, huge Mexican dollars, a fifty-dollar gold slug, and a scattering of nuggets. The camp at Rabbit Creek had rallied around Taylor in the contest with Dr. Robinson, or had strolled into the theater as the applause thundered. The resourceful little doctor was defeated and retired, leaving Mary Ann Crabtree to consider her child's success.

As things were, Mrs. Crabtree could come to only one conclusion. When Taylor talked excitedly to her of the profits to be made by a quick tour of the mining camps, of the necessity for more music, himself on the guitar, a violinist to be added to the little troupe, Mary Ann herself to learn to play the triangle, what could Mrs. Crabtree say? Her child's success had cast the die for her; the matter was out of her hands. From now on she would watch over Lotta, guide her, take care of her money, see that she did her job. But, child or not, it was Lotta who was important, and Mary Ann Crabtree saw that. Here at last, providentially, was her chance to engineer for herself and her daughter an escape from John Crabtree's ineffectualities. She simply could not let it go. They hurried preparations all they could. Taylor taught Lotta to sing "How Can I Leave Thee?" and rehearsed her in a few new dance steps. Then they were off on their great adventure. Mary Ann Crabtree left a note. Sooner or later her husband would return and discover that his wife and daughter had made up their minds they knew what was best for them.

Their tour led them up the lovely cañon of the Feather River to Quincy, then northward over the ridges to the lesser mining camps, including Rich Bar where Dame Shirley had lived only a few years before. It was hard work but splendid training for the child. Mary Ann learned how to get the best out of Lotta, when to coax and when to be firm; and Lotta herself discovered earlier than most actresses the exactions of life on the road. Sometimes they traveled by coach, often it was a matter of trails where horseback was the only method possible. Taylor knew his way about, and they missed no camp they could possibly cover, Mrs. Crabtree thriftily hoarding the profits, playing the triangle, occasionally doing a brief imitation or a monologue of her own to round out the show. At one small camp, the story goes, Mrs. Crabtree and little Lotta were compelled to lie on the floor of their hotel room in order to escape the bullets that ripped through the walls as a pair of drunken miners shot it out in the building and down in the street. Bidwell's Bar, Oroville, on northward even as far as Weaverville—the camps all knew Lotta that summer and autumn. She was to tour them again and again before she grew up and left for the East and newer, greater conquests. But it was that first scratched-together venture that really made Lotta in the mines. It made her and her mother independent, too, for Mrs. Crabtree knew how to hold on to money; she had seen little enough of it in her time. John Crabtree drifted into their lives and out again more than once, then out for good and all. By that time Lotta was enjoying triumphs in the East and abroad, growing rich, having the career that Mary Ann Crabtree had dreamed for her when she first found Lola

Montez teaching her tiny daughter a pirouette and a song. Never a great actress in any true sense of the word, Lotta conquered her audiences by being herself—a self which was unlike any other in the world. Her childhood in the California mines had taught her the trick; she had learned to handle a dozen or a thousand rough miners in a crowd, and after them no audience could be difficult. And Lotta remembered the country that had made her what she was. Several times, after she had become a noted star in New York, she returned to California, played long engagements in San Francisco, acknowledged the plaudits of men who had seen her and roared their approval when they—and she—had been much younger. Though she retired in the East finally, in the low, rolling New Jersey hills at first and later in Boston, she never forgot California. Lotta's Fountain, her gift to the city she loved best, still stands in San Francisco, the city that represented to her all the enchantment of the California she had once known, the California that had given her her chance and taken her to its heart. Few people remember that she lived to be nearly eighty years old, dying alone in 1924, leaving to hundreds of carefully specified charities the fortune of something over four million dollars which had had its origin in those Mexican dollars and Rabbit Creek nuggets so carefully hoarded and managed by Mary Ann Crabtree who had seen the road her daughter was to follow and courageously chosen it for her.

7.

====

The Cow and the Quartz

GRASS roots gold is not inexhaustible. Stream-beds, however richly sprinkled with the yellow metal, peter out some day; even the richest dry diggings may be washed down to nothing. Gold, after all, does not renew itself, and there were miners by the tens of thousands combing every cranny of the foot-hills, probing the granite and gravels of the cold mountain streams. It was not long before the boom camps began to dwindle. Men surged restlessly up and down California, looking for new diggings, fresh rivers. Sometimes they found them. When they did, they worked them out in short order and moved on again. The placers were going; that was the truth of it. More than one miner made up his mind that California's gold hills were done for. And the word began to get around. But for a lucky accident all the newly minted Californians might have gone home again, leaving Captain Sutter to pick up the pieces.

It was a cow that brought about the accident. Like the famous beast of Mrs. O'Leary in a later day, this Californian animal merely behaved in proper bovine fashion; the cow-consequences in both cases were happenstance, no more. Mrs. O'Leary's cow, in a moment of maiden meditation, waved her tail; a lamp went crashing, and Chicago burned. The cow of George McKnight (or "Knight") of Grass Valley did nothing so rash; she simply went for a walk. Because she walked farther than was her wont, Mr. McKnight, in something of a temper, was compelled to follow her almost as far as Boston Ravine outside of town. On a hilltop, just before dropping down into the arroyo, Mr. McKnight stubbed his toe on an outcropping of white rock. He stubbed it hard enough to break off a fragment of the quartz. Even his understandable irritation, however, was not sufficient to make him lose his head entirely. The broken piece of white rock was seamed and veined with what was unmistakably gold. Mr. McKnight may or may not have caught his cow; no historian seems to have been interested in pursuing the subject. But he was miner enough to take the bit of rock straight back to his cabin, pound it to powder in an iron Dutch oven and wash the grit in his pan. The result was amply convincing. If he could only keep his discovery quiet, Mr. McKnight had stubbed his toe on his everlasting fortune.

At this point McKnight vanishes from the record. But the white quartz on top of what immediately became known as Gold Hill was only a beginning. For such discoveries can not be kept quiet. Within a few months, McKnight's lucky find had touched off a new kind of boom.

There had been quartz mining in California before. Down near Mariposa, Frémont's agents had gone so far as to import a steam mill to pound the rock they found in the rich ledges of the Frying Pan Grant. In Tuolumne County, a hunter had killed a grizzly, only to have the dying animal, in its final throes, roll over the edge of a cliff, its carcass stopping part way down on a projecting shelf of rock. Following to skin the animal, the hunter saw that the rock was gold-bearing quartz. There is even a tall tale, by no means authenticated, about a miner shooting it out with a robber, thereafter noting that a bullet which missed him had creased the rock at his shoulder, exposing a vein of gold. The Mexican miners, too, knew about quartz; their *arrastras,* crude arrangements of rock-paved bowls in the ground and a mule walking round and round hitched to a long lever-like pole with a granite boulder on its end to grind the quartz, were in operation from the earliest days of the rush. But this Grass Valley discovery put the others in the shade. By the early months of 1851 the Gold Hill Company had built a mill and was in full operation. Other stamps, crude at first but developing fast as the miner's ingenuity led him to improve his machines, were soon at work. Gold-mining in California was no longer a haphazard affair of pick and pan, rocker and Long Tom, a matter of individuals or small groups panning or sluicing readily accessible deposits in river or bank. Almost immediately it became a business of machinery, of drilling and blasting, of engine and mills and amalgam and a whole new technic, one that demanded capital and plenty of it. Moreover, it was not any longer a question of quickly booming mushroom camps, here to-day and gone to-morrow. Where there was a deep hole in the ground and a hundred thousand dollars' worth of hoists and cars and stamps to fix a population to the spot, a camp turned into a town and men stayed put. The mines had moved ahead another notch. California's gold was demonstrating that it could hold men in the hills as well as bring them there.

There were disappointments, of course, along with the new riches. Even the broadest and finest veins had a trick of suddenly thinning out, sometimes vanishing utterly, like the veriest will o' the wisp. The hills were full of water, too, and it was not always where the miner wanted it. Often a deep shaft would fill overnight from some hidden spring unexpectedly tapped by a blast. Then pumps must be bought, transported to California, carried up into the hills, installed, and put to work. That was often a matter of months, and in the meantime, pay-rolls had to be met, and expenses mounted. Syndicates, companies, and individual miners learned the truth of the aphorism about a gold mine's frequent habit of absorbing more gold than can be squeezed out of it. And, while California's quartz was to contribute far more to the state's riches than the placers ever had, hundreds of treasure-hunters were ruined in the development period. Some lost more than their money. There was, for instance, the case of Michael Brennan, president of the Mount Hope Mining Company on Massachusetts Hill.

Brennan with his wife and three children had been in Grass Valley a year and a half; and, at first, had done very well with the mine, which was financed partly in New York, partly in London. At first everything went smoothly. The Company paid good dividends and there was every indication that greater depth would bring increased reward. Expensive machinery was installed, the shaft was driven down; Messrs. Thallon and Satterthwaite of Throckmorton Street and the Hanover Bank in New York were pleased with their investment and with the conduct of their Dublin-trained Mr. Brennan who had been entrusted with the management. A dozen or so Grass Valley citizens who had been let in on the venture had visions of a pleasant independence on their profits, and they liked and admired Michael Brennan, who was managing the enterprise on Massachusetts Hill with such eminent success. Then the vein disappeared, broke off and ceased to be.

Michael Brennan was a mining man and knew these things happened. He remembered all he had learned about geology.

Rabbit Creek, Sierra County, California
There was plenty of gold in the hills surrounding Rabbit Creek,
but it is probably better remembered as the raw mining camp where

Lotta Crabtree was launched on a career that would bring her world fame and fortune.

He recalled the classic examples of veins that had stopped abruptly and picked up again, better than ever, when the operators found the other end of the break some ancient convulsion had made. It would mean spending some of the stockholders' money without immediate return. It would mean some scientific planning and some guesswork, and perhaps a little luck. But the Brennan luck had always been good. Any business had its ups and downs, mining in particular. Michael Brennan did not worry unduly.

Things didn't go quite that way. The other end of the break in the vein was astonishingly elusive. There were weeks of drifting, of sinking the shaft deeper, of consultation and argument. The weeks ran into months, while the pay-roll went on and the local investors began to ask Mr. Brennan whether he thought everything would be all right. Mr. Brennan did not know; he could only do his best to reassure the anxious men whose money was in his mine. Meantime his devoted young wife, Dorinda, took good care of the house and their three small children and did her best to keep smiling. Grass Valley women respected her courage and loved her for her sweet temper.

Then the worst happened. In their frantic efforts to blast a way to the elusive vein, Brennan's men broke through into a gushing underground torrent down in the bowels of Massachusetts Hill. That was the end of it. There was some hopeless foolery with pumps; the gesture had to be made. But the men on the job knew that it was all over. So did the investors in Grass Valley who had put all they had into the Mount Hope mine.

Michael Brennan knew it too. On Sunday evening, February 21, 1858, prolonged quiet in the Brennan house led two neighbors to break down the locked door of the parlor. Inside the room were the bodies of Michael Brennan, his wife, Dorinda, and Ellen, Robert, and little Dorinda, the two-year-old. Dr.

McCormick and Dr. Cleveland sniffed the lips of the five dead and examined the empty vials scattered about the room. They agreed that there could be no doubt about it. The Brennans had come to their deaths by means of prussic acid administered by the fond husband and father.

The tragedy made an enormous sensation in the Grass Valley papers, which printed the story in full detail and quoted from several letters left by the dead man. If his motive had not been clear enough, the letters would have explained it. After leaving detailed instructions to his friend, Walter Martineau, Michael Brennan set down in simple direct prose his reasons for acting as he was about to do:

"Massachusetts Hill," he wrote, "has fairly beaten me, and I am tired out and doubtful of the future so that I take a sudden leave of all. No man knows what I have suffered the last few weeks, meeting so many I owed and unable to pay. I have, in all, done what was right and honorable as far as I could see it at the time. The proof is to die. No other would ever clear me; did I live and ever do well, many would believe that I had acted basely here, and this would make life bitter."

It was quite plain. Michael Brennan, for all his Trinity College education, had seen no way around a set of circumstances he had been unable to alter. He had considered his course of action and taken his way out. Only one grim afterthought came to him, and he put it into a postscript: "Do not bury us until you are sure we are dead," he wrote. "Let decomposition take place."

Presently there were no more details to print, and the California papers forgot about Michael Brennan, merely observing as they dropped the case that the search for gold had claimed yet another victim. One editor did take pains to say that something should be done about the pharmacist who had sold such a quantity of deadly poison, but the shop was in San Francisco and nothing seems to have come of the suggestion. No journalist of the day was enough of an amateur psychologist to note two points which, though perhaps of no direct importance, may at least be said to hold some interest. One is the matter of the date. Michael Brennan committed his final dreadful act on a Sunday, when there was no work to occupy him, only time in which to brood; moreover, the next day was February 22, Washington's Birthday, and therefore twenty-four hours more of holiday emptiness stretching ahead. The other point is the weather. Three lines in the Sacramento paper tell the story: "There were thunder and lightning on Saturday night and Sunday throughout the north." Even though Michael Brennan had his vials of prussic acid ready, who can say that the ominous rolling of the thunder, the heavy and electric air, were not the determining factor in his dark, unhappy deed?

As for the note of irony, it was present and plain enough for those who cared to look. The same newspapers that carried the first reports of the tragedy were full of good news about gold. At Yankee Jim's, said the Placerville *Courier,* the Golden Gate tunnel was now producing $5,000 a week. Over at Michigan Bluff the dealers were buying from $1,200 to $1,500 worth of gold a day. At Whiskey Hill near Jamestown, Alexander Brooks had found a rich vein thirty feet wide; near Saw Mill Flat, Conner & Co. had discovered a new vein where they were realizing $2,500 for one day's work "with fine prospects ahead." And the little camp of Brown's Flat was in a positive fever of excitement. "The old Italian lead there," said the *Union,* "which has yielded so immensely during the past year, now bids fair to surpass anything heretofore found. On Saturday last they took out about $25,000 there and have taken out a larger amount since." There was gold still in the California hills, plenty of it. Californians were just beginning to understand the new methods of finding and developing it from the rock of the great Mother Lode itself.

All this did not come about without enormously costly trial-

and-error methods, failures, booms, and their consequent collapses. Such a situation always provides a field day for inventors and there were hundreds of wild schemes tried out when it was realized that the big profits in gold would henceforward come from quartz mining. There was, for example, that notable humbug, the Bunker Hill Company.

The Bunker Hill operation had its day near the beginning of the quartz fever, and those who lost their money were chiefly citizens of Nevada City. When Mr. McKnight's cow first showed the way to riches underground, everybody in the area began tunneling, crushing quartz, subjecting the rock to all kinds of new processes to extract the gold. Most of these were in principle the same; the thing was to reduce the quartz to fine grit, the gold along with it, and then to separate the two. Stamps and rollers accomplished the first step; washing, chemicals, mercury accomplished the second. But the Bunker Hill plan approached the problem differently. It was a plan to "roast" the quartz, no less. Smelted in a specially designed furnace, the rock would be dissipated into the air in gaseous fumes and the gold would automatically drop into a receiving chamber below, where it would be run into appropriate molds and appear at last in the form of large and luscious ingots of the pure metal. It sounded like a perfect scheme; the idea of pure gold in bars, just like that, was something even the most ignorant could understand and appreciate. The financing, therefore, was no trouble at all; the Bunker Hill Company got its funds almost overnight, and the construction of the plant began.

A hill in the Deer Creek area was chosen as the site for the new mine and the magical smelter that was to make everybody rich. It took time, and the equipment was extremely costly, but no one was troubled about that. After all, this was science; this was the new thing. Wasn't it true that men were living in a scientific age now, and that the inventor was always the man who knew? No question about it. Citizens of Nevada City could hardly wait for the first batch of rock to be dumped into the furnace, for the significant vapors to begin pouring from the stack, and particularly for the gold to begin running off into its special lower chamber, there to flow into the carefully designed molds and to appear, soft and rich and yellow, in those fine, heavy bars.

Eventually the new mill was ready. With a magnificent clatter and roar, truckloads of broken rock slid down into the smelter where the inventor's fiery furnace waited to receive it. A glorious metallic stench spread over the hills, making the miners cough and sneeze even in the saloons where they had gone to celebrate to-morrow's golden reward. All day the iron trucks dumped their rock, the fire burned and the yellow smoke wound through the pines. It was easy to see that the wise ones who had supported the Bunker Hill Company with their cash were going to be very rich indeed. All that was necessary now was to wait for the furnace to cool.

The great moment came, and all Nevada City but a few old-fashioned miners whose imaginations had not been up to the progress of science trooped out to Bunker Hill to watch the receiving chamber opened and feast their eyes on the purified gold.

Strangely, the molds were empty. Some ash had sifted down into the waiting forms, but that was all.

The heads of the company were momentarily disturbed, but they saw immediately what had happened. Obviously the channels had become clogged. The gold would be found above, spread on the furnace floor. Of course. But all their poking in the cold leavings brought them nothing. There was a good deal of fine ash. There were assorted chunks of exceptionally handsome slag and some large, reddish clinkers. But there was no gold, none at all.

The promoters rallied wonderfully; promoters have the rallying temperament. The trouble, they volubly explained, was in the design of the furnace. Unfortunately, the gold must have gone off with the fumes from the rock and the inventor's secret acids. It would be a simple matter to make a few adjustments. Next time there would be no difficulty.

The inventor made his adjustments, keeping their nature to himself, and the experiment was tried again. Once more the smoke poured from the stack; again the Nevada City miners lined up at the bars to toast the wealth that would be theirs. For the second time the town waited for the furnace to cool.

There was no gold in the molds that time either, nor in the ashes. Sadly the promoters admitted that there was something wrong; in the most scientific language at their command they published a statement to the effect that there must be "inherent defects in the philosophy of the process." Then they went away. Nobody went after them. The new scheme had cost the stockholders $85,000, but it was clear that the men behind it had got none of the money. It was right there in Bunker Hill, sunk in the shaft, in the hoists, in the trucks and most especially in the scientific furnace with its cold bed of ashes and clinkers and its empty, virgin molds. It was not until some weeks after the whole affair was over that a miner with a practical turn of mind thought of trying out the rock on Bunker Hill by the approved, stamp-mill-and-washing method. A few still hopeful stockholders put up the money, built a water-wheel to run the stamps from the power in a near-by flume, and a mill was knocked together. Results showed a very excellent grade of quartz, but no trace of gold.

That was the end of Bunker Hill. The stamp-mill was taken apart and removed to a spot where it might find genuine gold-bearing rock to work on. The furnace was gradually torn down for scrap iron. Only the great overshot wheel remained for years, a monument to the ready gullibility of human beings who want to make a fortune in a hurry.

There was one amusing aftermath, however; a delightful

demonstration of the Yankee sense of humor. This final work was an announcement in the columns of the Nevada *Journal* to the effect that the Munchausen Quartz Rock Mining and Crushing Company, with a capital of $2,000,000, was ready to begin operations. Its president, so the notice said, was General Napoleon B. Gulliver. Its secretary was Mr. Junius Quien Sabe, its treasurer Mr. J. Squander Swartwout. Listed as members of the Board of Directors were P. T. Barnum, Guy Fawkes, and Robinson Crusoe.

There is one notable point about the desire to get rich quickly; it is no respecter of persons. All men, of all races, are affected in the same way by the idea of gold, particularly gold lying about free for the taking.

From the beginning of the gold rush, California's rich hills were the goal for thousands of foreigners as well as for Americans who flowed across the plains and sailed by way of the Isthmus. French, Germans, and Italians came in shiploads. Mexicans swarmed up from below the border to swell the number already in California. South America sent its quota of Chileños, Peruvians, Bolivians. Englishmen drifted in and out, most of them finding that the greatest profits were to be had by supplying cash for new ventures through their unmatched organization of world finance that had its headquarters in London. Even the Orient sent its quota, and out of the growing yellow flood arose some of the most difficult problems Californians had to meet. Out of it, moreover, came two of the most bizarre occurrences of the whole gold-rush era —the two Chinese Wars which took place within the boundaries of the state, which involved no white men (except on one occasion when a stupid and brutal Swede asked for trouble and got it), and which were conducted throughout with the beautiful formality and precision peculiar to the Oriental mind. In neither case were the fatalities important; indeed, the Chinese Wars were notable for lack of slaughter. But because the Chinese were at the front of every Californian's mind, the battles took on a significance far greater than they deserved. They have, in fact, become a part of the great legend of the Gold Days, and so deserve a place in this chronicle.

Before the discovery of gold there was little to bring the Chinese to the delightful cattle-and-grain Arcadia that was Spanish and Mexican California. Chinese were notable for neither riding nor roping, and while they were an agricultural people, there was ample opportunity in their own country for the practice of that art, wherefore they remained there and practised it. There is a charming fairy-tale about one Hee-Li who sailed his junk across the Pacific in 217 B.C., explored the Bay of San Francisco, traded with the natives, and returned to China to be the first man anywhere to spread the gospel of the California climate. His visit, so the fable goes, was all an accident, the result of a cockroach having crawled into his compass and jammed the needle so that it consistently pointed due south instead of north. There is also a story of a Chinese cabin-boy aboard the brig *Bolívar* which sailed into the Bay in 1838, but sailed out again presently, cabin-boy and all. Better authenticated is the arrival of the merchant, Chum Ming, who is said to have been the only resident Chinese when gold was discovered. In his *San Francisco's Chinatown,* Charles Caldwell Dobie discusses all three of these early visitors and puts forward his own opinion about them.

Thoroughly demonstrable, however, is the arrival of two Chinese men and one woman, servants of Mr. and Mrs. Charles V. Gillespie, visitors from Hongkong in the American brig *Eagle* which entered the Golden Gate on the second of February, 1848. And there is little question about the exotic

Madame Ah Toy who established herself in San Francisco in the same year, and by 1849 was involved in a court dispute with some miners who, she said, had paid her—"for the privilege of gazing upon her countenance" as the modest record of the time puts it—not in the gold-dust specified but in mere brass filings. One would like to know much more of the tall, handsome Madame Ah Toy in apricot satin jacket and green silk pantaloons who charmed the rough and ready miners into the dizzy error of mistaking brass for gold-dust. The record yields little more than the depressing information that after the trial she abandoned jacket and trousers and adopted American costume.

On two points, however, the facts are incontrovertible. At the end of 1848 there were only seven Chinese registered in what was to be the State of California. By the middle of 1852 the new state showed 20,000 Chinese on its rolls. Most of the 20,000 were up in the mines, as was no more than natural. The Chinese kept coming. In the end, their presence led to violent riots, to a whole political philosophy based on the simple slogan, "The Chinese Must Go." But this was later. In the Fifties real trouble had not yet begun. There were sporadic, usually ridiculous efforts made to limit the number of incoming Chinese. Every now and then some newspaper editor would lament the Oriental addiction to prostitution and gambling. Once Governor Bigler imposed an entry-tax, and once it was fantastically suggested that the Chinese be kept out by a law requiring their precious queues to be trimmed "within one inch of the head." But nothing came of the queue-clipping idea and excessive taxes merely cut into state and county revenues. The yellow men, most of them, were not arriving entirely under their own power, but were being brought in by Chinese companies as contract labor. And a great organization is always able to turn off and on the tap of such importation as the occasion requires. When it was seen to be a choice between incoming Chinese and state income in cash, the revenues won. Wherefore, though there was some resentment against the Chinese among the whites in California who did not like Oriental competition, in the Fifties it was not organized opposition. The Chinese were still a matter for jokes among the miners. Inoffensive, quiet, self-effacing, the Chinese immigrant went about his business, ran his laundry or little shop in the city and camp, and contented himself with working over gold-claims that white men had abandoned. This, in fact, was his specialty. Placer claims, tailings, mine-dumps that the Chinese had sifted were empty of gold; one could be sure of that. As a newspaper editor of the day put it, "Anything that escapes their keen vision and painfully laborious assiduity is hardly worth having." In the opinion of miners who knew, the word "hardly" might as well have been "not."

By 1854, then, the Chinese in California were an important factor but still not sufficiently disturbing to the white man to bring about any sustained effort to banish them. To be sure, the Chinese laborer was consistently the butt of the white miner. He was beaten and robbed; he was at the mercy of any one who felt like fleecing him. Entries in tax-collectors' notebooks show that the law winked at almost any sort of shenanigans where the Chinese were involved. Wrote one such deputy: "I was sorry to have to stab the poor fellow; but the law makes it necessary to collect the tax; and that's where I get my profit." Noted another: "I had no money to keep Christmas with, so sold the Chinks nine dollars' worth of bogus receipts." As has already been pointed out, thieves in the mines found the Chinese their easiest victims and had little compunction about murdering them; it was the notorious Three-Fingered Jack, said to have been Murieta's first lieutenant, who was reported to have hung six Chinamen up by their queues, slitting their throats one after the other for the fun of watching them die. Nevertheless, by and large, John Chinaman was still a jest, something to laugh at rather than to grow serious about. Undoubtedly that was why so much was made of the two Chinese Wars. Each was in its way a circus, a performance put on by an alien and obviously inferior group of creatures for the entertainment of the white man, who was certainly going to see that he got the most out of it.

Weaverville, up in its little valley in mountainous Trinity County, was finding 1854 a prosperous year. There was a large Chinatown which included four stores, four gambling saloons, and a restaurant, and the Chinese were arousing envy by their fine clothes and high living. Chicken and eggs were staple articles of diet with them, and since the latter, fried, cost $1.25 per pair at any regular restaurant in town, the Chinese were considered to be a good deal more well-to-do than was fitting. Now and then a white man would try one of their gambling games, though not often, since the Chinese maintained no bars in such establishments, merely side-tables on which were served tea and long paper cigars. When a miner did try to guess odd or even among the coins shuffled and hidden under their tin cover, he was usually wrong and went away far more profoundly irritated by his losses than if he had dropped his dust in a sensible game of stud poker in his own part of town. Many said openly that the Chinese were getting a bit above themselves, riding for a fall.

The month of July had begun auspiciously in Weaverville. There was the Independence Day celebration, of course, with a public reading of the Declaration followed by a resounding oration on the subject of life, liberty, and the pursuit of happiness. There were fireworks in the evening, and the French residents, resolved to be in no way backward, festooned the Diana Saloon in red and blue calico and held a dance at which every one in town was welcome. There were no serious fights and the citizens of Weaverville agreed that no camp in the mines could have put on a better show. If there were headaches for a day or two afterward, that was merely the natural aftermath of making one's patriotism plain in the correct way.

But the Fourth was only the beginning. Hard on its heels came the sitting of the District Court, an event which called for long nights of exchanging gossip in the bars. Almost immediately the Whigs held their political convention, followed by the Democrats, an even harder-drinking lot, if that were possible. It was small wonder that Weaverville was in a mood to prolong its two-week spree of excitement when the chance offered. That chance became clear when the blacksmiths, iron-workers, and hardware merchants of the town suddenly found themselves swamped with orders for curious and outlandish implements whose purpose they could not mistake. The customers were all Chinese and the implements were of two classes —offensive and defensive weapons. Within an hour the word went around. The Chinese were going to fight a war.

Even at the time no one was able to say with certainty what the fight was about. Some believed that the Celestials were grouped into two factions representing the Imperial and Rebel parties in China. Others said that the argument had begun when one "Company" or society of Chinese had insulted the other. One newspaper hinted that the source of it all was a disagreement at the gambling-tables over a matter of six bits' worth of gold-dust. The Chinese themselves kept their own counsel. All that was clear was that extensive preparations were being made for bloodshed.

A reporter of the day went to some pains to describe these arrangements, and his story is the best source still. According to his account, one group dressed its members in red, with long scarlet cloths wound around their heads, and carried a large white banner with the inscription "Yangwah Company" on it; at any rate, the ideographs were so translated for the white man by a Chinese of whom he inquired. The other group wore hats of sheet-iron resembling tunnels and carried a red and black banner inscribed "Canton City Company." On both sides the chief weapon was a fifteen-foot pike. John Carr, local blacksmith, made hundreds of these for both factions at good prices. Indeed, when Sheriff Lowe remonstrated with him, threatening to have him indicted for manufacturing weapons intended to do bodily harm, Carr told him to go ahead. The $500 fine prescribed by law would still leave him a respectable profit. Since Carr was only one of many working day and night to arm the warriors, the Sheriff let it go. As for the other weapons, these ranged from three-pronged spears to horrid swords five feet long, set in six-foot handles of wood, which the Chinese swung about their heads with both hands. On both sides the fighters who were to occupy the front ranks had short stabbing-swords and round shields, some of iron and some of thickly plaited straw. All week both parties paraded the streets of Weaverville, practising jabs and sweeps, making the nights hideous with their warlike yells. Oddly, from the white man's point of view, there were no physical encounters. The battle had been set for Saturday, July 14, and it would have been contrary to Chinese etiquette to go farther than the proper, formal boasting and challenging until the correct moment arrived.

On Friday night, the two factions left town and set up camp about a mile from Weaverville, at a place known as the flats of East Weaver. Early on Saturday morning there were nearly two thousand whites assembled to see the fight—something like four times the total number of Chinese engaged. They might have taken their time with their breakfasts; the soldiers of both Chinese armies knew the right ritual and were not going to be hurried into combat until the requirements had been fulfilled.

According to the rules for warfare *à la Chine,* there must first be the correct marching and countermarching, each side endeavoring to impress the other with its superiority in tactics. Sometimes the whites thought the battle was actually going to begin, especially when the Red Cap army, numbering about one hundred and fifty men, staged a kind of parade in company front facing the enemy, gongs beating and horns blowing, their pikes held at the shoulder-arms, a squad of specialists with huge squirt-guns maintaining these implements at the ready. No one knew what fearful liquid the squirt-guns contained, nor has any commentator on that first Chinese War ever risked a guess.

But the Red Cap demonstration was not an attack. After some wheeling and drilling on their side of the Flat, the army paused to give the Canton group its chance.

The Cantons were far more numerous; estimates at the time ran from three hundred and fifty to five hundred. Likewise their show was much more impressive. Their specialty was a species of helter-skelter charge across the Flat, with spears held before them. At the moment when spectators concluded that this was at last the real thing, the entire army would stop dead, members of the front rank dropping to one knee with shields held before them, forming a gleaming wall of iron bristling with the pike-points that protruded from the rows in the rear. However, in spite of these military maneuvers, the general opinion was that the Red Caps would win. It is necessary to report here that there was good ground for this opinion. For the Red Caps had concluded a secret agreement, secretly arrived at with the white men. It was a simple enough matter, and showed the Red Caps' leader, one "Charlie," as a very superior strategist. The whole point lay in Charlie's disposition of his forces. He had drawn up his little army of a hundred and fifty men so that his flank was protected on one side by a sharp rise of ground. Facing him across Five-Cent Gulch, a depression in the Flat, was the Canton army, at least three times the size of his own. Clearly, Charlie's other flank was his weakness. It was concerning this matter that Charlie had made his deal. The agreement was

Grass Valley, California, 1858
The discovery of gold-bearing quartz brought the boom to
Grass Valley in 1850. By 1853, it was a city of five thousand

miners. In 1855, the city was burned out in a brief two hours
of holocaust. To rebuild the city, most of the surrounding hills
were stripped of their trees.

simply that when fighting finally commenced, his white friends would see to it that the spectators crowded in on that side. Thus, under the guise of getting a better view of the battle, a thousand or so white men would protect his only exposed flank. None of the Cantons would dare to force their way through the close-packed miners from the rear.

It happened exactly as Charlie had planned. By three o'clock on Saturday afternoon, both sides had got through the prescribed formalities and were ready to get down to business. Charlie's forces began it, charging across Five-Cent Gulch and up the other side with what observers afterward admitted to be "unexampled ferocity." Unexampled or not, the violence of the attack was enough to break the Canton Company's front, which gave way, fighting hard. Perhaps the Canton leader had planned this break; a shrewd captain might well have ordered a maneuver of this kind, knowing that the pursuing Red Caps would thus leave themselves open to attack from the rear. Indeed, there is some ground for believing that this was the plan of battle, for a detachment of Cantons immediately attempted to sweep in on the Red Caps' flank. But Charlie's strategy was perfect. The Americans who were in on his scheme raised a cry of "Fair play!" and the unthinking crowd joined with them. The flying squadron of Cantons was in no way anxious to get into a fight with the white men and, when it was clear that they would not be allowed through, fell back and attempted to join the rest of their army. But by that time it was too late. The main body, seeing that its plan of battle had failed, was in complete rout, and that was that. The entire operation had lasted perhaps ten minutes.

When it came to totting up the damage, it was found that the casualties had run to something like fourteen. Eight Chinese were dead. Half a dozen more were wounded severely enough to require a doctor's care. Of these, one report states that some died later. Surprisingly, one white man had been killed, and the miners were inclined to be incensed about it until a dozen bystanders came forward with the facts. The dead miner was a Swede from a camp near-by, an individual known to be surly and particularly disagreeable when in his cups. He had expressed himself as disgusted with the ritual marchings and demonstrations, and when the Red Caps actually commenced the attack, he had drawn his pistol and fired at random into the little army to "get them going." Some one—and the best evidence points to a miner standing beside him—had shot him through the head for his wantonly cruel act. When this was known, the crowd decided that the Swede had got what he deserved. One American who saw the whole affair and later wrote an eyewitness account said plainly it was too bad that about a dozen more white men had not been served the same. He added that as to the morality of the proceedings, that was another matter, but the general sentiment of Weaverville was that "if the Chinese wish to fight among themselves and kill each other, the people here are perfectly willing."

That was the Weaverville Chinese War, a seven days' wonder in the California press. Details vary; there was and still is debate on such questions as whether the Red Caps were really the anti-Canton faction, one writer stating positively that they were the "Cantons" and that the "Hongkongs" were the losers. Another who was there called the Red Caps the "Young Wos" and the defeated army the "Ah Yous." It does not matter a great deal. There was a battle, such as it was. The Chinese on both sides spent the next day burying their dead with appropriate ceremonies, including a brand of music which distressed the reporters present sufficiently so that several of these mentioned the "yowling and squawking tunes" in their dispatches to the papers. A follow-up story to the Shasta *Courier* notes that the War settled nothing for the Chinese: "Their differences are no further composed now than they were in the beginning. Neither side dares to go to work."

But the trouble was smoothed over, at least well enough. Until the 1880's when Weaverville began to fade, there were many Chinese in and around the town, and there were no more wars. In fact, there was only one other Chinese War important enough to deserve the name. The doubtful honor of conducting that enterprise belongs to some two thousand Chinese of the Southern mines who found themselves, a little more than two years later, unable to compose their differences without resorting to the same proclamations and violent threats, the same solemnity of ritual marchings and counter-marchings, that had distinguished the quarrel of their northern brothers.

In September, 1856, the settlement of Chinese Camp, not far from Sonora, was titillated by the appearance, in the Columbia *Gazette,* of a reading-notice somewhat out of the ordinary run. It bore the heading, "Challenge from the Sam-Yap Company, at Rock River Ranch, to the Yan-Wo Company at Chinese Camp," and readers of the *Gazette* were interested to note that it minced no words. It read, in part:

There are a great many now existing in the world who ought to be exterminated. We, by this, give you a challenge, and inform you before-hand that we are the strongest and you are too weak to oppose us. We can therefore wrest your claim, or anything else from you, and give you notice that it is our intention to drive you away before us and make you ashamed of yourselves. You are nothing compared to us. . . . You won't stand like men; you are perfect worms; or, like the dog that sits in the door and barks but will go no further. If you won't accept the challenge, we tell you, by the way, to go and buy lots of flour, and paint your faces; then go in your houses, shut the doors and hide yourselves, and we'll kill every man of you that we come across. Shame! Shame!

There was more of it, including the poetic declaration that the challengers were durable as stone while the challenged were pliant as sponges, but the general tenor throughout was that of the sample quoted.

This, as the reader will observe, was no mere local squabble. So challenged, all Yan-Wos within reach were practically bound to join in the fight against the Sam-Yaps or lose face. For that matter, with the honor of the society to uphold, all Sam Yaps that could get to Chinese Camp must report for duty; such a challenge once issued must be upheld.

As in the case of the Weaverville battle, there are conflicting accounts of the origins of this later war. Apparently the most reliable is that of one James Hanley, who subscribed himself a "Chinese Interpreter" and stated in a communication to the Sonora *Union-Democrat* that the whole business began when some Yan-Wos, working side by side with a group of Sam-Yaps at Two-Mile Bar on the Stanislaus River near Knight's Ferry, rolled out of their way a large rock which came to rest on the Sam-Yap claim. Only eighteen miners on both sides were involved in the original dispute. But the all-important matter of "face" made it necessary that neither group should give in. Before many days had passed, the quarrel grew to such dimensions that nothing less than a proper war could settle it, wherefore the formal challenge.

Preparations were much like those in the north, with a few extra trimmings. Pikes, swords, and salmon-spears were ordered in quantity, and the blacksmiths of the towns round-about profited as their colleagues in the north had done. Their gross take was greater, however; reliable estimates place the number of warriors involved in this fracas at somewhere close to two thousand in all, including a troupe of Chinese actors who closed their theater in San Andreas and came down to Chinese Camp to be in on the fight.

Nor were these traditional weapons all of it. The Sam-Yaps sent to San Francisco for muskets, powder and ball, so that some of their soldiers, at least, might have the advantage of the white man's weapons. There was one minor difficulty here; the Chinese could not seem to learn the trick of shooting a gun. On the Sam-Yap side this difficulty was met by hiring white miners, at ten dollars a day and whisky, to act as instructors. Indeed, fifteen of these are said to have painted themselves yellow, hung three-foot horsehair queues from their heads and actually marched into battle, at what rate of pay does not appear. They could not have been very good shots, or perhaps they fired into the air. For although, on September 26, the day of the conflict, a witness reported that something like a hundred shots were fired, the casualty list stood at four dead and four wounded. A deputy had his horse shot from under him when he attempted to prevent the two factions coming together. His timing was bad, that was all. For when the two armies had had their fill of marching, poking, slicing, and thrusting, Sheriff Stuart and his aide, Mr. Cogswell, had no trouble disarming both factions and sending them along home. Interpreter Hanley, who went down next day to Rock River Ranch to make sure that all weapons were given up, reports that each Chinese to whom he talked confessed he had been a fool to fight and would not do so again for anybody. Very likely by that time the face-savers had had a chance to reflect that they had been taxed the considerable sum of forty dollars a head for the war chests on both sides, and that the performance had not been worth it. As for the white miners' view of it, this was best expressed by the bored journalist who recorded the affair for the San Francisco *Bulletin:* "It was a very bad battle," he wrote, "as so few were killed."

The Chinese Wars were one more demonstration that the mining area was losing its random character; it is only after men have begun to settle into a new country, to build up a consciously developed society of a sort, that planned conflict occurs. War is proof of the civilizing influence at work; it can only be conducted through organization of a kind which can not be brought into being until men have got together, worked out schemes in common, agreed to submit to specific disciplines. Not that the yellow man was the only one privileged to illustrate the increasing civilization of the new Californians. Even the red men, infected by the notion of regulation in all things, contributed their small bit to the developing urge for order, for exactitude, for labeling, pigeon-holding, getting things done according to rule. Their endeavor along this line, oddly enough, involved the Chinese and provides one of the most charming examples, in California or elsewhere, of the results of a passion for precision carried to extremes.

The incident took place down near Mariposa, where the Indians of that region, only barely accustomed to the idea of men with white faces, found themselves puzzled anew by the appearance of men whose complexions were distinctly yellow. Such an apparition was confusing; it required to be classified, ticketed, put in its place. Conferences were held under the dappled shadows of Mariposa County's scrub oak; higher in the hills, groups met beneath the tall pines and seriously argued it out. It was important that the decision should be the correct one. Here were men neither white nor red-brown. Where did they belong? How were they to be considered? In short, were these Chinese white men or were they Indians?

It took time to debate the matter, and in the end words were of no avail. The tribes were split. One faction held to the belief that the yellow men were Indians. Their hair was black and straight and coarse; their skins were not white; there were no blue eyes among them. The other faction opposed this conclusion with bitterness. Did these yellow men dress like Indians? They did not. Were their habits Indian? By no means. They grubbed, just as the white man did, for the golden metal that could neither be eaten nor used to keep the body warm. They lived in wooden shacks, transacted business, conducted themselves in all ways precisely like the whites. Clearly they were a species of Yankee, or *Boston*. The argument grew heated. If there had not been a latter-day Solomon among the Indians, it might have come to a serious split.

There was such a Solomon, though his name is lost to us, and he proposed a test which would settle the matter once and for all. Indians, he reminded his people, could swim; brought up on the banks of the rushing mountain streams, they understood the water from childhood. On the other hand, as was well known, white men could not swim; every Indian had watched the awkwardness of the miner in his heavy boots, battling the chill rivers in his search for gold. Very well, then, could the yellow man swim or couldn't he? If he could, he was an Indian. If he could not, then, manifestly, he was a white man. All agreed that here was wisdom.

The test could not be made at once; the rains had not begun. Down near the Mariposa settlements the rivers were low, and farther up in the hills there were no Chinamen conveniently at hand. But the Indians could wait. There was no reason for haste. Indeed, it was pleasant to have a few months in which to savor the beautiful logic of the trial that was to come.

The tribes waited until spring, when the snows melted and even the dryest arroyo became a swift torrent. They waited until one evening two Chinese miners stepped in single file on to the narrow foot-bridge that spanned the Merced, near General Frémont's Benton Mills. Perhaps the yellow men wondered for a moment at the odd demeanor of the Indian who did not wait for them to cross but walked out of the bushes on the opposite bank and on to the planking toward them, when there was hardly room to pass. They may even have turned, to see the second dark and menacing figure behind them on the bridge. They could not have had time to do more.

They had no way of knowing that a few minutes later two soft-walking braves would report to their chief that the vexing question was settled. Chinese were white men.

Two factors had contributed more than any others to the development of the foot-hill mining area into a chain of prosperous, stable communities. One was the discovery of quartz gold and the working out of improved methods for extracting gold from the rock. The other was the determination of the miner to compensate for the unproductive dry season by bringing water down from the high Sierra so that work might be carried on all year round.

By the latter 1850's the ingenuity of the miners and their extraordinary capacity for grueling labor had brought about miracles. A survey of the mining regions made in 1858 shows, in the northern mines, some 1500 miles of ditches and flumes constructed, in the central mines 2175 miles, and in the southern mines (roughly from Mokelumne Hill to Mariposa) 796 miles of earth moved, rock blasted, and boxes built to carry the all-important water. Altogether 731 companies or more loosely organized groups had been formed to carry on the work. Sometimes, when a company failed, public associations or water districts were set up and funds pooled to put the job through. In Nevada County, for example, the camp of Rough and Ready made the first plans to bring water to its area, attempting to divert and bring down to its gulches a large portion of the flow of Deer Creek. When the enterprise began to lose ground, two competitors were interested; the Deer Creek Mining Company and the Coyote Water Company. The latter were involved in a long dispute about priority rights but concluded to settle the argument by joining forces and swallowing the original organization. Meantime the Middle Yuba Canal was begun, to conduct the flow from Grizzly Canyon to San

Juan, Sebastopol and other camps, and though the route was difficult, the Company met with sufficient success to be able to take over both the Deer Creek and Coyote Companies. So mergers and combinations were built up. One way or another, the water had to be brought in, and if one set of men could not manage it there was always another group that could.

Certainly one of the most extraordinary feats in construction anywhere in the northern mines was that of the consolidated Rock Creek, Deer Creek and South Yuba Companies. Blocked by a granite promontory on the South Yuba, the workmen found it necessary to blast rock to a height of eighty feet for a stretch slightly more than a mile long—all this in order to gain a fifteen-foot level for the ditch. Through Deep Hollow Mountain they had to cut a tunnel some two hundred feet below the summit and 3100 feet long; it was practically solid rock all the way. But it was to ditches and tunnels like these that such important districts as North San Juan, Laporte, Camptonville, and many others owed their existence. Without the water there could be no mining, especially now that the placers were worth only what the patient Chinese could scratch out of them. Without the water, particularly, there could have been no hydraulic mining, and it was this latter type of wholesale washing that changed entire landscapes, tore down mountains, and filled the California rivers with red mud. Invented in California and first used by a miner named Matteson on American Hill near Nevada City, the method was ideally suited to the need of the time. As the water was developed and pressures were increased, new and bigger nozzles were manufactured, until the California "Monitors" came into general use. These giants had to be especially braced on a rig that permitted one man to guide a stream that could cut away half a mountain in a few minutes, exposing the gold-bearing strata for working. In the Fifties there were too few farmers to object when the silted rivers overflowed in the great Sacramento Valley; the hydraulic miners went on with their vast operations much as they pleased. Eventually it became clear that one small portion of the State was profiting at the expense of a far greater and more important group, and there was a widespread and general protest. It was almost thirty years, however, before the necessary laws were passed and hydraulic mining on the grand scale became a thing of the past.

The development of hydraulic mining, going hand in hand as it did with the extension of the tunnel method and the improvement of quartz mills, brought money to the mines. Because it brought money, it brought competition. And out of such competition between water companies has come one of the earliest tales of business skullduggery in California. Whether or not it is a true story does not matter. It could have been. Indeed, something like it must have happened, and more than once, in those days when water came close to being worth its weight in gold.

The story concerns a boom camp in the southern mines to which a private water company had brought a ditch, profiting magnificently on the high rates it charged for its imagination and enterprise.

The miners bore with the excessive rates for a year or so, giving due allowance to the company's claim that construction costs had made these necessary. For a few months more they grumbled but paid, the company promising that rates would soon be reduced, now that the original expenses had almost been absorbed. But when the company continued on its high-handed way, doing nothing about reductions and even going so far as to suggest that if the miners did not like the rates charged they were welcome to do without the water, even the most timid citizens of the town saw that something had to be done.

There was a meeting of the miners, and a new company was formed, toward which all who worked claims in the district contributed amounts based upon their holdings. A survey was made, a committee was appointed to handle the details of the new ditch, and the miners sat back to await the arrival of their own water and the time when they could tell the profiteering water company, exactly and in detail, where to get off.

The great moment came at last, and the miners assembled under the brand-new flume where it crossed the flats, just outside of town. To give point to the ceremony, a pipe had been dropped from the box, high overhead, and at the platform from which the speeches were to be made a valve was installed. An American flag was tastefully draped over this, and at the right moment the veil would be swept aside, the camp cannon (brought out from the fire house for the purpose) would be fired, the orator of the day would turn the valve and the clear stream would gush forth as proof that at last a decent, hard-working miner had his rights. It was all very symbolic and proper and eminently suited to the occasion.

No one thought of going to work on that great day; early in the morning crowds gathered in the bars, and a special committee of stockholders was appointed to clamber into the hills a matter of two miles or so to where the main valve was situated. At five minutes to twelve—and the leader checked his watch with that of the speaker of the day so that there would be no mistake—they were to open that great valve and allow the water to flow from the pressure reservoir into the new flume. At twelve o'clock precisely the Mayor would reach the climax of his speech, stoop and turn the symbolic valve on the platform, and from it would spurt the limpid stream, evidence of a task completed and a bandit water company well and thoroughly beaten at its own game. It is not certain that the Mayor planned to meet his great moment with the phrase, *"Finis coronat opus,"* but considering the oratorical habit of the day it is more than likely.

Everything went according to schedule. By eleven-thirty

the town band had swung into *Oh, Susannah!,* and by eleven-thirty-five the final cymbal-clash of *Yankee Doodle* had echoed from the hill. The president of the miners' association introduced the Mayor in a few appropriate words, and by eleven thirty-eight the latter was well into his speech. It was excellently timed. At one minute to twelve the Mayor looked down at his watch and raised his hand. He dropped it and the fire chief touched a lighted fuse to the breech of his cannon. It took perhaps fifteen seconds for the roar to die away down the little valley. Then the Mayor faced about, thrust away the flag, stooped, and turned the valve.

No crystal stream flowed from that pipe. The Mayor wrenched at the valve; it was stuck, of course; it hadn't opened properly. But no water came. With admirable presence of mind the Mayor signaled to the musicians to go into action, and while the music drowned out the murmurs of the crowd, the head of the association swarmed up one of the supports to the flume-box. He stayed there five minutes, ten minutes, while the miners watched from the ground and the band pumped and brayed its hardest. Then he slid down again. There was no water in the flume, either.

It took almost an hour for a hastily formed posse of miners to go up into the hills to the reservoir and return with the puzzled main-valve committee. There had been no mistake there; at eleven fifty-five precisely the big valve had been opened, the water had swirled through it with satisfactory violence into the beginning of the flume and around the bend out of sight.

It took the rest of the afternoon to discover exactly what had happened, but as darkness fell the camp surveyor and half a dozen volunteer assistants came back with the melancholy answer. They had followed the water from the reservoir along the flume, noting with astonishment the diminishing vigor of its flow, coming finally to the spot where it stopped,

229

lapping gently at the wooden walls and floor of the box. Obviously it had reached reservoir level. Unwilling to credit his eyes, the surveyor could not help believing the instruments that at last told him the story. There was no knowing when it had happened, but at some time during the construction of the long flume into town, somebody experienced in the water business had gone out along the route and raised all the stakes that marked the levels for the last mile. Not much, but enough.

Between them, the hydraulic process and the increasingly profitable quartz mining altered the face of the gold country swiftly and inexorably.

As the 1850's wore to their close, more and more camps of Chinese sprang up along the rivers from which the white men were moving away. Higher, where there was good rock, the stamp-mills pounded and shook the mountains day and night, and the gray-green dumps of waste grew and spread. In the valleys the monitors roared and the red hills crumbled and fell away, the rusty flood carrying all manner of detritus down the stream beds, altering the watercourses, often burying the stony bars and little flats that had seen the frantic activity of Forty-Nine. The towns themselves were changing again, too, this time taking on the aspect that was to be theirs, more or less, for the next three or four decades.

In the first years of the gold rush, Dame Shirley's description of Rich Bar would have fitted a hundred, perhaps a thousand camps. Raw lumber and red calico were the height of luxury. Out in the ravines and gulches miners often built their cabins of logs, chinked them with mud, stacked rough and ready chimneys out of the square-fracturing, slaty stone so abundant in the hills. Now and then, in some areas, the Mexican influence predominated; stores, inns and always the jails were built of adobe or of a combination of adobe and stone. There was little variety; men put their shelters together out of the materials at hand. There was something more important to do than worry about architectural niceties.

Now, however, two factors began to influence the physical aspect of the mining towns.

For one thing, the procession of ships around the Horn began to bring made lumber from the East. Windows milled in Maine were no rarity; doors and sills sawed from sound New England timber were a commonplace. Rough boards and colored cloth were no longer enough. Maybe the placer gold was going, but blasting-powder and the unceasing roar of the giant nozzles were ushering in a new era of greater and more solidly established wealth. The man who was anybody at all showed his standing by building himself a house out of materials that had come from his own home town "back East."

The second factor in the change was fire. Year after year, at the end of the dry season, fire swept the camps. And millwork from Boston burned just as brightly and as fast as homesawed pine from the Sierra. There was fire-fighting apparatus, of course. Indeed, because membership in a fire company was proof of definite social standing, many a town had—in theory—far more fire protection than it needed. Engines were ordered in San Francisco, sometimes in New York, and on holiday occasions trundled out for parade in all the pomp and circumstance of red enamel and immaculate brass. Rival companies, spick and span in tailored uniforms, held hose-coiling drills and races, practised setting up their apparatus and timing the run. Doubtless they turned out at fires too. In fact, the records show they did; newspaper accounts of the day made a habit of including in the story of a fire the number of minutes taken by competing volunteer companies to arrive, uncoil, and begin pumping. Fire drill was a show, but it was not all show. Nevertheless, with monotonous regularity the towns burned down. And eventually it became plain that some-

Chinese Camp, Tuolumne County, California

Chinese Camp, not far from Sonora, was the location of the

Chinese War of 1856 in which two thousand Chinese of the southern mines upheld their honor on one clamorous day of battle.

thing must be done about it. Brick was the answer—brick and the tall, heavy iron doors that still survive up along the Mother Lode.

By wood and fire, then, a new kind of mining town came into being. Along the main street the stores, banks, saloons, particularly the Wells, Fargo offices, were of brick. So were the breweries on the outskirts, the mills and the engine-houses at the mines. Partly for protection against vandals, partly because they would not burn, doors and window-shutters were of iron. As for the citizens' houses, wood was good enough; they were scattered, by no means the fire hazard that closely grouped business buildings constituted. Now and then some leading citizen would go to the length of building a brick dwelling. But for the most part wood was used—good Eastern lumber put together in the solid Colonial fashion that the builders liked because they had been born and brought up in such houses. Public buildings varied. In Mariposa the court-house, which still stands, might have been transported whole from some quiet New England village. Elsewhere brick or stone-and-adobe took the citizens' fancy. But whatever materials went into the making of these new towns that rose from the ashes of the old, they managed to reflect the new age. As far as the architectural idiom of their day permitted, they were planned towns. They had a look of permanence. They were solid, practical, made to stay put. Their citizens had begun to sense what they had not yet put into words. They would not have wanted to say as much, but in their hearts they knew it was true. Forty-Nine, the feverish early Fifties—those years were gone now. The gold rush was nearly over.

8.

The Mines Come of Age

FOR nearly a decade California had been the gold mines, and the gold mines had been California.

There was San Francisco; down by its magnificent bay the city had to be taken into account. But it had been chiefly a gateway. In through its narrows poured the ever-growing stream of new Californians; out of it flowed the vast wealth the mines produced. The city was gold; it was the mines in little. Its finance, its entertainment, its commerce and shipping depended upon the vital stream of gold pumped through its banks, its gambling palaces, its hotels and theaters. The money-wizards, the restaurateurs, the storekeepers looked to the miner for their profits; from those grubbing thousands away off in the foot-hills came the gold that made the city possible.

But such situations have a reciprocal side. And toward the end of the Fifties this began to be felt. The great arteries had carried the rich blood of profits down to the beating heart of the State; now the flow of influence, of significance, began to run the other way. In ten years California's mines had produced nearly six hundred millions in gold. They were still producing, still enormously important in the scheme of things, as they have been ever since. Nevertheless, other factors began to color the picture.

The gold miners were young men still. Those who had come across the plains, around the Horn, across the disease-ridden Isthmus of Panama were young men when they made their great trek; the average age was from twenty to thirty. Now, though the average was rising, it was not higher than approximately twenty-five to thirty-five. These were young men still, vigorous, imaginative, forward-looking. Moreover, thousands of them had found their feet, decided that, mines or no mines, they wanted to live in California and were going to do just that. The clerks began to gravitate toward the cities, San Francisco of course, and the lesser but rapidly growing towns such as Sacramento and Stockton. The farmers began to spread out, take up land, plant and cultivate and harvest as they had done in the country from which they had come. As early as the middle Fifties California was producing a large proportion of its own food, the cereals and potatoes and green stuff that the miners of earliest days had missed so greatly. By the end of the decade California had nearly twenty thousand farms. Sutter had been ruined, his great agricultural schemes rubbed out by the irresistible tide of Argonauts. But his guess had been right. There would be wealth in the hills for generations still, but there was wealth in the valleys too. More and more miners began to give up the unequal struggle for gold, which was every day becoming

more strictly a business, less a gambling game in which anybody might be lucky.

Moving into town, spreading out through the valleys, turning to the farm, however, could not rob the Californian of his
memories. He had been a part of the great epic of the century.
The gold rush was the biggest thing that would ever happen
to him. He didn't want to forget those wild years, and he was
not going to forget them. Sometimes he relished straight
factual knowledge of what had passed; after all, no man had
seen more than a minute part of the whole, and it was interesting to look back through another's eyes and learn what had
happened in Mariposa, say, in the southern mines, when you
had been frantically searching for your fortune up in Weaverville. At other times it was the yarn that counted; softened by
the passage of time, the rigors of early days seemed less severe;
it was pleasant to recall the odd and amusing circumstances that
had made life a bit more bearable then. It was even a pleasure
to look back, now and again, and ruminate on the less happy
aspects of that day. A gentle, controlled melancholy was the
fashion of the time, in literary matters anyhow, and Nature,
as is so often its habit, found itself imitating Art.

For these reasons the periodicals of the latter Fifties reflect extraordinarily well the change that was taking place.
Californians were settling back just a little and beginning to
think about the past. Ten years seemed like a lifetime, was a
lifetime, for that matter, if one counted by the events and
experiences crammed into those years. And the miner of yesterday, whether he was still mining or had decided to farm,
clerk it for a living or what not, found himself relishing an
opportunity to reminisce a little. It was one more sign of
adulthood, though the Californian did not stop to think of
that. Perhaps the editors of the newer magazines put it into
those terms; there were educated men among them quite able
to philosophize about the life of which they were a part. Or

235

perhaps, in the immemorial manner of good editors, they simply sensed what their public wanted and gave it to them. Whichever it was, Californians now began to take a look at themselves. It was San Francisco, quite naturally, that gave them the means by which to do this.

There had never been any lack of newspapers in the mines. Traveling printers had brought their presses and cases of type to the mining centers, set up shop and gone to work in every sizable concentration of gold-hunters. Often they had picked up and moved along when the notion took them. In San Francisco and Sacramento there had been a solidly established press almost from the beginning. Men far from home wanted news, and there was always some one enterprising enough to supply it. But for half a dozen years the newspaper filled the need. True, the more literary journal, *The Golden Era*, had flourished since 1852. Even as early as 1854, Ferdinand C. Ewer had tried to establish a monthly magazine, the *Pioneer*, in order, as he put it, to publish the work of those "desirous of distinguishing themselves in Poetry, Belles Lettres, and the more flowering paths of Literature." Mr. Ewer was by no means as naïve a navigator of those paths as his stilted announcement may make him seem. For two years his *Pioneer* did well, publishing such literary pieces as "An Epitome of Goethe's Faust," such thoughtful lucubrations as "Hints on the Moral Influence of the Commercial Spirit of the Age." It is to him that we owe the preservation of the excellent descriptive letters written by Dame Shirley; Ewer printed them all during the twenty-four months his magazine appeared. Nor did he ignore the lighter side. Stephen C. Massett, as "James Pipes, of Pipesville" contributed odds and ends of chit-chat and gossip to the *Pioneer;* so did Captain George Horatio Derby, writing under the nom de plume of "John Phoenix." A Harvard man, Ewer was an intelligent, sound editor; he knew how to give his public a full feast. His *Pioneer* might have lasted longer if it had not been for the depression of 1856, when San Francisco was more exercised about crime and the Vigilante activities than about reading and writing. Toward the end of the Fifties it was therefore left to others to furnish San Franciscans and miners alike with their reading matter. And though these may have been men and women of somewhat lower literary standards, because they sensed what their readers wanted their periodicals interpret the California of the time as well as any medium to-day's reader can discover. There was, for instance, *Hutchings' California Magazine*.

Mr. J. M. Hutchings was the gentleman who had patched together the rather labored humor of the "Miners' Ten Commandments" and suddenly found that he had a success on his hands. With the "Ten Commandments" broadsheet tacked up on every cabin wall in the mines and the profits rolling in at an amazing rate, Mr. Hutchings made up his mind to continue in the publishing business which was so evidently the field for which Providence had intended him. In the summer of 1856 the first issue of his Magazine appeared, and Californians learned what "boosting" meant. Mr. Hutchings appreciated the seriousness of the *Pioneer,* no doubt; very likely he had reflected on the fate of editors who try too hard to improve their readers. At any rate, whatever he thought of Mr. Ewer's venture, he had planned his own along slightly different lines. The epic spirit was all very well in its way, but there were more important things to consider. Hutchings, along with thousands of others, had made his money in the splendid State of California. Very well, then, he would do what he could to make adequate return. His magazine would be devoted chiefly to celebrating the glories of the state that had done so well by its people. As for literature, that would not be ignored, of course. *Hutchings'* would supply its readers with a due allowance of material appealing to the finer sensibilities; there would be no trouble finding contributors.

For five years, *Hutchings' Magazine* hewed to the line drawn by its founder; it lasted, in fact, until Mr. Hutchings himself was compelled by the state of his health to discontinue his publishing business and retire. He chose the Yosemite Valley, often the subject of long articles in the pages of his magazine, and settled down to hotel-keeping. Yet in its five years of vigorous life *Hutchings'* gathered into the fold an enormous number of contributors who—partly because they were not really writers but rather "inclined to be literary," in the phrase of the day—managed to reflect better than they knew the reading tastes of the people for whom they wrote. The "boost" articles were no more and no less than the same kind of thing two generations later, allowing for the difference in style and approach. They were perhaps less exaggerated; in that day even a booster-editor stuck close to the facts and influenced his writers to do so, wherefore the files of *Hutchings'* are an excellent source for the student who wants to know how the miner lived, how hydraulic mining was carried on, what vacation spots attracted the tourist of the time. It is in the files of *Hutchings'*, too, that the student has found a rich vein of woodcuts and lithographs depicting life in the mining camp and the city of the 1850's. But the clue to the tastes of the Californian, to his lively interest in the days so rapidly vanishing, his willingness to accept, under the guise of "literature," practically anything that reminded him of his romantic past, so close and yet so remote, is to be found in *Hutchings'* lighter departments. Stuffed with facts, the reader could turn the page to find essays, poetry, stories, a whole spiritual and emotional table set and groaning with viands for the not-too-exigent mind and heart. It is not too much to guess that it was this side of *Hutchings'* that kept its circulation in the profitable brackets. Indeed, to a regular contributor who coyly signed herself *"B"*—though sometimes admitting the reader still further into her confidence by confessing to *"Bessie"*—and to a

long list of writers of her general ilk, the reader of to-day
owes his knowledge of the kind of prose and verse the sentimental Californian liked best. Here, for example, is "B" in
one of her typical moments, writing of the lonely miners, who
(she felt) did not attend church on the Sabbath as often as
they might, but who were nevertheless to be excused, since
in Nature one might find an acceptable substitute for sermons:

> Even in the fields they may think and commune with beloved friends
> at home, and with their own hearts, for rather would they go forth
> alone, beneath the lofty dome of earth's wide temple, and there, amid
> the gorgeous drapery of the universe, in imagination hover round scenes
> and persons, far, far away, and which are to the soul, like the soothing
> sounds of distant music—the bright links of memory's chain, that binds
> them to the past—and the scenes of the day, the affections, speak to
> man's better nature, and he goes forth a better man on the morrow
> after these communings and aspirations.

What aspirations? Which bright links and soothing music?
Never mind. This is what passed for literature, if not with
the better educated, at any rate with the large list of subscribers
to *Hutchings'*.

There was *"Dr. Dot-It-Down,"* too, whose verse appeared
frequently in the magazine. It is sheerest doggerel, worse for
what it is, even, than the overripe prose of *"B"*; yet oddly it
does convey something of the feeling it sets out to impart.
Witness this extract from "Christmas Carol in California," in
which *"Dr. Dot-It-Down"* honored the holiday season of 1857
for his editor:

> Visit we now the lonely miner
> (Fresh comer or the Forty-niner)
> With head and hand on knee reclining
> He shuts out once all thoughts of mining.
> With eye fixed on a log that's burning,
> Thoughts of dear home and all its yearning
> Burst fresh and vivid on his mind,
> Of all that's dear, left far behind—

> Takes from his breast the last long letter,
> His glistening eyes still growing wetter,
> Reads o'er again his mother's blessing,
> His father's hopes, sweetheart's caressing!

The reader will agree that this is a good deal to find in a single letter, but *"Dr. Dot-It-Down"* was not troubled by the idea. He passes on quickly to registering the effect of this three-in-one correspondence:

> The letter falls—down drops his head—
> Between his hands 'tis buried;
> Now Nature's tears flow thick and fast,
> Remembrance, tribute of the past!

The poem concludes, properly, with an apostrophe to Divine Providence to make it up to the poor fellow somehow. The reader will appreciate the practical quality of the poet's mind, as evidenced in the final line:

> Almighty God, spare Thou his tears;
> Grant him success in later years;
> Let not his sweat be thus all spent,
> Without a hope, without a cent!

Here, also from the pages of *Hutchings'*, is another view of the miner:

Noble-hearted, generous, and hospitable even to prodigality, sharing his last slice of bacon or his last dollar with the worthy unfortunate, he has been the liberal patron of every monied institution of the State, from the ten-pin alley up or down to the banking business—[this may be a fine roundhouse swing at banks or bankers or it may be merely another example of the seemingly limitless confusion in which most contributors to *Hutchings'* seemed to find themselves the moment they set pen to paper]—he is a great reader, and exhibits much sagacity in his selections of books, papers and periodicals, for he always reads all he can get.

The *non sequitur* here is the rule rather than the exception in *Hutchings'*. And the writer concludes:

The miner has been California's heart. Indefatigable in everything he has undertaken appertaining to his vocation, with money or without, he has turned the river from its ancient bed and hung it for miles together in wooden boxes upon the mountain's side, or thrown it from hill to hill in aqueducts that tremble at their own airy height; or he has pumped a river dry and taken its golden bottom out. He has leveled *down* the hills, and by the same process, leveled *up* the valleys. No obstacle so great that he did not overcome it; "can't do it" has made no part of his vocabulary; and thus, by his perseverance and industry, were the golden millions sent rolling monthly from the mountains to the sea!

True enough sentiments, these, if slightly overwritten. Hutchings, himself, as well as his contributors, had seen it all, and knew. And the miner of yesteryear had no objections to being reminded what a splendid fellow he had been. Hutchings unquestionably knew that too.

A trifle lighter, more delicate in sentiment, was *The Hesperian,* which defined itself as "A Journal of Literature and Art," stating its motto to be: "We Will Stand By the Rudder that Governs the Bark, Nor Ask How We Look from the Shore."

Launched in the spring of 1858, it named Mrs. A. M. Schultz as Editress and Mrs. F. H. Day as Associate Editress. Mrs. Schultz lasted four months. By July of that year Mrs. Day, quite evidently a firmer soul, had her name at the masthead, and *The Hesperian* was fairly started on its career of making it plain to the women of California that some one was looking out for their interests, that woman's influence was the main thing, and that every Pure Home is an Altar. One of the chief contributors—evidently the homey quality of his verse hit Mrs. Day right where she lived—was a Mr. E. G. Sproat who appeared regularly in *Hutchings',* but found his muse so prolific that he aimed his overflow at *The Hesperian.* Mr. Sproat ran particularly to verse, though he occasionally made excursions into the essay form, fiction, and even little parables for children tailored to fit Mrs. Day's romantically named juvenile department, "Youth's Casket." It was Mr. Sproat who contributed to this young people's section the poem entitled "Little Margaret, the Lost Child," which began—

> The sun was set, the sky was dark;
> Dark were the woods below,
> As little Margaret wandered on,
> Not knowing where to go.

Fortunately for the peace of mind of Editress Day's child readers, Little Margaret was found, and though she had spent a night in the open was apparently none the worse for it. Indeed, she had had a very happy dream, to the effect that her father had come to find her, which, sure enough, he did. The poem ends quite gaily for that age of melancholy in verse, with the simple lines—

> And so her father took her hand
> And led the Lost Child home!

It was Mr. Sproat, too, who discoursed poetically on the subject of a child bidding its father good-by in the morning. His first quatrain sets, better than anything else that ever appeared in *The Hesperian,* the general tone that industrious and confident Editress Day was trying to achieve. Wrote Sproat:

> Oh, happy is the loving father's heart,
> For though his soul be proud, his physique burly,
> His eyes grow moist with gladness when he hears
> Those young lips utter, "Papa, tum home early!"

Yet they were not all *"Bessies"* and Sproats writing for *The Hesperian,* nor for *Hutchings',* either. Both magazines published many articles by men then well known in California. Bret Harte and Mark Twain belong to a later age; in the heyday of these periodicals the former was driving stage over in Union, near the coast, trying his wings with an occasional practice flutter in anonymous contributions to newspapers, and Clemens was still soaking up atmosphere along the Mississippi. But there were others—Massett, of course, and James Bowman, J. S. Hittell, later to become one of California's noted historians, John Rollin Ridge, remembered now chiefly for inventing the Murieta later writers have innocently swallowed whole, but in the Fifties a prolific and clever poet, editor, and political writer. "Joaquin" Miller had not thought of adopting a bandit's name; he was still Cincinnatus Hiner Miller, a lad of sixteen trying to get used to the wild Oregon frontier. Ambrose Bierce, a seventeen-year-old in 1858, was back on an Indiana farm, and John Muir at twenty-three had just arrived in California to inquire "where the wild part was" so that he might have a look at it. But there were Soulé and Nesbit and "Old Block," and dozens of others who wrote passable prose though their names have now been forgotten, and there were capable men like Nahl to draw pictures. Readers of California's magazines had no reason to feel themselves slighted in either quality or quantity. As for fiction, in an age of lurid serial stories *The Hesperian* and *Hutchings'* held up their end with the best of them. Subscribers might find Mrs. Sigourney herself in their pages. If one editor announced "The Law of Love" by "Luna," the other came forward with a rival author, "Cloe," in a new romantic tale, "The Countess of San Diego, or The Bishop's Blessing." As for uplifting counsel and solid fact, these were never neglected. If *Hutchings'* offered "The Moral Power of the Family Hearthstone" or perhaps a lighter sketch such as "Our Chowder Party," Mrs. Day was ready to cap both with a solemn essay on "Confucius, the Great Chinese Moralist" or a piece on "The Birds of California" with exceptionally fine plates in color. Once Mrs. Day definitely scooped her rival. Her series of memoirs of such famous Californians as Thomas O. Larkin, Jacob P. Leese and Peter Lassen is still valuable reference material for the student. In purely literary matters, you could take your choice of book reviews; both editors furnished them for their readers. *Hutchings'* reviewer, in fact, offered, on publication of Oliver Wendell Holmes' *Elsie Venner,* as safe an opinion as a man of his trade has ever put forward: "This book," he wrote, "is one of the most singular novels we have ever read." And Mrs. Day, in *The Hesperian,* afforded Californians their opportunity to note what *Punch,* across the Atlantic, thought of Professor Longfellow's new poem, "The Courtship of Miles Standish," offering the quotation without comment. Wrote *Punch's* reviewer:

Miles Standish, old Puritan soldier, courts gal, Priscilla, by proxy.
Gal likes the proxy the best, so Miles in a rage takes and hooks it:
Folks think he's killed but he ain't, and comes back as a friend to the
    wedding.
If you call this ink-Standish stuff poetry, *Punch* will soon reel you off
    Miles!

By and large, then, as the Fifties neared their end, Californians were able to look around them and take pride not only in their achievements but in their native literary reflection of the great deeds that had made the state what it was. They were less proud of the blackmailing scandal sheets that flourished sporadically in this age of the consolidation of wealth. There were several, but the leader, by all odds, was *The Varieties,* which called itself "A Chronicle of Life in California" and was edited by "The Recluse."

The Varieties was what it was, and with the utmost frankness. It carried chiefly the advertising of saloons, wines, liquors, hotels, and theatrical performances, puffing outrageously in its editorial columns the wares of those who bought space, never hesitating to castigate, even to libel, merchants who refused to play its little game. In the old files of *The Varieties* the reader of to-day may come across such curious bits of information as that "Our Rifle Whiskey Is Warranted to Kill at One Hundred Yards," that "The Newest Luxuries, Persian Sherbet and

Orange Wine, are Superb, Sweet, Sparkling, Simple, Safe and Sublime," and that "Dr. V. Gelcich, Physician and Surgeon, is now Sole Proprietor of the New Balsam of Santa Lucia, a Simple Extract of Herbs which is Regarded as an Efficient Remedy for All Kinds of Diseases of the Eye, Especially Chronic Cases." The occasional appearance in *The Varieties* of an entirely reputable advertiser, doing his best to come up to the rough humor of the medium, furnishes a charming contrast, as appears, for instance, in the pathetic forced gaiety of a firm that manufactured boots and shoes:

> In fact amongst importers, search where you will,
> From the first to the last on the roll,
> For workmanship, neatness, and moderate bill,
> No one can beat Holcombe and Dole!

The Varieties, however, would hardly be worth noting here for such commonplace cheapnesses. What gives the paper its claim to attention nearly a century later is its gossip column, in technic and coverage startlingly similar to those of to-day. The parallel is astonishingly exact, even down to the alliterative name with which the column was signed. "Paul Pry" was *The Varieties'* leading feature. He respected nobody and nothing—not even the canons of good taste. Observe, for instance, this sample, and note the remarkable likeness to the middle twentieth-century gossip-approach:

What ARISTOCRAT, on California St. between Dupont & Powell, keeps in a splendid mansion a BASE WOMAN whose acts disgrace the neighborhood? If he does not move her off I will furnish his name in the next issue.

It's all there, even to the assumption of the rôle of protector of the public morals. Wrote "Paul Pry":

What WOMAN, residing on Green St., visits the Nigger Assignation House on Broadway near Powell? Does her HUSBAND know she's out?

245

North San Juan, Nevada County, 1858

North San Juan was once an exceptionally rich camp, first
because of the surface deposits, then, when these were exhausted,

because of the gold washed out of the surrounding hills by the roaring monitors. After a disasterous fire, North San Juan was rebuilt with brick.

Even for subscribers in the foot-hill towns this was deliciously wicked reading, and hundreds of country mice must have thrilled to the sinfulness of their city cousins. Moreover, the editor of *The Varieties* knew a good thing when he saw it. Within a month of "Paul Pry's" appearance, Sacramento had two special correspondents lifting local lids for "The Recluse." They called themselves "Man About Town" and "Scorpion" and outdid the originator himself in the ardor of their peeping and the vigor of their style. So did the others who immediately offered to cover Marysville, Grass Valley, Auburn, Jackson, Mokelumne Hill and Sonora for *The Varieties,* writing under such names as "Special Watcher," "Viper," "Diabolo Colorado," "Night Owl," "Asmodeus," "Hog-Eye," and "Anti-Hypocrisy." True, *The Varieties* did not live long; but for the few months of its existence it furnished the ultimate proof that yesterday's rough miner was fast approaching sophistication. He was able to enjoy luxuries such as Dr. Gelcich's "New Balsam of Santa Lucia." His vigilante organizations had put down banditry, at least of the more overt sort. Mrs. Day's *Hesperian* supplied poesy and patterns for his wife and careful little fables for his children. *Hutchings'* gave him the stronger meat of solid articles on the advantages and resources of the great state he had helped to make, the reminiscences of fellow gold-seekers who had lived through the same kind of trial and tribulation that had been his own lot. Now *The Varieties* demonstrated that he was a settled citizen, a man of some account. He could be gossiped about.

San Francisco, made by the mines, did more than supply the miners with reading matter. There was the drama and its offshoots, and the city was the source for the entertainment of every conceivable variety that now poured into the mining towns.

It was a tiny gold-camp that had given San Francisco the inimitable Lotta Crabtree. Now the city made lavish return. George R. Stewart, in a little pamphlet, has set down the record of one theater in the mines, a playhouse in Nevada City which lasted only eighteen months before it was burned to the ground as the 1850's ended. The performances, of one kind and another, which took place in the Nevada Theater may be considered typical of those with which the miner-turned-citizen was privileged to amuse himself in any of the more prosperous towns of the gold country.

The house was opened with a performance of *The Merchant of Venice,* played by Mr. Warwick's company which was good enough to hold the stage successfully for five weeks. Its repertoire was large, including a farce called *The Widow's Victim,* a romantic drama, *The Corsican Brothers,* and the pageant-like *Forty Thieves.* Once, three days before Christmas, Mr. Hugh McDermott essayed *Richard III,* and the men of Nevada City went looking for old cabbages. They had heard of the self-styled "master tragedian," McDermott; San Francisco and Sacramento had already suffered under his habit of tearing a passion to tatters, and Nevada City was determined to be ready for him. Mr. Warwick himself played King Henry that night, and the bombardment of vegetables was so severe that, dead or not, he was forced to rise and run for it. High point of the evening, however, and even more delightful than the cabbage barrage, was the moment Richard bared his breast to Lady Anne. As she stood there, holding the sword and hesitating, the Nevada City pit roared as one man, "God damn him! Kill him!"

Early in the spring Mrs. Hayne put on *Camille* and her success was so great that she remained ten days, during which she staged *Romeo and Juliet, Lucretia Borgia, The Lady of Lyons, The Love Chase, The Hunchback, Griseldis* and *Camille* again for the last three nights. By that time Nevada City was sufficiently up-to-date to be amused by a critics' battle which resulted from one newspaper's remarking that in *Camille* the sick-chamber scene was "really painful to witness." The rival paper's critic rose to inquire, "Wonder what effect our neighbor thinks a sick-chamber scene should have?"

The Robinsons followed Mrs. Hayne with farces, vaudeville, and song-and-dance turns, but the audiences of the time seemed to like serious drama better, and the John S. Potter Company saw that they got it, presenting *Richelieu* and *Ingomar* and even *Hamlet*. The Potter Company broke the rule once, with a comedy called *The Young American Actress* by a rising young playwright, Dion Boucicault, but that was an exception.

Generally speaking, this was the kind of fare to which the mining towns were rapidly growing accustomed. Sandwiched in between proper dramatic productions, of course, were oddments of a lighter sort. In Nevada City, for example, the miscellaneous entertainment, for the period in which the theater stood, included three circuses, a "snake-tamer," a French Ballet, Jacobs the Wizard, and dramatic readings on Sunday evenings. The Nevada Minstrels, a local organization, appeared regularly, as did the school-children in skits and recitations, and Mitchell's Equestrian Company, specializing in performances which afforded a good opportunity for horsemanship and the discharge of firearms, played to a tent audience said to have numbered a thousand people. But the point is that the mining country, because it had grown settled, because its citizens had money to spend and pride to urge them in the spending, got pretty well the same thing, in dramatic and sub-dramatic fare, that San Francisco was getting at the time—or New York, for that matter.

Nor were the purely indigenous elegances ignored in this new scheme of things in the mines. The moment it became plain that the miner was no savage, even if he did still dress roughly when he was at work, hundreds of music-teachers, dancing-masters, booksellers, and librarians made their way into the hills. The latter Fifties in Grass Valley, for example, found Mr. and Mrs. J. B. Robinson respectfully announcing "A School for Teaching All the New and Fashionable Dances of the Age, Including the Quadrilles, Waltzes, Polkas, Schottisches." Mrs. Robinson and her husband further assured patrons that they had fifteen years of experience, and that there would be separate classes for Gentlemen, Ladies and Juveniles. Several years earlier an attempt had been made in the remote camp of Volcano to establish a public library; it failed, as a newspaper report put it, "because the Association had no power to compel the restitution of books." That kind of thing, however, was in the past; it belonged to the older, disorderly day when nobody knew where a man came from nor when he might pick up and go somewhere else. Now every mining town of any size boasted a library. As for bookstores, there was Sacramento not too far away, and E. B. Davidson's shop was well stocked, if not with the classics, at least with the kind of volume known as a "Gift Book." Mr. Davidson, to judge by his advertising in the Sacramento *Bee*, was especially proud of such titles as *The For-Get-Me-Not, The Philopena, The Ladies' Scrapbook,* and *Friendship's Offering.* He indicated, too, that he was prepared to furnish copies of *The Gentle Annie Songbook* containing sixty-four popular songs for as low as fifty cents in paper covers and seventy-five cents in cloth. Perhaps it was this collection which moved a prospector to name his mine, near Placerville, "The Gentle Annie."

The ladies and gentlemen of Auburn, of Jackson, San Andreas, Angels Camp, and Sonora, were doing themselves well along less intellectual lines too. The Sacramento stores spent large sums, even at the minuscule advertising rates of the day, reminding newspaper readers up in the mines that they might buy handkerchief perfumes in such exotic *odeurs* as Perfume of Paradise, St. Valentine's Nosegay, and Rondeletia, not to mention such familiar fragrances as Vervain, Frangipani, and Jockey Club. In soaps there were available such favorites as Coudray's Glycerin, while for those who wanted to chance it there was something called Jivers' Lettuce Juice Soap, said to be Excellent for the Complexion. If lettuce seemed a trifle far-fetched, the yearner after beauty might turn to Pistachio Nut Skin and Complexion Powder; the advertiser declared that this was Widely Admired. As for the gentlemen—and any one who smoked cigars was a gentleman —they were privileged to select from among such brands as Figaro, Salvador Montaro, Martinez y Hijo, and something called "Movimiento Continuo"—perhaps one of those dangerous looking torpedoes designed not to be lighted but rolled from corner to corner of the mouth. Not that there was no thought taken for higher and better things. In Grass Valley there was a night-school in full swing. For two dollars a week, or five dollars for three weeks, in advance, the earnest citizen who wanted to better himself might be instructed in the rudiments of Arithmetic, Mensuration, Mechanics, and Chirography. Latin, Greek, and Surveying came a trifle higher; Professor B. W. Crowell, A. M., found it necessary to raise his fee to ten dollars a month for these. It is hardly surprising that in such high-flying times there should have been a certain degree of irresponsible gaiety, and it was one such evening of innocent revelry that caused a complainant, writing under the name of "Good Order," to note bitterly in the columns of the local press that things had got to such a point that "If there is any moral force in the town it should be brought into active requisition" to put a stop to the goings-on. What was troubling "Good Order" was a "shivaree" that had waked him up the night before; worse, a shivaree during which the

M. E. church bell had been carried off and used to produce a "disgusting secular uproar" which, together with "tin pans, sheet-iron, and blackguardly noises of all kinds," constituted "an unmitigated nuisance and an intolerable outrage." It is clear that "Good Order" must have been one of the atrabilious sort which considers all spontaneous expression of good spirits an outrage. To-day's reader can only look with tenderness upon the picture of those ladies and gentlemen, by no means old yet not quite young, trained in the Polka and the Schottische, in Arithmetic, Chirography, and Surveying, their handkerchiefs perfumed with Vervain and Rondeletia, their clear Havana Figaros drawing well in the sharp night air, full skirts modestly lifted and tall hats firmly fixed on heads, wishing their newly wedded friends God-speed with tin pans, sheet-iron, and a good hearty secular uproar beaten out of the M. E. church bell.

One of the first manifestations of organized society is the tendency to get together in groups, with varying degrees of secrecy and mystery. The mines were in no way behindhand here. Early in the Fifties the Masonic order had established lodges up and down the Mother Lode. The Odd Fellows were close on their heels, as was the Order of United Americans whose purpose was not purely social but "the support and encouragement of labor, and sustaining the prices of the same." The Order of Druids had chapters in the gold-towns. Even the Knights of the Golden Circle, founded in the South, had branches in California; frankly an outgrowth of the filibustering days, its members came together to further "the conquest of certain countries in order to spread over them the genial influence of our institutions."

Most popular of all were the organizations devoted to the promotion of Temperance. Pioneering Americans everywhere were hard drinkers, but in California the habit had become a cause for genuine concern. In San Francisco, an Inebriates' Home had been built, and newspaper editors, when there was space to be filled, wrote essays on "Temperance: A Living Issue," and "Alcohol, Enemy of Man." The Sons of Temperance were earliest in the field; in 1852 the *Alta* declared that in San Francisco the temperance idea had become a veritable fad. Lodges sprang up quickly throughout the mines, and the Grand Division held conclaves in San Francisco and Sacramento with the avowed object of influencing legislators. The lawmakers were cagey about it; after all, the liquor business was an important factor in California's commerce. Not all of the Press supported the temperance view either; editors were sometimes inclined to make game of the matter. In 1856, for instance, the Placerville *Mountain Democrat* was so bold as to print a "Topers' Soliloquy," the work of some anonymous contributor who plainly had experience:

To drink or not to drink, that is the question; whether 'tis nobler in the mind to suffer the slings and arrows of outrageous thirst or take up arms against the Temperance League and by besotting frighten them? To get drunk—to sleep it off no more. To get drunk without a headache, and to walk straight when drunk—'tis a consummation devoutly to be wished. To get drunk—to sleep in the street; to sleep! Perchance to get "took up"—ay, there's the rub! And thus the Maine Law doth make sober men of us all; and this, the ruddy hue of brandy, is sicklied o'er with the pale cast of water—to lose the name of Drink!

But in general the newspapers stood behind the temperance principle; it cost nothing to take up a righteous attitude, and nobody's feelings would be hurt since, where alcohol is concerned, it is an ancient rule that it is always the other man who drinks too much and needs exhortation. Now and again the gentlemen of the Legislature obligingly introduced measures of one sort or another as the various temperance groups produced drafts of bills they thought might help to mitigate the evil. They never by any chance permitted any of these proposals to become law, but perhaps the temperance societies did not really expect so much.

Most of these organizations for the abolishment of drink were national in scope; chapters and lodges were brought to California by the gold-seekers when they found the new state so fertile a field for their brand of missionary work. One of them, and for some time the most successful, was California born. It sprang full-panoplied from the aching brow of one, Frank E. R. Whitney, appropriately on the second day of January, 1859, when he and eighteen of his friends made up their minds that they would never suffer through another New Year's Day like the one they had just experienced. Mr. Whitney christened the Society "The Dashaways," explaining that: "The basis of the Society rests upon a mutual resolution to 'dash away' the use of alcoholic liquors as a beverage."

The Dashaways attracted adherents by the thousands. Membership in the group became fashionable almost immediately. The Society built assembly-halls and chapter-rooms, staged lavish entertainments, often persuading well known actors and musicians to perform gratis for the good of the cause. In part, its success was doubtless due to the energy of its founder and president, who missed no opportunities to spread the Dashaway gospel and make public its aim and methods. As for the latter, the Dashaway plan had certain points, notably the brilliant scheme of making members each other's watch-dogs. As President Whitney put it, "The distinctive principle of the Dashaway Association is a *reciprocal pledge* to abstain from all intoxicating liquors, recognizing a mutual responsibility and, by exacting the duty of *mutual surveillance,* enforcing a rigid observance of the obligation under penalty of forfeiting the confidence of their associates." This method, Mr. Whitney believed, would enable the Dashaways to show "results summed up in a vast aggregation of human

happiness and prosperity." He added in his statement to the
press that the good to be attained was unquestionably above
estimate and beyond price. In conclusion he said he was convinced that this organization of men and women banded together against intemperance was "one of the most sublime
spectacles the world has ever beheld."

Sublime or not, the Dashaways flourished for nearly a quarter of a century throughout the mines. Down in San Francisco
the Society had a hall which seated a thousand people and
boasted a stage fifty-five feet wide. On its second floor
were ladies' and gentlemen's reception rooms and hat-rooms,
and one smaller chamber, fitted up at the expense of a well-to-
do member, for use as a meeting room for the Trustees of the
Home for Inebriates. The third floor was occupied by a "commodious reading room, library and billiard table." To this
hall Mrs. Judah brought the entire Lyceum Company for a
benefit show. In it the Nelson Sisters performed, that the
Dashaway coffers might be filled for the execution of good
works. From its stage Julia Hayne, Mrs. Frank Mayo, Miss
Lawrence, and a supporting cast presented, on one historic
evening, a musical interlude entitled *The Honeymoon* and a
farce, *To Paris and Back for Five Pounds,* followed by a dance
for which, by special permission of General Wright, the Ninth
Infantry Band furnished the music. Notables of the time
lectured to Dashaway audiences on every conceivable subject,
among them being the well-known Dr. George W. Beers, who
chose as his topic, "Creation, Vitality and Animated Existence," adding rather pointedly that his talk would be "Of
Particular Interest to Heads of Families." When Mr. Horace
Greeley consented to appear for the cause, the Dashaway
Hall was not large enough to contain those who wished to hear
him. For that one occasion the Forrest Theater was leased,
and Mr. Greeley spoke to a packed house, discussing "in his
peculiar style" (as the Sacramento *Union* described it) the

evils of intemperance, "comparing himself with hundreds of his contemporaries who had fallen victim to the alcoholic poison, while he, at the age of forty-eight, was as healthy and vigorous as when a boy." At the close of that affair, which must have partaken somewhat of the nature of a revival meeting, no less than twenty-two persons signed the Dashaway pledge, "among them a lady who would not leave the house until her husband had also signed."

Unfortunately, the affairs of the Dashaways passed into hands less capable than those of the earnest and talented Whitney. By the early 1880's the management was divided, and constant squabbles undermined the society. Perhaps the chief trouble was that the Dashaways had been altogether too successful, had grown too rich. On February 15, 1884, the editor of the *Union* spoke his mind: "A more disgraceful diversion of a public trust," he wrote, "is not recorded than the breaking up of the Dashaway Association and a division of the property of the corporation among a few greedy men. By a system of persecution and bulldozing, these drove real temperance workers out, in order that the remnant, composed of peculators, might line their pockets with money contributed by the public for a continuing and benevolent trust."

That was the end of the Dashaways—or almost the end. Two months later their obituary was written, and punctuated by a bullet. Half a dozen tragicomic lines in the *Union* tell the story:

DASHAWAY DIFFICULTY:—San Francisco, April 15, 1884:— At a meeting of the Dashaway Association this evening, in which the two factions were represented, a dispute arose between Isaac Abbott and Amasa Thayer over the disposition of a trifling sum of money. Thayer finally pulled out a pistol and shot at Abbott, missing him but hitting a bystander, one Edward Frodshaw, in the leg.

No mention of lodges, secret orders, and such matters in the mines can be complete without some account of what was in many ways the most powerful society of them all, in spite of the fact (or because of it) that the members steadfastly refused to take themselves, or any one else, seriously.

This was the Ancient Order of E Clampsus Vitus, whose members were popularly known as "Clampers." Invented, no one quite knows where or by whom, the order was plainly a burlesque of all such secret societies. Its head was the "Noble Grand Humbug." Its members were called together by the braying of the "Hewgag," and gathered in the "Hall of Comparative Ovations." Members were taken in at every opportunity; indeed, one of the order's chief purposes was to take in others. Once thoroughly taken in, the new Clamper had to put a good face on it; on the principle that his pleasure would now derive from seeing his successors sold as he had been, he was glad to keep his mouth shut and did. As for the name of the society, no one has yet been able to decide upon any plausible translation of the hog-Latin of which it consists. From beginning to end, the whole affair was one enormous hoax, an expression of the crotchety-humorous gigantism that characterized the age, the kind of typical American Davy-Crockettry that still survives in modified form.

The curious thing was that E Clampsus Vitus in the end amounted to far more than it had ever set out to be. Its members were part of a huge joke; well and good. But having had their joke, they were good citizens, too. Assembled in solemn conclave for the taking-in of a "Poor Blind Candidate," they enjoyed their belly-laughs. Then they sat down and discussed whether the family of the preacher in the next town didn't perhaps need a benefit, or whether maybe some youngster who showed a talent for fiddling oughtn't to be sent down to San Francisco to get better instruction. Having made up their minds, the Clampers proceeded quietly to see that these things were done. The newspapers of the Fifties are full of notices of just such charities being carried out by the society. It made no difference whether the beneficiaries were Clampers or not; those in distress, the deserving in any way, were sure of aid from E Clampsus Vitus. Here, for example, is a letter from the "Correspondence" column of the Placerville *Mountain Democrat* for January 19, 1856:

EDITOR DEMOCRAT:—It has always been my belief that the good deeds of individuals or societies should be noticed.

A few days ago I visited a sick and destitute family in the suburbs of our city, and accidentally witnessed the noiseless and unostentatious but liberal manner in which some societies perform their mission of charity.

The head of this family has been unwell for some time and unable to work, and they were greatly distressed and desponding. Ere my visit ended, a wagon, loaded with provisions, drove up to the door. In a few minutes, without a word of explanation, the provisions were transferred from the wagon to the house of the suffering family. With tears of gratitude the generous donors were blessed. Nor did their charity cease here. A few days subsequent I again visited the family and noticed with pleased surprise that clothing had been furnished in the same mysterious manner.

With the curiosity of my sex, I resolved to penetrate the mystery, and at length learned that the society or order of *E Clampsus Vitus* had furnished the provisions and clothing. May the blessing of Heaven rest upon them.

A LADY

It was natural that the order should thrive; the whole atmosphere of the mines was suited to its nicely balanced program of horse-play, nonsense, and good works. The Clampers sponsored fancy-dress balls, picnics, benefit shows of all kinds. In the middle and latter Fifties chapters of the society sprang up in almost every town in the mines. Not all of them followed precisely the same ritual; there was always some inventive member who could think up new ways to torture and bedevil the next neophyte. But the general principle of the initiation and the ceremonies of meeting remained the same. From Weaverville in the north to Hornitos in the south, the Hewgag brayed for the regular weekly gatherings; the Noble Grand Humbug explained to the brothers, new and old, the reason for the Clamper motto, *"Credo Quia Absurdum,"* the importance of the order's Clampatron, St. Vitus, the significance of the society's emblem, the Staff of Relief, and asked them the ritual question, "What Say the Brethren?" to receive the thunderous reply, "Satisfactory!" And the outsiders, though their good judgment told them this was all nonsense, were impressed just the same. They had to be. All the big men in town—any town—belonged to E Clampsus Vitus. What if common sense whispered that, after all, it was hardly likely that Solomon, George Washington, Henry Ward Beecher and Captain John A. Sutter had all been Clampers as the members of the order claimed? When the judge, the doctor, the most able lawyer in town, and both bankers belonged to E Clampsus Vitus, you got in too, if you could. That this sort of reasoning was based on straightforward realism is proved by the story of the initiation into the order of one, Lord Sholto Douglas, head of a company of touring actors. True, the noble Lord Sholto was taken in some years after the society had lived through its great days, but this does not alter the value of the anecdote as a demonstration that it paid to be a Clamper.

The Marysville *Appeal* carried the story. The company, with the peer at its head, was scheduled to play Marysville for two nights. It was evident that Marysville citizens had heard about Lord Sholto, and that what they had heard was hardly favorable; gate receipts for the opening performance totaled seventy-one dollars. Since this would come nowhere near meeting expenses, the company was ready to forget the second evening, write off its losses, and go back to San Francisco. But somewhere, very likely in the hotel bar, Lord Sholto met a Clamper, who saw instantly a chance to help out a discouraged man, enhance the prestige of his order by initiating a British peer, and furnish the brethren with an evening of first-rate sport. Writes the reporter for the *Appeal:*

Last night after the performance at the theater, the sonorous tones of the Hewgag floating over the city warned all good Clampers that a stranger was to be initiated into their order. Presently 500 men had assembled within the walls of the Hall to witness the ceremony of the initiation. The Clamp Petrix announced that he who sought admittance was no less a personage than Lord Sholto Douglas. When he had been blindfolded, the shoe removed from the right foot and the pants-leg rolled to the right knee, the work of introducing him to the mysteries of the order was begun.

His ride in the wheelbarrow over a ladder, and the elevating influence of a blanket in the hands of 40 stalwart brothers were appreciated by the candidate. With three cheers for England and America, the meeting adjourned.

The proof of the pudding was the next night's audience. Lord Sholto Douglas was one thing, but a brother Clamper was another. The theater was filled: Lord Sholto made a very effective curtain speech, introducing his wife who sang and danced, to the great edification of the brethren in the audience who rewarded her with roars of "Satisfactory!" When the curtain was finally rung down, Lord Sholto made straight for the box-office. The take was slightly over $300. Before he left town the next morning the noble Englishman told the press that he did not understand Marysville, but that he would never forget the city or its people. It is fair to assume that he meant both.

For a golden decade the mines had poured their riches down into the State of California and through San Francisco's Golden Gate to the rest of the world. Some six hundred millions of dollars had been lifted from stream-beds, washed from dry diggings to which water had been painfully brought, crushed from the hard quartz, sluiced down from the hills

Auburn, Placer County, California, 1857
In 1848, the diggings at Auburn ran from eight hundred to
fifteen hundred dollars a day for a miner willing to work.

Auburn owed its eventual size to more than its mines. The town was a logical center for the area around it, and hotels, a Wells Fargo office, banks, and a stage stop sprang up there naturally.

by the giant nozzles. Yet all this vast wealth had occasioned extraordinarily little conflict. There had been some fights, limited bickerings of one sort or another. Thieves had nibbled here and there at this king's ransom in gold. In the middle Fifties there had even been an attempt or two at organized robbery; the reader will recall Tom Bell whose schemes for wholesale banditry came to such a sudden end. The Chinese had battled, though in all probability not primarily over gold, and there had been murder done often enough. But these were small matters, considering the tens of thousands, good and bad, that had come to make their fortunes in California. In the larger sense there had been no trouble of the kind that such great quantities of gold might have been expected to attract. In the main, the miners individually and the companies they formed to exploit California's treasure had been content to stay within the framework of the laws. As has already been suggested, this was more or less a matter of mutual forbearance. When men are dependent upon each other in the degree in which the miners found themselves dependent in the early days of the rush, a law of the highest common denominator seems to operate; for the time being, the best in each man contributes its bit to the average, and the ethical standard rises instead of going down. This state of affairs lasts until life grows easier. As this comes about, as civilization develops and men are not faced so starkly with forces against which all must stand, the once closely knit community begins to break up into groups. The ethical standard drops. A new kind of conflict comes into being—that of group interest. The motive, which is greed, is more easily concealed, more simply disguised under this or that covering of justice or right or legality. And things can happen between opposing groups which would have been impossible in the days when the same kind of conflict would have been frankly and openly between one man and another.

California's gold-rush decade had one prime example of this curious human weakness. But for good luck and a bit of quick action, the incident might have developed into a full-sized battle or series of battles, and this in the most literal and exact sense. The central figure in the struggle was one of early California's great men, John Charles Frémont. The incident which might have been so much more was the Mariposa War.

At forty-five, Frémont had already lived a remarkably full and varied life. Fortunate enough to attract the attention of Joel Poinsett, he had been chosen through the latter's influence to accompany Nicollet in his explorations between the upper Mississippi and Missouri rivers. Backed by Senator Thomas Benton, he had gone ahead with explorations of his own, mapping much of the Rocky Mountain area, visiting the Oregon country, and swinging across the Sierra Nevada into Mexico's California. He had become famous in the days of the Bear Flag revolt, met reverses when he could not get along with that tart soldier, Stephen Kearny, and had suffered the disgrace of court-martial, though his sentence was later remitted by President Polk. Married to Senator Benton's daughter, Jessie, he had made up his mind to begin a new life in California. In fact, when he left for the East for his trial, he had already made some provision for what he thought was to be his future. He had given Thomas Oliver Larkin, former United States Consul in California and after the American occupation a business man in the new territory, three thousand dollars with which to buy a ranch for him. Frémont had specifically requested that Larkin acquire for him a certain piece of property near Mission San José, down at the southern end of the Bay of San Francisco. There, he felt, he could settle down and lead a peaceful existence untroubled by the kind of pull-and-haul that went with public life.

To this day no one knows the ins and outs of the land deal

that Mr. Larkin made for his friend Colonel Frémont. It is known that when Frémont sat at Sutter's Fort waiting for orders to face his court-martial a messenger brought him, from Larkin, the deed to a ranch. It is known also that this deed had nothing at all to do with the site Frémont had chosen, but that it conveyed to him, from one-time Governor Alvarado, ten square leagues—approximately 45,000 acres—of land over where the San Joaquin Valley began its rise into the foot-hills a hundred miles or so to the east. Further, it has been established that Frémont indignantly sent back word that Larkin knew very well what land he had selected, and that he wanted either the ranch he had picked out, down near Mission San José, or his three thousand dollars back again. There is no evidence that Larkin did anything about this ultimatum. Jessie Benton Frémont, in some unpublished notes quoted by Reuben L. Underhill in his book, *Cowhides to Golden Fleece,* referred to Larkin's purchase as a "curious error," which it may have been. If what Mrs. Frémont added is true, the phrase becomes an obvious irony; wrote Jessie, "By another curious error, Larkin became possessed about this same time of the very olive orchard and lands Colonel Frémont had directed him to buy, and for which he had substituted the Mariposa property." At any rate, Frémont could do nothing about it at the time; he had to go East immediately to be tried by military court. As for the "error," it was not long before Larkin discovered how grave a mistake he had made, and Frémont learned that luck had been with him after all. On his way out to California after the court-martial, Frémont and his party fell in with a large group of Mexicans near the Gila River on the southern route. They were from Sonora, in old Mexico, and were headed north. Perhaps they would have liked to conceal their errand, but there is one secret that men can not keep. It was not long before Frémont and his band found out what was drawing the Mexicans to California. Gold had been discovered at Sutter's Mill.

The discovery changed Frémont's plans, and for that matter his life. The Mariposa Grant proved rich in gold. Frémont became a leading citizen of the new State, a Senator, in 1856 the presidential candidate of the young Republican Party. Defeated, he returned to California to look after his mining properties, and for a year or two shuttled back and forth between California, New York, and Washington, trying to settle some of his business and legal difficulties. The Mariposa mines were producing fabulously, but lawsuits about mining rights and the size of his grant, bad management and absentee ownership were costing him far too much. Eventually the courts found for Frémont, and his boundaries were definitely determined. It was out of this circumstance that the conflict came. Frémont's "floating grant" had floated too long. While the court decision was pending, individual miners and mining companies worked where they pleased in the Mariposa area. Who was to say whether they were on Frémont's property or not? No matter how the final boundary lines had been drawn, there would have been some to claim they had been unfairly treated. Now, with the limits of the grant definitely fixed, there were several large and influential operators hostile to Frémont and his group. One, the Merced Mining Company, brought suit, in the meantime threatening violent action. This was the moment, in the summer of 1858, that Frémont chose for his decision to move his entire family to the Mariposa Grant to settle down.

There were seven of them altogether: the Colonel and Mrs. Frémont, their three children, the Colonel's niece, and a young visitor from England, a bright, lively lad named Fox. They had moved into the former agent's house, a white, story-and-a-half frame building pleasantly situated on a slight rise of ground not too close to the little village of Bear Valley and not too far from the Merced River down in its cañon to the northward. The stamp-mills were producing something like two thousand dollars a week, and prospects were good; there were the latest English and French novels to read, and the Colonel made a point of keeping fine saddle-horses. It was hot in the summer, but there was always a breeze in the evenings; farther up in the hills the Colonel had built a rough summer camp under the pines where it was cooler. Frémont knew that the Merced Company was planning trouble for him but perhaps he felt that in such civilized times nothing serious could happen; at any rate, he said no word to his wife. It was a complete surprise to her, therefore, when a messenger rode furiously up to the house, calling to the Colonel that there was bad trouble at the Pine Tree Mine. Frémont knew what it meant. The Merced Company had fulfilled its threats. Now, unless everybody was extraordinarily fortunate, there would be bloodshed.

The Colonel and his men had seen what was coming and had done their best to prepare for it. At the Pine Tree they had built a miniature stone fort with thick walls behind which even a small body of determined men might hold off a large group of attackers. The Merced Company, taking advantage of a court decision which held that miners might take possession of any "unoccupied" claim, had already bribed the night-watchman at the Black Drift and barricaded themselves in its shafts and tunnels. They had also surprised the Josephine Mine and seized it. Now they had taken a longer step and tried to capture the Pine Tree, which was defended. For the moment, at least, matters were at a stalemate. The Pine Tree miners stood firm. The Merced Company's larger body of fifty or sixty heavily armed men did not quite dare to rush the defenders; to do so they would have had to approach without cover of any kind, certainly losing many of their number. Both sides breathed fire and slaughter, but both stayed where they were.

The first move was Frémont's. An old campaigner, he saw that it was possible to cut off the Merced Company's force from behind, and hurriedly got together twenty or thirty men for that purpose. The result was to immobilize all three forces. The defenders in the mine had no chance if they came out. The Merced Company's men had not felt like risking a quick rush; now the Colonel had them bottled up from the rear. As for Frémont and his group, there were not enough to break through and relieve the men at the mine. All they could do was sit tight where they were.

At this point the Sheriff arrived and did what he could. This consisted in reading the Riot Act and ordering the Merced Company's men to disperse. Their leaders told him flatly that this was something they would not consider. He went away and came back again with warrants. Three of the Merced group gave themselves up; the rest told the Sheriff he would have to come and get them. During the next night a few of Frémont's volunteers managed to sneak through the Merced Company's lines and make their way into the Pine Tree to reinforce their friends. Their daring did not mean much, for by morning it was seen that the Merced men had added several more to their ranks also.

The editor of the Mariposa *Gazette* had his opinion about all this. He made it clear in his paper that he considered the Mariposa War a disgrace to the county in general and to Bear Valley in particular. He scrupulously refrained from taking sides, but reminded his readers of Law and Order, concluding, safely enough, that though he would not pretend to say on whose skirts would be found the blood of the victims should any actual encounter occur, the public "must place its seal of condemnation upon the proceedings." As an editorial statement, this was a masterpiece of hedging. It does not appear that it had any effect whatever upon either party to the quarrel.

The amazing thing is that no one was killed in the whole five-day siege. One student of the Mariposa War tells a romantic tale of the English boy, Fox, who saddled the finest horse in the Frémont stables, somehow found a hidden trail around the mountain and down to a ford across the Merced into the town of Coulterville, whence messengers were sent via Stockton to the Governor, who at once ordered the militia to take the matter in hand. Whether or not these are the facts, the soldiers did arrive—some five hundred of them. They found Frémont standing his ground, cutting off the Merced Company's hired warriors, insisting that he would provoke no bloodshed, but that, on the other hand, he would not agree to the suggestion made by a nervous Citizens' Committee that he withdraw his men and wait for the courts to decide. Characteristically, Frémont made his statement with a flourish. "The demand you make upon me," he cried, "is contrary to all my sense of justice and what is due my own honor!" One of the Merced Company's men liked the sound of that, and deserted to Frémont, saying, "When I go gunning next time, I'll make sure first if we're after wild duck or tame duck!" When Frémont saw the State forces, however, and realized that they were ready to compel the Merced Company's withdrawal along with his own, he felt that his honor would not suffer. His wife and family had been threatened with physical violence; one historian goes so far as to say that Frémont's servants had instructions to shoot Mrs. Frémont and the girls rather than let them fall into the hands of the enemy. But now they were safe. Frémont himself had shown his mettle; so had his men. Perhaps, after all, it would be better to wait and see what the law had to say.

So ended the Mariposa War, in which, by miraculous good fortune, no shot was fired. Examined from this distance it may seem a ridiculous affair, an *opéra bouffe* performance of empty gestures and hollow rodomontade. It was much more than that. Though there had been no killing, the War had proved one significant thing. The California mines had now moved into the big-business stage. Men could be found to fight, not for their individual rights or desires but in groups at the behest of moneyed interests. That was what it came to. The mining country had at last become integrated with the wholly civilized, world, in which masses of men may always be persuaded to fight others in a matter which has nothing to do with the personal well-being of any of them.

When a gold rush is in progress no one has much time to think about riches elsewhere; there is something about the gold principle that excludes from the imagination everything but itself. But when a rush slows down—even before the participants have realized the fact—there is a chance for new rumors to catch the popular fancy. Now this began to happen in California.

Since the autumn of 1857 there had been whispers about gold to the north, up on British Columbia's great river, the Fraser. There had been no good evidence, but the word went around as such things do. All winter the whispers grew louder; the Fraser bars were richer than anything California had ever seen; the Indians of British Columbia wore solid gold ornaments exclusively; the Hudson's Bay Company was digging out millions. No one could be found to say that he had actually seen either the red men's bracelets or any bars of bullion in the company's safes, but the rumor grew just the same. California's surface diggings were pretty well cleaned out. Nowadays a man had to have capital, financing, a bank behind him and a stock company to join him in exploiting the deposits in the rock. A man could hardly sink a shaft half a mile with his own two hands, nor could he crush the rock profitably even if he had it. The idea of the Fraser sounded like something. Gold in the river bars; that had the right ring to it. That was the way the Forty-Niners had got rich. People began to repeat the story of the Fraser with assurance. It would be the next great strike, no doubt of it. Californians were primed and ready. All that was needed was one good bit of proof to start them helter-skelter toward the north.

Early in the spring of 1858 the proof turned up. The Governor of Vancouver Island, who was also head of the Hudson's Bay Company, sent down to the San Francisco mint about eight hundred ounces of fine gold. Nobody stopped to think that this was not so very much, all things considered. It was gold, and it had come from the Fraser River. California miners who remembered the placering days saw visions of rich bars, golden gravels, another chance to make their fortunes. The foot-hills began to seethe and boil. The Hudson's Bay Company didn't own the world, did it? Certainly not. Here it was again, anybody's gold, ready for the taking.

Perhaps the excitement would have died down. But one hardy band of prospectors had good luck. They outfitted and sailed for the Fraser, and they struck gold. At almost the same time a merchant named Ballou had an idea. He was shrewd enough to know that though miners might strike it rich the wise man made his money catering to the ones who did the hard work. Wells, Fargo & Company had proved it a decade before. Very well, then, he would get in on the ground floor this time. He made a trip to Victoria, saw the bustle and commotion, and rushed back to San Francisco as fast as he could, spreading the news that he was going to start an express business from California to the Fraser.

That was enough. The Fraser River rush was on.

There was gold in the Fraser and in its tributaries. A year or two later there was a rush up to the Cariboo, where even richer deposits were found. True, the country was far less hospitable than California; there were difficulties with the Indians, and there was nothing like the contact with civilization that had been possible even in the California of 1849. It was cold, too, and wet, and those who returned had unhappy tales to tell of the hardships, the taxes, the profiteering that went on. But the gold was there, though not in the quantities that had been dug and washed out of California's Mother Lode in the early years. And there were enough favorable reports so that Californians in ever-increasing numbers began to flow out of the state to try their luck.

The press was indignant. As the Grass Valley *Telegraph* noted in July, the rush was costing California good money. Wrote the editor: "Not less than 400 of our population in this city have started for the Fraser River in the last six weeks, and over $100,000 in hard cash has been taken from our midst by the new adventurers." That was where the shoe pinched. And apparently it was going to go on pinching. Said the San Francisco *Call,* at the same time: "California has so far lost nearly 6,000 miners to the Fraser River, and it is to be hoped that the depressing effect of the Fraser excitement will be only temporary." The *Mining and Scientific Press* was sensible about it. The editor wrote: "Whatever may be the ultimate value of British Columbia as a mining region, certain it is that we have as yet no reliable evidence upon which to base the propriety of any extensive mining emigration to that quarter." Nobody paid much attention. Had there been any more reliable evidence ten years ago? There had been samples of gold, that was all. There were samples of gold in this case, too. Who could say with certainty that the Fraser might not be as rich as the California hills, even richer, maybe? The rush northward continued, growing larger with every week that passed.

In the end none of the bitter paragraphs in the newspapers, no speeches nor scientific pronouncements did any good. Some thousands of California miners were bound to see what they could find, and they could not be deterred. The press grew more violent as subscribers and advertisers were drained away. One portrait photographer saw his chance and combined propaganda with business. His advertisement in the Grass Valley *Telegraph* is a beautifully balanced bit of copy, cleverly calculated to keep gold-seekers from going to the Fraser if possible but also to get their business if they insisted on making the long trip:

PHOTOGRAPH:—Persons about to go to the Fraser River gold mines will do well to call upon M. Wood at his Rooms on Mill Street, and leave a resemblance of themselves with their friends. Should they ever live to return, it will be quite a matter of curiosity to notice the ravages which time and hardship will have made upon them, and should they find a grave amid the frozen regions of the north, such a *memento mori* will be cherished by their friends as a priceless gift.

Ravages or no ravages, not to mention the prospect of frozen graves, Californians continued to head for the Fraser. The press grew more and more strident, louder than ever in its condemnation of this new folly. Editors spoke of the "base and nefarious swindlers, made up of steamboat and ship owners and land pirates of every species and class, that have been enticing so many foolish miners from California." They wrote feelingly of the misfortunes encountered by gold seekers in the north. "Thousands upon thousands," wrote one editor angrily, "are returning from their explorations disgusted and discouraged, with nothing but rags to cover their nakedness and scarcely a dollar to provide that sustenance which is doled out to them by speculators at enormous prices. Hundreds, we are told, have put a violent end to their existence, or sat themselves down to die after their last possible efforts to escape from this modern Golgotha." It made no difference. The newspapers of British Columbia had a better story to tell and told it. "We have here," said the *Colonist,* "a greater extent of gold-bearing country than any other place in the world!" The editor added, "Our good fortune is putting to blush the croakers who have come here and left. There will be good diggings on the Fraser and Cariboo for the next twenty years. Indeed, it will take five years merely to open them up!" In the face of such optimism what could a miner —himself by temperament an optimist—do about it? He could go and see; your true Argonaut can decide in no other way. In the end, California had to let the excitement die of itself. Altogether something like twenty-five thousand miners had left the foot-hills for the Fraser before the boom passed its peak.

The significance of the Fraser River rush, of course, does not lie in the truth or falsity of the stories told about northern gold. The point is that California miners could be drawn away. They were so drawn, and the fact underlined what every one had begun to feel. Though gold and the mines would continue to be an enormously important part of California's future, to-morrow's Californian would have to look in other directions. Already, up in the foot-hills, some towns had been practically abandoned. The early, smaller camps had been hollow shells for several years; now many good-sized ones were empty save for a few older citizens who had farms. Towns that had once held ten thousand and more had shrunk to a hundred or two; their streets ran from nowhere to nowhere, their store-windows were shuttered with iron. Where the hydraulic process was doing well, the towns still flourished, and near the big quartz mines solid cities-in-little had developed sturdily—Grass Valley, Nevada City, Jackson, Angels Camp, and the like. In regions where fruit and truck farming had proved profitable, particularly where main highways crossed and branched, other types of town carried on, dependent still on gold to some extent but fast growing into supply depots and county seats— such centers as Auburn, Placerville, Sonora, Mariposa, and many more. But scattered up and down the three-hundred-odd

271

miles of the foot-hill mining country were scores of fading camps and villages, on their way to the ghosthood that was to overtake them sooner than they knew. The Reverend Martin Kellogg of Grass Valley's Congregational Church understood what he was about when, in his Thanksgiving Day discourse, he observed: "The feverish excitement of the first mad years has now worn away. Gold-getting has assumed the form of a business, and is no longer a game of chance. We are entering upon a new kind of life in this State, and it behooves every one to realize this." Even Mr. Kellogg could hardly have known how dramatically the curtain on his State's gold rush was to be rung down, nor how close he and his flock were to the final scene of the last act.

In the spring of 1859 four prospectors who had wandered across the "hump" of the Sierra all the way into western Utah —now the State of Nevada—came to the conclusion that they had found something. Their names were M'Laughlin, O'Riley, Penrod and Henry Comstock. What they had found was a four-foot ledge of the richest gold-bearing rock any of them had ever seen, running to something over forty ounces a day apiece for Comstock and his partners. There was a little trouble getting it out; mixed in with it were masses of some tenacious, heavy mineral that none of the four knew about. They called it "that blue stuff" and tossed it contemptuously on the dump with the heavy, dark earth and rock.

But there was a farmer living near-by who had a streak of inquisitiveness. He picked up some of the "blue stuff" and sent it across the mountains with a friend who was going over into California. Maybe he would be good enough to leave it at some convenient assay office. The friend did what he was told, turning over the lumps of unknown mineral and rock to a firm of assayers in Nevada City. They made short work of it. The "blue stuff" contained gold in quantity. But it was incredibly rich in silver. The news got out, as such news invariably does. Next day a handful of the smarter citizens left town in a small pack-train, headed back over the pass the Donner Party had missed so many years before. On their heels, in wagons and afoot, riding whatever broken-down horses or mules they could buy, were several hundred eager miners. It was July, 1859, and the first great Washoe rush had begun.

What came of that great stampede is no part of this history. The Comstock Lode is a story by itself, and capable and imaginative historians have dealt with it colorfully and in detail. Its significance here is that the swing to Washoe administered the *coup de grâce* to the California mining country. By the end of 1859 some four thousand Californians had flooded into the Washoe. Virginia City had sprung up, repeating the pattern of the early California camps. Here again were the saloons, the gambling-houses, the sporadic violence, the excitement of riches in the making and a chance for everybody. By the summer of 1860, twenty thousand more California miners had been siphoned over the Sierra and were burrowing into the miraculous hillsides that held both gold and silver. Down in San Francisco the financiers were busy skimming the cream, printing beautiful certificates, conducting a roaring trade in stock issues. Here was the new thing, the greatest ever. Forty-nine? Forget it! This was *Fifty*-nine! This was the Big Bonanza! The California gold rush was over.

Virginia City, Nevada Territory, 1861

By 1860, twenty thousand California miners had been siphoned over
the Sierra to Virginia City where the miraculous hillsides held

both gold and silver. Here again were the saloons, the
gambling houses, the sporadic violence, the excitement of riches
in the making and a chance for everybody.

Epilogue

Postscript to Gold

THE whole mining game had been a gamble throughout; every one in it knew that. It continued to be in a sense a gamble all through the Sixties. It was a business, of course; the element of chance was not manifested in quite the same way. Individuals did not stake their all, to win or lose on the presence or absence of auriferous quartz here or there. A mining company pretty well knew what it was about, or at any rate did its best to eliminate chances as far as it might by employing experts, running tests, and such matters. During the Civil War, too, when California was pouring its gold, and Nevada its silver, into the Union coffers, there was less disposition to take risks when they could be avoided. The thing was to get out the gold and the silver, to keep them coming.

But with the War over, the golden spike driven at Promontory Point, and the two seaboards joined by the new railroad, the Sixties gave way to the Seventies and a kind of recklessness hard to match in any other period. Gambling in mines came back with a rush. Only this time it was a matter of gambling with pieces of paper representing shares in a mine. Where men had once wagered their time, their health, even their lives, on the chance of finding a rich placer, a new vein, a hillside that paid for the building of flumes and the cost of the monitors, now they wagered their fortunes, big or little, on the rise and fall of mining stocks on the Exchange in San Francisco. Hardly any one was immune; the fever caught them all. Cooks, bell-boys, coachmen, and laundresses were buying and selling their small odd lots while the big men sat back and managed the market. Mines were the fashion everywhere, and why not? Hadn't such men as William Chapman Ralston, George Hearst, Haggin, and a hundred others showed the way to millions? They had. And what was good enough for them was good enough for the little fellow, sequestering four-bit pieces from his wages to take a flyer on the Exchange.

Nor was this fever of speculation limited to California, though California and Nevada promotions furnished the basis for the stocks in which the people traded. France and Germany were at grips; London and New York were the world's great money centers. And both those great cities were arm-in-arm with San Francisco. Had not San Francisco demonstrated, time and again for two decades, that the magnificent resources of the West had no end? Of course. If there was one thing certain in an uncertain world, it was that out there in the new Pacific Empire the surface had hardly been scratched. It was a San Franciscan, Asbury Harpending, who opened the Seventies by floating in London, with the famous (some said infamous) Baron Grant, a new issue of stock in the mine known

275

as the Mineral Hill. The shares were snapped up so fast that Harpending never really got over it; forty years later he was still marveling, in his memoirs, at the instantaneous success of the Mineral Hill flotation, out of which he and the Baron turned a profit of something over three hundred thousand pounds sterling.

In such periods of almost universal speculation there is one rule that invariably holds true. Sooner or later the men who manage and control the hysteria for their own ends wind up by catching it themselves. In California, in the Seventies, there was one classic example of precisely this law. The public did not suffer; due to the promoters' anxiety to keep all the profits, the biters were bitten, that was all. Earnestly and devotedly they had spread the message that the mines of the Far West constituted a glorious and inexhaustible source of mineral wealth, that there was no limit to what the investor might expect to find in them. Now they became the victims of their own hypnotic powers. What happened to them was known, after the bubble burst, as the Great Diamond Hoax. And because the Great Diamond Hoax could never have succeeded if it had not been for the two fabulous decades that preceded it, the story of that fantastic swindle is the perfect postscript to gold.

Mr. Asbury Harpending, highly successful San Francisco promoter and real estate operator, a friend and colleague of Ralston and a hundred other of the city's biggest men, had moved his office to London in 1871. Part of his reason was the Mineral Hill stock issue with which he and Baron Grant had had such an immediate success. Part of the reason, too, was Mr. Harpending's sudden realization that the Baron was inclined to ride the wave too recklessly. He had taken on another mine to float—this time a bad one which Harpending knew was bad. Harpending was out to stop him if possible. He knew a hawk from a hand-saw, no matter which way the wind blew. And the Emma mine was not a good property; he had examined it from top to bottom long before.

The Baron, however, was not to be dissuaded, and this gave Harpending several things to think about. He subsidized a British financial paper and fought the Baron in its columns. He launched a private investigation into the affairs of the financial editor of the staid London *Times* whom he suspected of conniving, for his own profit, to forward the Baron's schemes. Harpending had these irons in the fire and a host of less important ones. He was in no mood to be interrupted when he received from his old friend, William Ralston, in San Francisco, a cable that made his hair stand on end.

It was more like a letter than a cable; at the rates then in force, it had cost the sender something over $1,100. And what it contained was enough to convince Asbury Harpending that his friend had taken leave of his senses.

The message was vague sometimes and at others astonishingly detailed. It told Harpending that somewhere in a remote section of the United States a vast diamond field had been discovered. The stones already turned up were of incalculable value, and more might be gathered in limitless quantities at very little expense. In this field the very ant-hills glittered with precious dust, and there was no doubt that it could be considered conservatively as a $50,000,000 proposition. Moreover the sender, Ralston, and a mining man named George D. Roberts, whom Harpending knew, were in practical control. The message ended with an appeal to Harpending to come back to San Francisco as fast as he could get there and take on the job of general manager of the entire enterprise.

The more Harpending thought about it, the more it seemed to him that Ralston must be laboring under some strange delusion. In any event, the various affairs in London to which he was committed left him little choice. He replied to Ralston that there was nothing he could do about it. His business in London made it necessary for him to stay there.

Perhaps Harpending thought that his answer brought the matter to an end. If he did, he didn't know his Ralston. Cable followed cable. Harpending simply must not think of staying in England. There was only one man to handle a promotion of this magnitude, and Harpending was that man. He must and should come to San Francisco immediately.

As far as Harpending was concerned, it might have ended there. But rumors began to get about. Financial men began to come to him and ask him what he knew about this discovery that W. C. Ralston was reported to have made; something about diamonds, wasn't it? Harpending kept his mouth shut, but began privately to wonder. Was Ralston on the track of something really big after all? And when no less astute a banker than the Baron Rothschild himself came to call, Harpending could hardly help taking the matter seriously. The Baron had inside information, he said. He knew that Mr. Ralston and several others were going into this matter of western diamonds. What did Mr. Harpending think? Mr. Harpending showed the Baron the cables he had had from Ralston, saying that while he had always had the greatest confidence in his friend he felt that somehow this time Mr. Ralston had been imposed upon and that it would all come to nothing. The Baron shook his head and told him not to be too sure. America was, after all, a very large country. It had furnished the world with a few surprises already. It might have others in store. Then he went away, leaving Mr. Harpending to his thoughts.

It was something to think about. Harpending got out the cables again and read them over. They were positive, assured, confident. Mr. Ralston nowhere mentioned possibilities or chances; the diamonds were a fact; a sackful of them, taken from the new fields, was in his possession. On the other hand, here was Harpending's London office in full blast, a seven-year lease to consider, a financial paper to be managed, a struggle with a high-powered promoter, Baron Grant, actually going on. Yet—well, Baron Rothschild was not noted as an idle dreamer. He had seemed to think Ralston knew what he was about. At that moment one last cable arrived from San Francisco begging Harpending to come at once, even if he could stay only sixty days or, at the most, ninety. He turned for advice to an old friend, Alfred Rubery, a nephew of John Bright, with whom he had shared adventures in the old privateering days of the Civil War. And Rubery's advice decided him. It was nonsense to stay in London wondering what this was all about, Rubery said. The thing to do was to go back to San Francisco and find out. Two or three months of absence from the London office would make no serious difference. As for himself, he was bored to extinction with London and everything in it. He would be delighted to have such a good excuse to accompany Harpending to San Francisco. Maybe the two could stir things up again in the Far West as they had done half a dozen years earlier.

Harpending cabled Ralston that he and Rubery would make the trip as quickly as steamer and train could carry them. They arrived in San Francisco in May, 1872, ready to look at irrefutable proofs of the greatest diamond field in the world or to get back to London again as fast as they had come.

These were the facts spread before Harpending and his friend, Rubery, when they went down to see Mr. Ralston at the Bank of California.

A few months earlier two weather-beaten men, typical miners by their look, had come into the bank with a package they wanted put in a safe place. It was exceptionally valuable property, they said, and they would like to be sure it was well taken care of.

In the natural routine they were asked the nature of this property, and, after some hedging, they unrolled a bundle and displayed some stones which they said were uncut diamonds. Asked where they had found them they showed no disposition to explain, but were at length prevailed upon to admit that they had picked them up "in the desert." They would say no more, took their receipt, and left.

The secret leaked out, of course. The first man of importance to learn it was George D. Roberts, who found that one of the men, Philip Arnold, had done some prospecting for him some years before. Roberts insisted that Arnold and his partner, John Slack, come with him to meet Mr. Ralston. With Ralston at the time was William M. Lent; for some weeks only Ralston, Lent, and Roberts were let in on the find. At the meeting Arnold did the talking for his partner, Slack; it was Arnold, also, who handled all the negotiations afterward.

From Arnold and Slack the three financiers got the impression of two simple-minded old-timers, bewildered by their good luck. Yes, they had picked up these diamonds themselves, out in the desert, exact location unspecified. Arnold said vaguely that it was "a long way off." An interesting side-light here is that shortly after this meeting several groups of men were known to have departed quietly for Arizona looking for diamonds. It does not appear which of the three, Ralston, Lent, or Roberts, was responsible for sending out these scouting expeditions on his own, though it must have been one of them.

In any event, Arnold and Slack stuck to their determination not to reveal the location of their fields. Would they take in any others in order to help finance their venture? Well, perhaps. They were not eager, but eventually they were persuaded to part with a small interest in the fields in return for a hundred thousand dollars, which, they explained, they had to have in order to make sure of claims to the land surrounding their find. Ralston and his friends had at least got one foot inside the door to riches.

Here, however, the deal bogged down. Neither Arnold nor Slack could be persuaded to sell a further interest. In fact, they appeared to expect that the hundred thousand dollars would be turned over to them merely on the strength of their unsupported story. Ralston told them carefully, in simple language, that he did not do business that way. Some one would have to see the diamond fields. There had to be some good evidence that they actually existed.

Arnold and Slack admitted that this was fair. After some thought they said they believed they could work it out. They would conduct two men, no more, to the location of their claim; Ralston and Roberts might choose whom they pleased. Once on the ground, these representatives might satisfy them-selves in any way they wished that the diamonds were there. But there was one proviso. At the point where Arnold and Slack would lead them off the beaten track, the two investi-gators must submit to being blindfolded for the duration of the trip into the desert. The same would hold true on the re-turn trip. Ralston agreed for his fellow-promoters. The trip was made, and the investigators came back with more dia-monds and enthusiastic reports of the ease with which they had been found. They had even a ruby or two. Ralston, Lent, and Roberts were sure that they had hold of something bigger than they had ever come up against in their lives. It was at this point in the proceedings that Harpending and Rubery arrived in San Francisco.

The first thing Harpending wanted to do was to talk to Arnold and Slack. This was impossible; the men were out of town. Ralston was a trifle secretive about it, but the explana-tion went down well enough. Lacking the men themselves,

Harpending inquired in the city and learned that Arnold had a good reputation among mining men. Nobody knew Slack, though some thought that he was a connection of Arnold's by marriage. Next, Harpending went over the notes of the conferences Ralston, Lent, and Roberts had had with Arnold. The story checked at all points; in repeated quizzings Arnold had never contradicted himself. Harpending had to admit that everything seemed to be open and above board. Still, there was the matter of the hundred thousand dollars Arnold and Slack had asked for. Their request made sense; it was obvious that options should be secured on the land surrounding such valuable property. But such a sum could hardly be handed over without a guarantee. Harpending began to wonder if there was any way to keep the deal from dying where it stood.

Then Ralston told him where the two prospectors had gone.

Before Harpending's arrival, Arnold and Slack had suddenly come forward with a solution to the impasse. The small package of diamonds they had put in the bank's vaults had been valued by such experts as were available in San Francisco at approximately $125,000, as nearly as rough stones could be figured. The rubies were included in the estimate. If the bankers did not feel this to be sufficient security, they, Arnold and Slack, would make another trip to their claims and bring back, as they put it, "a couple of million dollars' worth of stones." These they would hand over to Ralston's group as a guarantee of good faith. Ralston approved, and the men had left for their field. They were due to return any day now.

That put a different face on the matter. Harpending had to grant that two million dollars' worth of diamonds would be adequate security for a paltry hundred thousand in cash. More, he would very much like to look at two million dollars' worth of diamonds; it should be a sight worth seeing. As though it had been carefully timed, a telegram arrived at that moment from Arnold and Slack. They had reached Reno on their way back. Would Mr. Ralston, or some one he could trust, meet them at Lathrop to share in the heavy burden of responsibility? Harpending jumped at the chance. When the train pulled into Lathrop station, he boarded it and found his men without difficulty. Both were travel-stained and weather-beaten and looked extremely tired; in fact, Slack was asleep. He awoke, however, when Harpending sat down and Arnold began to tell him his story.

They had had a little trouble, Arnold said. They had luckily struck a spot which was enormously rich in stones, and selected enough to be worth, at their guess, about the two millions they had set out to get. These they had done up in two packages, one for each. On the way back they had been forced to build a raft in order to cross a river which was swollen with a sudden rain. This raft had been upset in the current, and they had very nearly lost both bundles of diamonds. One, indeed, had been swept into the water. They had thought of fishing for it, but since the remaining bundle must contain something like a million dollars in stones they had decided it would do. Their tale apparently sounded all right to Harpending. He said that he thought a million dollars' worth of diamonds ought to be fairly satisfactory, and when the two miners explained that they wanted to leave the train at Oakland in order to get some rest with friends, he scribbled them a receipt and took charge of the bundle. It must have seemed an eternity before the ferry reached the San Francisco shore where the Harpending carriage was waiting. None of the group had been able to bear the thought of delaying their meeting as much as one day. They were assembled at Harpending's house, ready for him to arrive. Some one found a sheet and spread it on the billiard-table. Then Harpending cut the fastenings of the bundle, took hold of the lower corners of the sack, and upended it. Arnold and Slack's million dollars' worth of diamonds tumbled out on to the white cloth. This time there were other rough stones mixed in with the diamonds. They had no trouble identifying them as emeralds and sapphires.

Matters moved quickly after that; Ralston and his friends were old hands at promotion and organization, and they went swiftly into their accustomed routine.

Arnold and Slack were called in and told that this kind of business was far too big for them. After some debate they agreed. Hundreds of millions would be made out of the new diamond fields; there could be no doubt about it. Even a small share would make them rich men, and they would have none of the trouble of financing that was bound to come with a promotion of such magnitude. Finally they said they would be content with a quarter share. Ralston and the rest congratulated them on their perspicacity, drew up the papers, and arranged for payment to them of cash sums amounting in all to something over $600,000 in return for three-quarters' interest. That took care of the two miners. The gems the syndicate held would be ample security for that much.

Next an outline of a corporation was sketched. Ralston, Lent, Roberts, and Harpending were owners of three-quarters of the property. Between them they would hold enough to retain control; the remainder would go to friends who deserved to be let in on such a good thing. The capital stock was set at $10,000,000, and the allotments of shares were defined. General Dodge, a mining partner of Lent, bought an interest at once, and Maurice Doré acquired a holding. Others were to be permitted to buy stock as soon as details were taken care of. By way of letting the world know what they had, the syndicate arranged for a display of the marvelous gems in a downtown office. The final step was to send a sample lot of the stones to Tiffany's in New York for appraisal. If Tiffany agreed with the San Francisco experts, then a mining authority was to be found in New York and brought out to examine the fields.

Arnold and Slack agreed to conduct this authority to the scene of their operations.

Harpending, as general manager, took the sample stones to New York. His first move was to retain Samuel Barlow, a leader of the New York bar, as counsel. General B. F. Butler was also added to the corporation's legal staff. There were good reasons for this; General Butler was influential in Washington, and could aid the company materially in legislation needed to acquire the lands adjacent to the diamond fields. Then Mr. Tiffany was invited to meet with Harpending and his lawyers at Mr. Barlow's house to view the gems. There was no harm in making it a social occasion too while they were at it; the secret did not have to be kept any longer. Among those invited to the preview were General McClellan and Horace Greeley, who stood and watched while the great authority on precious stones sat down and allowed Harpending to open the treasure-sack.

Mr. Tiffany viewed the display gravely, sorted the stones into little heaps, held them up to the light. Then he spoke. In his memoirs, Asbury Harpending sets down his words. "Gentlemen," he said, "these are beyond question precious stones of enormous value. But before I give you an exact appraisement, I must submit them to my lapidary. I will report to you further in two days." Mr. Tiffany's lapidary was not quite as enthusiastic, though he did well enough. He said the stones that Mr. Harpending had brought would be worth $150,000. At that rate the total on hand would come to something like a million and a quarter or thereabouts. As general manager of the company, Mr. Harpending was satisfied. Only one step remained. They had to find a mining expert and take him to see the actual diamond fields. That part of it was easy. There was one man, Henry Janin, whose reputation was head and shoulders above all the rest. It was said of Janin that he had examined six hundred mines without having caused a single client to lose a cent through his bad judgment. If he had any failing, it was on the side of conservatism; there had been complaints that Janin never took a chance. Manifestly he was the man they wanted. He agreed to make the examination for a fee of $2,500, all expenses, and the right to take up a thousand shares of stock at a price. It was not a low fee, all things considered, but with hundreds of millions practically in sight, Harpending was not one to boggle. He closed with Janin.

The party would have started for the diamond fields without further delay but for one minor difficulty. This was Arnold's restiveness. He was plainly not satisfied, and when Harpending asked him he admitted as much. He had paper agreements, he said, but paper was not cash. So far, he and his partner had received a hundred thousand dollars. It seemed to him now that they ought to have another hundred thousand before revealing the location of the claims. He would be glad to let the amount remain in escrow pending Mr. Janin's report, but he did think that some such settlement as he suggested ought to be the next step. It did not occur to Mr. Harpending that this weather-beaten miner appeared to possess unusually good knowledge of business methods. Still less did he realize that Philip Arnold was exhibiting throughout an almost uncanny sense of timing. It was true that Tiffany's man had appraised at $150,000 the diamonds that Harpending now had in his possession for the company. That security alone left a healthy margin over the hundred thousand that Arnold was asking. After some consideration, Harpending concluded that Arnold was not being unreasonable. He communicated with Ralston, back in San Francisco, who sent on the cash by telegraph. The important thing, he wired Harpending, was to get the expert out to the diamond fields and have the examination made. Harpending saw the point. He wasted no time in getting Janin, Rubery, General Dodge who had come along, Arnold, Slack, and himself on to a train headed West.

286

It was a long, hot, dusty ride out to Rawlins Springs, in Wyoming Territory, which was the place where Arnold said they must leave the train. There was one bit of confusion on the way which helped to pass the time. This was a telegram from George Roberts whose enthusiasm, now that Janin was hired and on the way, was too great to keep in check. His wire contained the information that he and a party of friends would leave San Francisco headed east and meet the Harpending party at Omaha, so that all might visit the great discovery together. Here Arnold flatly rebelled. He pointed out that this constant changing of arrangements was not good business, that he had fulfilled to the letter all his agreements, and that he expected the Ralston group to do the same. There were still obligations for the syndicate to meet, he said (which, from his viewpoint, was quite true), and until these were taken care of he did not wish to expose all the details of the great find to the world at large. Harpending perforce agreed with him, and wired Roberts and his fellow-enthusiasts to stay where they were.

At Rawlins Springs the party left the train, rented the necessary mules and horses, and struck off into the wilderness, led by Arnold and Slack. If they had expected to reach their goal quickly they were sorely disappointed. Arnold himself often seemed uncertain about his directions; sometimes the whole party would have to wait an hour or two while Arnold climbed a high peak to find his landmarks. There were three days of this. On the fourth day, Arnold suggested the party remain in camp while he set out alone to "get his bearings." About noon he returned and said they might follow him. By evening they were encamped on the diamond fields they had heard so much about.

Next morning every one was up early and ready to begin the examination. The place to which Arnold had brought them was at an elevation of about seven thousand feet, so Harpending estimated. It was a gently sloping basin, comprising from thirty to forty acres of land, littered with rocks, through which a small stream ran. Arnold pointed out several ant-hills in which he had dug and found diamonds, and suggested that members of the party try these or any other places that took their fancy. In Rawlins Springs they had bought picks, pans, and shovels, and with these implements the party set to work, each member anxious to be the first to find a diamond. It was Rubery who won; within a few minutes the party heard him yell and joined him to see the rough stone he had uncovered. After that, all of them were lucky. For more than an hour they dug, turning up diamonds in profusion, many rubies, and a few sapphires and emeralds. Often jack-knives were sufficient to dig the gems from the mounds that sparkled with ruby and diamond dust. Harpending confesses in his memoirs that he and his friend Rubery frankly admitted that they felt "the intoxication that comes with sudden accession of boundless wealth."

The next day prospecting was resumed, Janin wandering farther afield than on the first day but finding diamonds wherever he went. He insisted upon taking a third day to extend his investigation, but at the end of that time he professed himself satisfied. He did point out, Harpending says, that the wise thing for the syndicate to do would be to see that it also had control of adjacent lands. He was assured that this would be taken care of; General Butler had been retained as counsel for that very purpose. On the fourth day they all spent their time staking off a wide stretch of country in all directions from the little basin in which the chief concentration of stones had been found. That was all that could be done. The next move was to get to civilization as soon as possible and start the wheels rolling. Slack and Rubery were left to guard the field, and the rest of the party headed back for the railroad.

Back in New York, Harpending set up an office, arranged

with Baron Rothschild in London to handle the British end of the financing, kept in touch with Mr. Ralston, who had insisted that the main office must be in San Francisco. The corporation was named The San Francisco and New York Mining and Commercial Company. Its powers were of the widest; it was not alone to engage in the business of mining and owning mines and their accessories, but also to engage in every class of commercial business including the preparation of precious stones for the market. It was this last definition of its powers that had the widest repercussions. Those in the business deduced that it was the intention of the Company to move the great lapidary establishments of Amsterdam to the Pacific Coast. The news caused quite a flurry of excitement in the Low Countries.

The business of organization went on, Harpending keeping in constant touch with Ralston, who scorned ordinary correspondence and used the telegraph constantly. In San Francisco twenty-five friends of the Ralston group were permitted to subscribe for stock in the amount of $80,000 each, and this initial capital of $2,000,000 was paid in to the Company's account in the Bank of California. A stockholders' meeting was held and directors elected. New York was given two on the Board, Samuel P. Barlow, the Company's lawyer, and—for front—General George B. McClellan. One of the San Francisco members was the Rothschild representative for the Far West. There remained but one point to be settled. That was taken care of by a final payment of $300,000 to Arnold, who had a properly executed power of attorney to act for his partner, Slack. Finally, on July 30, 1872, the articles of incorporation were formally filed and the report of Mr. Janin was made public. Handsome offices were engaged, and David D. Colton, who had left his position with the railroad to take on the general managership of the Company, was installed in them. Mr. Harpending, as an owner, was glad to let Colton take over.

On the wall of the office hung an enormous map showing the three-thousand-acre field with the relative positions of Discovery Claim, Ruby Gulch, Diamond Flat, and Sapphire Hollow. The plan was for the company to hold and work Discovery Claim. The other locations were to be placed as concessions on a basis of so much cash down and a royalty on the gems recovered.

The San Francisco newspapers had a high time with the story, now that it was out. Said the *Alta:* "The Company has 100,000 shares of stock, which have been selling at $40 a share. This price indicates great expectations. The superintendent expressed the opinion that with twenty-five men he will be able to take out gems worth at least $1,000,000 a month. The stones will be brought to San Francisco and cut here."

The New York papers did even better, a contributor signing himself "Old Miner" writing, in the *Sun,* that the Company had in its possession a single gem larger than a pigeon's egg, of matchless purity of color and worth at a low estimate $500,000. Since he had not seen the map in Mr. Colton's office, "Old Miner" added that the great new diamond field was in Southeastern Arizona, which was not more than eight hundred miles too far to the south. The San Francisco *Bulletin* declared: "The implements used by the discoverers in extracting the diamonds were ordinary jack-knives. If so much wealth can be turned up by such primitive means, what might be accomplished by shovels and pickaxes? Little else is discussed in California Street but diamonds and rubies."

For three months San Francisco, New York, and London buzzed with talk about the new diamond fields. Fifteen *bona fide* offers were made by concessionaires who were anxious to pay as much as $200,000 down and return a royalty on gems to the amount of twenty per cent to the parent company. Three subsidiary diamond and ruby companies were organized, one of them placing on view a large reddish stone known as the

"Staunton Ruby." Officials were deluged with letters asking to buy stock. Fortunately no one in the organization was willing to part with any. For on November 11, 1872, Mr. Lent, the President of the San Francisco and New York Mining and Commercial Company, received a message. It was from a small station in Wyoming and was signed by Clarence King, a geologist and engineer in the service of the United States Government. Mr. King stated, flatly and uncompromisingly, that the diamond fields were plainly "salted," and that the entire affair was a colossal swindle from beginning to end.

Ralston, Harpending, and the rest must have felt in their bones that their dream was over. It had all been too good to be true anyhow. But they had to go through the motions. A committee was appointed and hastily sent to join King at the diamond fields. Mr. King was waiting for them, only too glad to show them what he had learned.

For one thing, the "ant hills" in which so many of the stones had been found—those dazzling mounds that had sparkled so with diamond dust and ruby powder—were not ant-hills at all but had been artfully constructed by human hands. At the base of each, holes had been poked with a stick, and at the bottom of each hole reposed a diamond, now and then a ruby or sapphire. No one had disturbed the ant-hills, perhaps because they looked so pretty gleaming in the sun, perhaps because there were so many diamonds to be picked up elsewhere. That is, no one had touched them until Mr. King came along with his German assistant. They had done some kicking and poking and exposed the artificial nature of the mounds.

Another point the company investigators had missed was the presence of several stones—rubies and diamonds both—on the top of a large flat rock. They were pressed into crevices so that they would stay in place, which was puzzling to Mr. King and his helper. But the clincher had been a discovery

291

the German made. Harpending reports his remarks verbatim. He doesn't say how he learned the precise words the man used, but his rendering is in all likelihood close enough. The German had been working by himself, when all at once he stopped and called to Mr. King. "Look here, Mr. King," he had said. "This is the bulliest diamond field as ever was. Not only it produces diamonds, but it cuts them also!" King looked at what his helper held in his hand. It was a diamond, no doubt of it. Any one could see where the lapidary had worked on it.

The party returned to San Francisco, and on November 25th the general facts were given to the press. The Great Diamond Hoax was exposed, and two dozen rich and influential business men were the laughing stock of half the world.

There was nothing left but the dreary business of winding up the affairs of the San Francisco and New York Mining and Commercial Company.

Mr. Ralston's instant reaction, so Harpending writes, was to see that none of the twenty-five men he had led into the scheme should suffer loss, and to this end he repaid them all their original investment, framing their receipts to hang on the wall of his office in the bank. The net loss of something close to three-quarters of a million dollars fell upon the owner-promoters—Ralston, Harpending, Roberts, General Dodge, and Lent. There was an investigation, during which a man by the name of Cooper came forward and said that the whole idea of the swindle had been his, and that he had suggested to Arnold and Slack the method of salting the field, but that the two partners had refused him any share in the booty when their scheme succeeded. Since this testimony was plainly given in revenge, it was discounted. More to the point was the information turned up by a private detective agency which found that Arnold and Slack had made something like $50,000 in a mining deal in 1870, that Arnold had made two trips to

Amsterdam and London to buy coarse stones, sailing each time from Halifax rather than from an American port, and that one of his London purchases had been a large quantity of the poorer grade South African stones known as "niggerheads." If there had been any doubt about it, a double confirmation arrived from London. The firm to which Baron Rothschild had submitted some of the sample diamonds for appraisal recognized them instantly as coming from the lot it had sold to the uncouth American. The firm was rather surprised to receive, shortly afterward, a photograph from a detective agency in the United States, but its manager was glad to identify the likeness as that of the same American, although since the purchase had been for cash he was unable to say whether or not the man's name was Arnold. That might have concluded the investigation but for the determination of Mr. Lent to follow Arnold on his own hook and see if he could not run him down.

It proved very simple. Arnold had gone back to his old home in Hardin County, Kentucky, bought a fine piece of land, a house, and a safe. He carried a good balance at the local bank, but it was common rumor that most of his wealth was kept in this strong box at home.

The rumor was confirmed when Mr. Lent of San Francisco arrived in Hardin County, hired a lawyer, and proceeded to file suit against Arnold for $350,000. Arnold's reply through the newspapers was vigorous, even abusive. He did not, he said, owe Mr. Lent or any one else a cent. He had half a million dollars in his safe, if anybody was interested. That money he had made by his arduous labors as a prospector and miner in the Far West, and this attempt to gain possession of it was no more and no less than a decent man might expect from a "shark from California," an outrage of the grossest sort. Further, this accusation that he had ever salted a claim was the purest fabrication. He had turned over to Mr. Lent's company a perfectly good diamond field; the report of Henry Janin proved its quality, as did the valuation put by Tiffany's of New York upon the stones he had extracted from it. If there had been any salting it had been done later; in fact, such skullduggery was about what one could expect from practically any "California scamp." Mr. Lent might put that in his pipe and smoke it. As for himself, he, Philip Arnold, would stand off the whole of California, if necessary, in order to protect his rights, and he was certain that his fellow-Kentuckians would support his position.

Arnold understood his Hardin County and his friends. Even those who knew nothing about him declared themselves on his side as against the stranger from California where, as every one knew, any kind of jiggery-pokery could be put over. Mr. Lent was beaten even before his suit got under way. For some reason, never quite clear, however, Arnold indicated privately his willingness to compromsie. Harpending writes that he acted as go-between in the deal, and that in the end Arnold paid Lent $150,000 on consideration of immunity from further litigation. Whatever the arrangement, Arnold went his own way from that time forward. As it happened, he did not live long to enjoy his prosperity. Within a year he got into a shooting scrape which landed him in the hospital. He was on the way to recovery from a severe shoulder wound when pneumonia finished him.

As for Slack, Arnold's partner, he remains perhaps the greatest mystery in the whole affair. Always a silent man, preferring to let Arnold do the talking, he disappeared as silently as he had played his part in the hoax. The last one to see him was Harpending's friend, Rubery, who had been left with him to guard the hundred-million-dollar claim in the mountains. When they were relieved of their watch they had gone together to the railway station at Rawlins Springs. Rubery left for San Francisco. Slack said he would wait for the eastbound train.

Despite an active and prolonged search, nothing was ever heard of him again. More than one student has wondered how it came about, since Arnold and Slack had always represented themselves as partners, that all the profits turned up in Arnold's bank account and iron safe.

That was the Great Diamond Hoax, California's postscript to gold.

Shrewdly as Arnold handled his part in the affair, the swindle could never have succeeded if it had not been that even the smartest business men were half-blinded by the incredible wealth that had already been found in the new West. Diamonds, rubies, emeralds, and sapphires were not customarily found in the same fields; that was true. But who could tell about this vast western empire? As Baron Rothschild had said, America had produced many surprises already; why not another? Tiffany, after all, had said no more than that the stones shown him were diamonds. They were diamonds. The business Tiffany conducted was confined to cut gems; he and his local staff were no experts on uncut stones. Janin had the Tiffany report to go on. He was not concerned with the genuineness of the stones, nor with their quality; it was his affair only to check the presence of the diamonds in the place where Arnold said they were. And they were there, plenty of them; Janin picked them out of the ground himself.

Nevertheless, the promoters had to take the ridicule. They had even to suffer the accusation that they had been in on the swindle, that even though they had sold no stock they were probably planning to do so in one gigantic operation. Rumors always fly about in such cases; there is no escaping them. In the end, it was Harpending who bore the brunt of it. He had made enemies in London, and these, through the columns of the London *Times,* accused him directly of acting in complicity with his friend Alfred Rubery to stage the entire diamond fraud. Rubery sued and recovered heavy damages. Harpending, disgusted with business, mining, and finance, turned most of his holdings into cash, left California, and retired to his home state. Oddly enough it was Kentucky. Californians of a later generation had almost forgotten him when he returned to San Francisco in the first decade of this century to dispose of a mine he still owned on the Mother Lode and to write his account of the Great Diamond Hoax. To-day's reader can only smile in sympathy at the old man's tart denial of the charge that the salting of the diamond claims was so crudely done that diamonds were even found in the crotches of the trees. "This," wrote Asbury Harpending, "was not true, for the very good reason that there were no trees there." He added wryly that he could still remember how beautiful the diamonds, emeralds, rubies, and sapphires looked, but that he had been wondering for forty years why a few pearls had not been thrown in too.

INDEX

A.B. LAFORGE. PRIVATE RESIDENCE.

B.V. SARGENT.

L. SOHER.

HODAPP & FRIEND.

J. WEBB.

G. LEGER.

W. RATZ.

J. HODGES.

PINK SMITH.

H.M. STURGES.

COURT HOUSE.

Drawn from Nature & on Stone by Kuchel & Dresel, 146 Clay St. S.F.

Entered according to Act of Congress in the year 1856

MOKELU